Elephants
in the
Church

GEORGE BLOOMER

Elephants
in the
Church

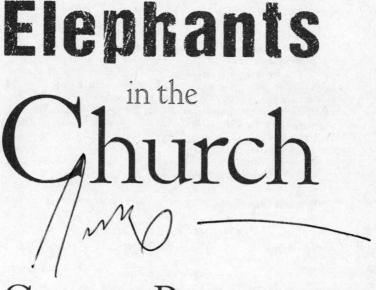

GEORGE BLOOMER

ELEPHANTS IN THE CHURCH:
Courageously Confronting Today's Tough and Controversial Issues

George G. Bloomer
Bethel Family Worship Center
515 Dowd St.
Durham, NC 27701
www.bethelfamily.org

ISBN: 978-1-62911-235-0
eBook ISBN: 978-1-62911-236-7
Printed in the United States of America
© 2014 by George G. Bloomer

Banner Publishing
1030 Hunt Valley Circle
New Kensington, PA 15068

DEDICATION

To all those brave enough to face the truth, live the truth, and then make the world a better place by speaking the truth in love.

"Outside the mainstream, outside the Big Apple, outside the box, Bishop George Bloomer is a fresh thinker, a truth seeker, and a genuine visionary. Listen to him. He is transparent; his life is one triumph over another. His fingers are firmly placed on the pulse of what we must know to confront the "elephants" coming toward us in our future. *Elephants in the Church* is a best-seller must read!"

—*Eldrin Bell*
Former chairman, Clayton County Board of Commissioners
Former Atlanta Police Chief

"There are only two places where elephants exist: in the wild and in the captivity of a zoo or circus. In the wild, the elephant operates by natural intent, as God created it; in captivity, it is reduced to performing. The church has become acquainted with mass performances, susceptible to the tricks of the ringmasters in a three-circus. Bishop George Bloomer's book, *Elephants in the Church*, exposes the church—the performing elephant—and places it back into its natural habitat and rightful position. Once again, Bishop George Bloomer nails it. Every believer should read this book."

—*Jamal Bryant*
Jamal Bryant Ministries
Pastor, The Empowerment Temple
Baltimore, Maryland

"Bishop Bloomer provides important insight regarding the 'elephants' of race and human dignity that are still challenges for people of color and faith in our country."

—*Michael McBride*
Director, Urban Strategies and Lifelines to Healing
Berkeley, California

"Bishop Bloomer takes on a series of subjects that are often ignored by the body of Christ. He offers tremendous insight, while always using the Word of God as a foundation. Issues like gay marriage, welfare, women's rights, and gun control are not always black and white but include many shades of gray. Bishop navigates these with love, compassion, and an insightfulness in a way that is both refreshing and thought provoking."

—*Paul Crouch Jr.*
Director of Project Development, The Word Network

"The elephant in the room: a major problem or controversial issue that is obviously present but is avoided as a subject for discussion because it is more comfortable to do so."

—*The Oxford Dictionary* (U.S. English edition)

"Our lives begin to end the day we become silent about things that matter."

—*Martin Luther King Jr.*

CONTENTS

PART I:

A New Paradigm for Transforming
Our Nation

INTRODUCTION:

WHERE ARE THE TRUTH-TELLERS TODAY?

"There was truth and there was untruth, and if you clung
to the truth even against the whole world,
you were not mad."

—*George Orwell, 1984*

Would you like to make the world a better place? Of course
you would.

However, in order to bring about cultural change you have to
be willing to confront the status quo and be politically incorrect
at times. Instead of pleasing people at all costs, you must commit
yourself to speaking the truth and going after sacred cows when
necessary.

Speaking the truth is definitely a "road less traveled" these days.
Most of us would rather "get along" instead of make a difference.

However, change agents throughout history were willing to
speak truth to power. In every case, they paid a price—but they
did so willingly.

+ Jesus was crucified.
+ Dietrich Bonhoeffer was executed by hanging while imprisoned in a Nazi concentration camp.

* Gandhi died when an assassin shot him in the chest at point-back range.

* Martin Luther King Jr. spent time in jail because of his non-violent protests, and ultimately he was assassinated.

* Nelson Mandela spent twenty-seven years behind bars for his opposition to apartheid—during the prime of his life.

And though I'm certainly hesitant to put him in the same category of any of these world-changing leaders, there's the strange case of Phil Robertson. As you probably know, Phil is the patriarch of the Robertson family that stars in the popular *Duck Dynasty* TV reality series on the A&E network.

Phil hasn't been crucified, assassinated, or even thrown in jail for his views, but he *has* faced lots of ridicule, criticism, and animosity for the stands he has taken on cultural issues.

When A&E decided to add "bleeps" to the *Duck Dynasty* program to spice it up, Phil Robertson told the network they shouldn't make it seem like the family uses profanity, since they do not. More trouble ensued when A&E chose to edit the family's prayers to delete "in Jesus' name." When the network explained to Phil that they didn't want to offend the Muslim population, he responded by asking, "What year is it?" The network execs said "2012," and Phil pointed out that the year was 2012 AD, meaning "in the year of our Lord." He asked why they would take someone out of the program, when the whole calendar was based on Him.

The argument about offending Muslims didn't carry any weight with Phil either. "How many Muslims have been watching our show anyway?" he asked A&E.

On December 18, 2013, A&E announced the indefinite suspension of Phil Robertson from the network because of an interview with Drew Magary of GQ magazine. In the interview for a feature article GQ called "What the Duck?" Phil was asked what kinds of behavior he considered sinful. Never one to mince words, Robertson replied: "Start with homosexual behavior and just morph out from there. Bestiality, sleeping around with this woman and that woman and that woman and those men." Then, paraphrasing the apostle Paul's words in 1 Corinthians 6:9–11, Phil continued: "Don't be deceived. Neither the adulterers, the idolaters, the male prostitutes, the homosexual offenders, the greedy, the drunkards, the slanders, the swindlers—they won't inherit the kingdom of God. Don't deceive yourself. It's not right."

Most of the firestorm of criticism from this interview stemmed from Phil's categorization of homosexual conduct as sin—even though he was simply quoting the Bible and articulating the position nearly everyone held just a few decades ago.

Was Phil being a bigot toward gays? Was he self-righteously setting himself up as a judge? Phil responded to the criticism by saying he doesn't judge anyone, but leaves that up to God: "We just love 'em, give 'em the good news about Jesus—whether they're homosexuals, drunks, terrorists. We let God sort 'em out later, you see what I'm saying?"

When A&E suspended him, Phil released a statement, saying, "I would never treat anyone with disrespect just because they are different from me." *Duck Dynasty* supporters raised such a stink about Phil Robertson's suspension—including a Facebook page that gained 1.5 million likes—that A&E quickly lifted the suspension before any episodes were affected.

What Can We Learn from Phil?

My purpose in this book is not to make you a disciple of Phil Robertson, even though that may not be such a bad thing. Nor is my primary focus going to be on a single issue, such as homosexuality, abortion, income inequality, or race relations.

But Phil's experiences can teach us a lot about ourselves and the society we live in. Ask yourself: Would you be willing to take a public stand on the issues Phil Robertson addressed—whether in agreement with him or in refuting his positions? And are you troubled at all by the way our politically correct culture seems intent on stifling public discourse on the hot-button issues of our day? Do we have to all agree in order to be respectful? In specific, do we all have to be supporters of the LGBT (Lesbian, Gay, Bisexual, and Transgender) agenda and gay marriage in order to avoid charges of intolerance and bigotry?

However, perhaps there's another question that should be more troubling to us than any of these: Why would a backwoods reality TV star have to be the main spokesperson for traditional and a biblical worldview? Where are the preachers who will stand up and declare what the Bible teaches about the difficult subjects of our day?

Even Pope Francis seemed squeamish when asked to weigh in on the subject of homosexuality in the church. "If someone is gay and he searches for the Lord and has good will, who am I to judge?" he replied. While one of the cardinal sins of today's politically correct society is to be "judgmental," the pope's answered missed a very important distinction. Of course we are not to be judgmental in the sense of imposing our own preferences and opinions on others. But what about moral issues that are clearly addressed in Scripture? Shouldn't Christian leaders be able to declare what the Bible says without apology?

And you've probably heard of a similar 2013 interview when the pastor of one of America's largest evangelical churches joined Josh Zepps on *HuffPost Live* to discuss the pastor's current best-selling book. Zepps read this statement directly from the book: "It doesn't matter who likes you or doesn't like you, all that matters is that God likes you. He accepts you, he approves of you." He went on to ask the pastor if homosexuals were included in this apparent unconditional acceptance from God.

"Absolutely," the pastor insisted, "I believe that God breathed life into every person and that every person is made in the image of God and you have to accept them as they are, on their journey. I'm not here to preach hate or push people down."

In a similar interview by Larry King, this same megachurch pastor and best-selling author replied when asked his views on homosexuality, "I believe that Scripture says that it's a sin, but I always follow up by saying, you know what, we're not against anybody."

When King pressed him further to explain this seemingly mixed message, the pastor said it was a subject he just didn't want to address: "There are a lot of things, Larry, that I don't understand, so I just don't want to preach on it."

Hmmm...is that explanation good enough for a national and worldwide spokesperson for the Christian faith? Do I have to "understand" every precept in the Bible in order to teach them as true? Is it acceptable to God that Christian leaders choose to duck the issues they feel uncomfortable with?

What are we to make of this common reluctance by pastors to address moral issues like homosexuality? Is such an approach simply the prudent thing to do these days? Do we have to avoid the "hard sayings" of the Bible so we can focus on the good news of the gospel message? Or have we just succumbed to a cowardly desire to be accepted by the prevailing culture, caring more about pleasing people than pleasing God and being true to His Word?

But before we are too hard on the pope and the megachurch pastor I've described, perhaps we should take a good look in the mirror. When was the last time *we* were willing to take a clear stand on a controversial issue, knowing that we would face ridicule and rejection as a result?

In the Lion's Den

As Christians, we increasingly find ourselves in an unfamiliar and hostile environment. Not many decades ago, even most unbelievers gave lip service to biblical morality. You would have had a hard time finding people who advocated the right to sodomy or to homosexual marriages. And scarcely *anyone* would agree that bisexual or transgender conduct was anything but abnormal.

But in a shockingly brief period of time, everything has changed. Assisted by a mainstream news and entertainment media that has readily embraced the LGBT cause, the culture now condemns those who still hold to traditional concepts of marriage and sexuality.

The book of Daniel paints a similar picture to what we are experiencing as Christians in today's increasingly secular culture. Daniel and his friends—Shadrach, Meshach, and Abed-Nego— had been taken exile from their homes in Judah to the pagan world of Babylon.

You probably know the stories. When Shadrach, Meshach, and Abed-Nego refused to bow down and worship the golden image set up by King Nebuchadnezzar, they were thrown into a fiery furnace. And when Daniel later disobeyed King Darius' edict not to pray to anyone but him, he was thrown into a lion's den.

The good news is that God protected and preserved His people even amid the fiery furnace and the lion's den. In the same way, He can come to our aid when we face repercussions for taking a stand for Him against the twisted cultural norms that are sweeping our nation and the world.

But perhaps the real question in these stories is this: Where are the courageous people today like Daniel or Shadrach, Meshach, and Abed-Nego? Are we willing to refuse the edicts of our society in order to stay true to our God?

A "John the Baptist" Generation

Before Jesus' first coming, He was preceded by John the Baptist, a fiery, straightforward preacher of righteousness and repentance. John came as *"the voice of one crying in the wilderness: 'Prepare the way of the* LORD: *make His paths straight'"* (Matthew 3:3).

Jesus is coming again. And before He returns, I believe that God will raise up a similar "John the Baptist" to prepare the way. This time the prophetic message won't come just from one lone voice, crying out in the wilderness. This time the preparatory message will come from a new generation of radical followers of Jesus—bold men and women who are willing to speak God's truth to a world that has lost its way.

This kind of audacious faith will put us at odds, both with the humanistic secular world and also with lukewarm Christians who prefer the praise of men to the praise of God.

John the Baptist wasn't a very accommodating kind of fellow. He called the religious leaders "snakes" and warned them to *"flee from the wrath to come"* (Matthew 3:7). Those who claimed to follow the ways of God were challenged by John to *"bear fruits worthy of repentance"* (verse 8).

John even addressed sin in the personal lives of the politicians of his day, challenging Herod about his immoral marriage to his brother Philip's wife. (See Mark 6:17–18.) And there was a heavy cost to challenging political correctness: Herod had John beheaded.

You see, there is a cost to embracing and proclaiming the truth. Are we willing? Or would we prefer to live in some safe stained-glass ghetto of comfortable Christendom?

The Fear Factor

The answer to these questions will be largely shaped by whether we fear God or fear people, as Solomon warns in Proverbs 29:25, *"The fear of man brings a snare, but whoever trusts in the LORD shall be safe."* No wonder we so often find ourselves ensnared and tied up in knots when called upon to explain our faith and address the central moral issues of generation.

But the late author and preacher Leonard Ravenhill said it well: "A man who is intimate with God will never be intimidated by men." If we truly spent time standing before God, it would be no big thing to stand boldly before people. Why? Because those who fear the Lord will have nothing else to fear!

Pastor and author Rick Warren addressed the "fear factor" in a 2013 CNN interview with Piers Morgan. After conceding that Rick is a Christian man and even "a great man," Morgan nevertheless was incredulous about his stand on homosexual relations: "How can you espouse genuine equality if you don't allow gay people the same right to get married as straight people?"

Rick Warren showed real wisdom when he replied, "I fear the disapproval of God more than I fear your disapproval or the disapproval of society." That kind of undaunted perspective is an indispensable ingredient for those who would be a part of the John the Baptist generation arising before Jesus' return.

We can't afford to keep ducking the issues and ignoring the elephants in the room! But this isn't an easy calling. Fair-weather preachers will be too faint of heart to engage in the cultural battles ahead.

Yet I love this observation by Catherine Booth, who founded the Salvation Army with her husband William: "If we are to better the future, we must disturb the present." So, what about *you?* Are you ready to "disturb" the status quo? Are you willing to address the "elephants in the room" that most people would rather ignore?

Then let's get started on this important journey. Not only will we ourselves be transformed by this "reality check," but there's a good chance that the church will be changed as well. Maybe even a nation.

1

THE CONSCIENCE OF A "CONCERN-ATIVE"

"The world will not be destroyed by those who do evil,
but by those who watch them without doing anything."

—*Albert Einstein*

When people hear that I'm concerned about the condition of our nation, they always want to know my party affiliation. Then they want to ask whether I'm a conservative, a libertarian, a liberal, or a progressive.

I hate labels sometimes, don't you? I understand that it's human nature to want to define people, but I just don't find any of the political labels to be very satisfying today. Liberal? Conservative? Progressive? Libertarian? Green? Tea Party? Do you really want to brand yourself 100 percent with any one label?

To make the "label game" even more bewildering, the definitions often change. The meaning of *liberal* a few centuries ago was totally different from what we mean by liberal today. Conservatives are supposed to be against the expansion of government, but there hasn't been one "conservative" president to actually reduce the size of the federal bureaucracy. And did you know that Abraham Lincoln—liberator of the slaves and opponent of "state's rights"—was a *Republican*?

The only label I'm truly comfortable with is "Christian," but at times I get embarrassed by how some other people act who carry that label. And they probably get embarrassed by *me* at times too.

Yet my greatest desire is to be a faithful follower of Jesus. He said *love* would be the major characteristic of His brand of followers, so that is my aspiration. (See John 13:34–35.) And I can't really picture Jesus waving a flag for any one political party or movement. He had a brand all His own, after all.

Who Do You Listen To?

If you tell me where you get your news, I can tell you a lot about your worldview and your political philosophy. You may argue that your favorite cable news network is "fair and balanced," but let's get real: *Every* network has a slant of some kind. And perhaps that's not entirely bad. We need to have a robust debate and hear all sides on the issues. However, that only happens if you expose yourself to different news outlets.

Can you name any news anchors from CNN, Fox News, MSNBC, CBS, or ABC? Are you familiar with both conservative and liberal radio talk shows? Do you read any publications or books that promote a certain political mindset? Or do you prefer to stay uninvolved and intellectually lazy?

Perhaps you read George Orwell's famous novel *1984* when you were in school. Orwell painted a bleak picture of a dystopian world where "Big Brother" was in control of everything and constantly watching your every action. All news came through a single source, the Ministry of Truth, which gave the government complete ability to shape people's worldview

Fortunately, we don't have a single source of news today. In fact, the Internet has given us access to more viewpoints than ever before. However, if you confine yourself to just one stream of "newspeak" information, you will end not much different than the brainwashed citizens of *1984*.

As a preacher, I know that some folks are too "spiritual" for any involvement in the political and cultural debates of our day. They love to sing, shout, and dance in our church services, but they could care less about the fate of our nation. These super-saints proclaim that "Jesus is coming soon," and they use that fact to excuse them from working to make the world a better place today.

Hey, I love the church. I even love most *people* in the church. But I also love my nation, and I believe God has called us to be "salt and light" to make a difference in every way we can. (See Matthew 5:13–16.)

Yet well-meaning Christians have fundamentally different views on which direction is best for our country. You need to have some familiarity with these viewpoints in order to be a well-informed, engaged citizen. Ideas have consequences, and we need to do the best we can to have God's perspective on the issues. Like the sons of Issachar, described in Scripture, *"who understood the times and knew what* [their nation] *should do"* (1 Chronicles 12:32 NIV).

Who's Shaping YOUR "Conscience"?

Someday I want to write a book called *The Conscience of a Concern-ative*. We should all "vote our conscience," after all. But I'm concerned that many voters haven't taken the time to *inform* their conscience with the facts. And often this requires a deliberate choice to expose yourself to a variety of viewpoints—even ones you strongly disagree with.

Over the past several decades, a number of "conscience" books have been written. One of the first was *Conscience of a Conservative*, written in 1960 by Senator Barry Goldwater, who became the Republican presidential nominee in 1964. Goldwater's book is notable for a number of reasons. Many of its arguments were later reflected in the views of Ronald Reagan and the Tea Party movement.

Goldwater promoted "freedom" as the highest value in American society. In radical, uncompromising statements, Goldwater said government often is the enemy of freedom. Preaching self-reliance and individualism, he said you should pretty much be free from anybody else's vision but your own. When you read some of his bold statements, you can probably see why he lost the 1964 election in a landslide:

> I have little interest in streamlining government or in making it more efficient, for I mean to reduce its size. I do not undertake to promote welfare, for I propose to extend freedom. My aim is not pass laws, but to repeal them. It is not to inaugurate new programs, but to cancel old ones that do violence to the Constitution, or that have failed in their purpose, or that impose on the people an unwarranted financial burden. I will not attempt to discover whether legislation is "needed" before I have first determined whether it is constitutionally permissible. And if I should later be attacked for neglecting my constituents' "interests," I shall replay that I was informed their main interest is liberty and that in that cause I am doing the very best I can.

When you work on formulating your own political "conscience," you need to wrestle with some fundamental issues raised by Goldwater and his successors: Is government a friend or an enemy? Does a society truly do better when there is less government and people are left free to their own devices? Or do we need government to take a more activist role—ensuring that there's a level playing field and providing economic security for the neediest citizens?

ELEPHANTS IN THE CHURCH

Before you answer those questions, you may want to look at some other books on the subject. In 2007, *New York Times* columnist Paul Krugman wrote *The Conscience of a Liberal*, an attempt to galvanize progressives in the same way Goldwater's book had stirred right-wingers. Krugman claimed that the rise of America's post-WWII middle-class society was directly related to the progressive policies of the Franklin Roosevelt administration, not an automatic product of a free-market economy.

Krugman's book praises labor unions and advocates increased taxes on the rich to fund redistributive social programs like food stamps, Medicare, and Social Security. According to Krugman's perspective, the New Deal consensus was narrowing the income gap and lifting the working class out of poverty until conservative Republicans hijacked everything. The Republicans, he says, advanced the interests of the wealthy, cut funding for social programs, and sought to diminish the influence of labor unions. The result has been greater income inequality and a heightened racial divide.

While Goldwater painted government as the main enemy of freedom and prosperity, Krugman promoted the rosy view that government is the only thing that can stave off the special interests and bring about economic fairness. Without a robust government and strong social safety net, income inequality will continue to soar, and low-income people will increasingly suffer.

You may not agree with all of Krugman's conclusions, but he makes a strong case that laissez-faire economics is neither practical nor beneficial. Similar arguments can be found in Ernest Partridge's insightful online book: *The Conscience of a Progressive*.

We the People?

Finally, in order to see where the political debate stands in America, you may want to look at *The Conscience of a Libertarian*, by Wayne Allyn Root. With the subtitle *Empowering the Citizen Revolution with God, Guns, Gold & Tax Cuts*, Root's 2010 book echoes many of Goldwater's themes fifty years earlier. He argues for a return to the constitution, lower taxes, smaller government, states' rights, an end to the Federal Reserve, and "a return of power to the people, just as the Founding Fathers intended."

There's a lot to like about the "power to the people" argument of libertarians like Root. But what if "the people" deny fundamental rights and liberties to each other? Should we go back to the Jim Crow days when "the people" could keep blacks from eating at their lunch counters or riding in the front of their buses?

And while we should rightfully honor our Founding Fathers as amazing, visionary leaders, would we really want to go back to those days? Have we forgotten that most women and blacks couldn't even vote back then?

Our founders were truly all about freedom, but some people were clearly less free than others. It has taken many years to free the slaves, empower women, and give everyone the same basic economic rights.

Conservatives paint an idyllic picture of an American that never was. Yes, we've had high aspirations for liberty and justice all along. But we can't deceive ourselves by forgetting what a struggle it has been to get to this point.

Does that mean I'm a "progressive"? No, I don't really care for that label either. I'm concerned that some people's *progress* may be taking us in the wrong direction—not toward greater freedom and prosperity but toward increased regulation and economic stagnation.

However, I'm hopeful that "hope and change" is still possible. It's not too late for our country to experience better days than ever before.

My optimism is not based on being a conservative or a progressive—it's because I'm a Christian and preacher of the gospel. I believe the Scriptures where God promises to heal our land when we turn to Him. And I love the fact that our spiritual lives are meant to be "progressive" in their ever-increasing impact: *"The path of the righteous is like the light of dawn, that shines brighter and brighter until the full day"* (Proverbs 4:18 NASB). We may not agree on all the issues anytime soon, but we still can love each other and let our light SHINE.

2

SUPERFICIAL SOLUTIONS TO THE WORLD'S PROBLEMS

"They have healed the brokenness of My people superficially, saying, 'Peace, peace,' but there is no peace."

—*Jeremiah 6:14 (NASB)*

Last winter a friend got a bad case of the flu, and she was simply miserable. Her head and throat ached, she was badly congested, and her cough was horrific. So she asked me to get her some cough drops among the other medications she needed to relieve her distress.

I virtually cleaned out the local CVS store, trying to find anything that might help, and I didn't forget the cough drops. After researching the ingredients on the labels of several different brands, I found the highest potency cough drops I could find.

When I returned with my bag of over-the-counter remedies, she was grateful for my efforts. But the cough drops weren't the kind she had really wanted. Luden's Wild Cherry Cough Drops were the ones she had in mind.

Of course, I was quite familiar with Luden's Cough Drops. As a kid, they were my first choice whenever I got a cold or sore throat. And they tasted so good that I sometimes bought them simply as candy.

So I returned to CVS to buy the sp

I noticed that their name has changed

longer even called "*cough* drops," but Lud

"Great Tasting *Throat* Drops." Instead of

or open nasal passages, the only active

product is *pectin*, the same component

jellies. And, of course, the "great tasting

mostly comprised of sugar and corn syru

My encounter with Luden's Throa

ture of why America's fiscal and moral

improve. You see, our tendency is to

Drops—something that tastes good

kind of real cures. And we're terribly

and governmental leaders who will give

stantive solutions.

When problems in the nation or

better, we express surprise that the Lud

work. It turned out that they weren't tru

least they *tasted* good.

How bad will our national "flu" have to

for true solutions, no matter how unpleas

When will we cry out to God in national

tion, asking Him to apply the healing bal

the candy-coated solutions of the politician

The "Fat Cream" S

Have you noticed how prone we are

ficial solutions instead of embracing the

to really solve our problems? Several ye

named James got hoodwinked by an in

According to the impressive claims in

unsightly inches" just by applying the cream to your belly at bedtime. With no effort at all, you would wake up each morning to a trimmer waistline.

In retrospect, James realizes that the promises in the infomercial were simply too good to be true. But hey, the fat cream came with a money-back guarantee, so what did he have to lose?

So James called the 1-800 number and paid $29.95 plus shipping and handling for his started jar of fat cream. He had about fifty pounds to lose and was hopeful that this would be an amazing, effective alternative to all those nasty weight reduction plans that required real lifestyle changes.

Soon the fat cream arrived—a soupy pink lotion in a white cold cream jar. Just as the directions said, James religiously applied the lotion to his protruding midsection before going to bed each night. His wife Jackie, who only weighed about a hundred pounds, couldn't help giggling as she watched the spectacle.

When Jackie wondered aloud if the gooey stuff would do any good, James replied firmly, "Sure, honey, it *has* to work. It's even guaranteed!"

But after a week or so, the results—or lack of results—were pretty evident. The extra inches were still there, just a little oilier than before.

When James told me his woeful story, I jokingly tried to console him, "Well, man, at least you probably burned some extra calories by rubbing that slimy cream on your gut every night!"

Is There a Lesson?

Fortunately, we can learn an important lesson from James' ill-fated experiment with fat cream: *It's easy to fall for schemes that promise easy and painless remedies to very difficult situations.*

Modern-day Americans seem especially guilty of this tendency. Somehow we've bought the line that the only things in life worth pursuing are quick, easy, and pain-free. Magazine headlines promise that just about anything can be remedied in "5 Easy Steps." Grocery stores seem increasingly dominated by microwavable dinners that require no preparation.

In stark contrast, the Bible never promises fast, sugar-coated solutions to individual or cultural problems. Biblical leaders like Jeremiah rebuked people for being fooled by false remedies: *"They have healed the brokenness of My people superficially, saying, 'Peace, peace,' but there is no peace"* (Jeremiah 6:14 NASB).

Just as in Jeremiah's day, people in America and around the world are still suffering from incredible brokenness today. The world is a fallen place, and no one has gotten by unscathed by sin, violence, or perversion.

Fat cream solutions won't do the trick when people are broken and undone. We need more than some new religious platitude or some expanded government program. We need the kind of deep transformation that only a widespread spiritual awakening can bring.

Why don't superficial solutions work? Because they don't recognize and address the true root issues of the problems. Most human problems stem from a very specific disease, and it is spelled S-I-N. But, tragically, neither the world nor even the church are fond of discussing the sin problem these days. As a result, we propose solutions that are no better than Luden's Cough Drops or fat cream—soothing the surface, but never bringing lasting transformation.

Many churches are little better than the world in this respect. We offer "3 Keys to a Happy Life" or "4 Steps to a Better Marriage," all the while ignoring the reality of sin and selfishness that is the root of people's misery. If we truly understood the desperateness of humankind's fallen condition (see Romans 3:10–18), we would realize that only a radical solution can ever suffice as the cure. We would discard our humanistic, ineffectual fat cream answers and put our full reliance on the power of the cross and the Holy Spirit.

Dr. Phil's Question

We need to face a fact: America is at a crossroad. We're in the valley of decision, and there's no guarantee we will get it right. For far too long, we've been in a state of denial.

Perhaps we need a visit from Dr. Phil.

Although I'm not sure his counseling tips are particularly original or profound, I love one question Dr. Phil commonly asks his guests. After they give him a rambling explanation to justify their boneheaded or ineffective actives, he simply asks:

"And how's that working for you?"

It's a brilliant question. Instead of directly confronting the guest and saying what he *really* thinks: *You must be crazy!*, Dr. Phil causes them to face the *fruit* and *consequences* of their actions. His question forces misguided guests to reflect on why their situation is going from bad to worse if their actions and motives are truly so noble.

If Dr. Phil interviewed America today...

+ When we described President Lyndon Johnson's good intentions when he launched America's "War on Poverty" more than fifty years ago, Dr. Phil would listen intently but ask, *"And how's that working for you?"*

+ When we explained why we voted for "hope and change" in the past few elections, I'm sure he would be sympathetic, knowing that hope and change are both good things. But in the end, he would surely have to ask, *"And how's that working for you?"*

+ When we described all the stimulus plans and bailouts to rescue the economy and create jobs, he would again inquire, *"And how's that working for you?"*

+ When we told him of our sincere hopes that by electing our first black president, America would finally bridge its economic, racial, and gender divisions, he would probe, *"And how's that working for you?"*

+ When we described America's efforts to project a more humble image overseas, apologizing for past mistakes and reaching out to Muslims in particular, he would inquire, *"And how's that working for you?"*

+ And in case you think I'm letting the Republican administrations off the hook, I'm certain Dr. Phil would *also* want to know if we're satisfied with the outcome of our country's decision to go to war in Afghanistan and Iraq: *"And how's THAT working for you?"*

We can have legitimate arguments as to the true intentions or motives of our leaders. But even if we deem them to be sincere in their vision for a better America, Dr. Phil's sobering question remains. He's not swayed by people's feelings, nor impressed with their lofty intentions if there isn't positive fruit in the *real world*.

Living in Denial

Just as many of Dr. Phil's guests want to remain in a world of denial, the same is true of many Americans and many of our politicians. We desperately need a *reality check*—and the sooner the better.

While the underlying issues of our society are rooted in sin and morality, some of our nation's problems also have common sense remedies. For example, how about this follow up question from Dr. Phil: "How long can an individual, a family, an organization, or a nation last, if they borrow 40 percent of every dollar they spend (as the federal government is now doing)?" This obviously isn't a sustainable policy, is it? And yet presidents from both parties have tolerated deficit spending for *decades*.

Many other questions are likewise no-brainers, yet subject to partisan blinders. Can we truly claim "progress" on unemployment when more and more people are simply leaving the job market and relying on the government for their support? And when debating what people's "fair share" of taxes should be, how can it be considered fair for half of American's citizens to pay no income taxes at all?

Sadly, partisanship and allegiances to special interests are preventing the nation from taking the needed action on such matters. And where is the church at this perilous time in our nation's history? Instead of being able to proclaim God's wisdom on the issues of our day, many of us have been blinded by politics too.

The Bible says believers will *"judge the world"* (1 Corinthians 6:2) when Jesus returns, so we're supposed to have some wisdom and discernment to deal with matters in this present life as well. The apostle Paul was bewildered when the Corinthians were taking each other to court instead of applying the wisdom and justice of God to their disputes: *"Can it be that there is no one among you wise enough to settle a dispute between the brothers…?"* (1 Corinthians 6:5 ESV).

Instead of Christians being helpless, disengaged bystanders regarding the events unfolding in our world, God wants to use us to reveal His wisdom: *"God's purpose in all this was to use the church to display his wisdom in its rich variety to all the unseen rulers and authorities in the heavenly places"* (Ephesians 3:10 NLT).

It's interesting that Paul says here that God's wisdom has *"rich variety."* Perhaps it's not a stretch to say that the Lord's wisdom is not just right wing or left wing wisdom, nor just Republican or Democratic wisdom. True wisdom is a "many-splendored" thing, full of rich variety and an ability to see all sides of an issue.

Pragmatic not Partisan

Dr. Phil's question isn't designed to be partisan, but merely *pragmatic*. The question should not be "Who wins?" but rather "Will this policy actually work?"

I'm certainly not against every government program. Many of them are doing a lot of good. However, some programs have outlived their usefulness—if they ever worked at all. And other programs are completely redundant and inefficient. Who will trim the fat in our bureaucracy, courageously willing to get rid of "sacred cows" if they aren't really working?

Of course, there's enough blame to go around for both major parties. But one thing is clear: "The same old, same old" clearly isn't working.

Meanwhile, our country seems dangerously poised to fulfill the old definition of insanity: Doing the same things over and over, but expecting different results.

3

ANGRY GOD OR SMILING GOD— DO YOU GET TO CHOOSE?

"Although God loves us unconditionally, He does get
angry at sin, wickedness and evil. But He is not an angry
God. God hates sin, but He loves sinners! He will never
approve of sin in your life, but He always loves you and
wants to work with you to make progress in living a holy
life in Christ."

—*Joyce Meyer*

A woman named Gail grew up in a church that had a very dis-
torted view of God. It gave her the impression that God was
angry all the time. Since He was angry at pretty much *everything*,
it ended up being hopeless to relate to Him or please Him. No
matter what you did, at the end of the day He would still be angry.

Fortunately, Gail eventually met the true God, and it turned
out He wasn't mad at her after all. In fact, He embraced her, wel-
comed her home, and threw a big party for her. (See Luke 15 for
the details.)

Although I'm generally an admirer of 18th century preacher
Jonathan Edwards, I'm not a big fan of his most famous sermon
title: "Sinners in the Hands of an Angry God." Can you imagine putting that on a church sign or billboard *today?* Definitely
wouldn't be politically correct.

But the main thing I don't like about Edwards' sermon title is that it gives the same false impression as Gail's former church—that God doesn't just "get angry" from time to time, He's angry *by nature*. Instead of just being mad at those who sin, He's mad at everyone, all the time.

What could we call this warped view of God? As Edwards practically says in his sermon title, this is the *angry* God. Since His anger never changes, you could put a scowling portrait of God on your wall. No matter what you did, the angry scowl would remain.

But oh how the pendulum has swung in our day. Thankfully, there are fewer and fewer churches that promote the angry-God theology. But sadly, we've adopted a perspective that is not much more accurate, replacing the *angry* God with a *smiling* God.

Just as the angry God never is happy about anything, the smiling God never gets angry and never frowns. Everyone and everything is quite okay with Him. "Different strokes for different folks" is the theology of the day, and God could care less about people's lifestyle choices. People's behavior is their private, personal choice, after all, and who is God to interfere with their pursuit of happiness?

So if you're a member of "The Church of the Smiling God," you probably have a very different portrait on your wall—a God with a huge, unchanging grin.

How did we ever get to such a place, where we adopt a picture of God with an unchanging expression on His face? Is it because He's actually an *unknown* God to us, like the God of the Athenians in Acts 17:23?

You see, if we don't really *know* God, we're prone to paint His picture with some kind of fixed expression that we've picked up from our church or some TV preacher. But that kind of God is not a real person, just a caricature.

The *real* God can be seen in the *real* Jesus. He certainly wasn't the angry God, but He *did* get angry at times—mostly at the hypocrisy of religious people. And despite some of the pictures of Him that we hang on our walls, Jesus wasn't the smiling God either. Yes, I'm sure He smiled, and I bet He smiled quite a lot. But He wasn't *always* smiling, and I don't think He's always smiling at the smiling church today.

The God described in the Bible is a God who has *emotions*. He's not angry about everything—far from it. But He's not happy about everything either.

We may be uncomfortable with the fact that God has emotions. We'd rather put Him in a tight, predictable box. But He's calling us to discard our tidy boxes and draw near to get to *know Him* better.

Be wary of any preacher who gives the impression that God is either angry or smiling at every person and every lifestyle present in a massive congregation or TV audience. Draw near, and find out what God is saying about *you*. He definitely will smile when you do.

Keepin' It Real?

We don't get to choose what God is like—our only choice is whether we will believe what the Bible says about Him. If we reject the scriptural revelation and try to make God into our own image of Him, He becomes nothing more than an idol or a graven image. (See Exodus 20:3–5.)

We live in a day when the truth about God is under attack. In fact, the very *concept* of truth is under attack. Many people would rather believe a lie and walk in unreality than embrace the true and living God as He really is. (See Romans 1:18–25; John 17:3.)

Why all the fascination with *Duck Dynasty* and other "reality" shows these days? Is it just another example of mindless cultural fluff, or is a profound spiritual message somehow involved?

Who would have believed that *Duck Dynasty* would become such a blockbuster hit series for the A&E Network? Why have so many people become captivated by the chronicles of the Robertson clan's rags-to-riches story as they've turned making duck calls into a lucrative company called Duck Commander?

On a media blitz in New York City, the bearded stars were asked by Matt Lauer on *The Today Show* whether *Duck Dynasty* episodes were "real" or scripted. Family patriarch Phil Robertson replied, "Most of the time we ad lib. Think about it: Some TV producer out of L.A. is fixin' to put words into our mouth? Gimme a break."

Jase, one of the Robertson sons, described the culture shock between the TV producers and the fiercely independent Louisianans: "They come up with ideas, and we just get to be ourselves in the situation."

Is that the secret to the amazing success of the Robertsons, after all—the fact that they "just get to be themselves"?

In various other interviews, the Robertsons have discussed how crucial it is for them to "keep it real," even in the face of constant pressure to compromise their faith and values. Success has its own temptations, but it would be deadly to the show's success if the family tried to fit into some mold set by TV gurus.

Walking in Reality

But if you're anything like me, you probably don't always like "reality." Yes, the truth will set us free (see John 8:32), but first it often brings pain and dismay. I can see why some people prefer to live their whole life in a fantasy world.

And have you ever wondered what people would see if *your* life was a TV reality show? Would it be the most boring program ever, because you never do anything heroic or adventurous? Would you be embarrassed if hidden cameras caught a behind-the-scenes look at what's really going on in your family or career?

Perhaps the reality show cameras would reveal that your public persona is far different from who you truly are. As Jesus described the Pharisees, maybe you're a hypocrite…a play actor… wearing a religious mask or "happy face" to hide your inner reality.

Jesus once told a Samaritan woman who had bounced from one immoral relationship to another, *"God is* Spirit, and those who worship Him must worship in spirit and *truth"* (John 4:24 ESV). There's an important message here about whether we're living lives that are authentic or phony.

The Greek word translated as *"truth"* is *aletheia.* In addition to meaning *truth* in terms of what is right and wrong (e.g., the *truth* of Scripture), *aletheia* has a much broader meaning. It can be trans-lated as "reality," and one Bible dictionary defines it as "candor of mind, which is free from pretense, simulation, falsehood, or deceit."

Many people today are yearning for reality. Perhaps they've never classified themselves as a "seeker of truth," but they're tired of the phony, the fabricated, and the hyped.

Yet, sadly, not everyone is ready to face the truth. Jack Nicholson's character in the movie *A Few Good Men* may have been right when he famously said, "You can't *handle* the truth!"

Let's be honest: At the same time as we applaud the "reality" of a program like *Duck Dynasty*, millions are also watching the *un-reality* of *Keeping Up with the Kardashians*. Do we even have a clue as to what is "real" anymore? Do we even care?

As you've probably guessed, my concern isn't whether the Robertsons or the Kardashians are living in reality or phoniness. My concern is for you and me.

I pray you have some true friends who are helping you "keep it real"—people who refuse to allow you to drift into unreality and self-deception. Even though it's unlikely you'll ever be offered your own TV program, may the *reality of Christ* be evident in your life. Although people will be impacted little by what you *profess*, they can be impacted greatly by the reality of what you *possess*.

While the Robertson clan has made a mark on the world through manufacturing duck calls, you probably won't be attracting any ducks through your sincere walk with Jesus. But I predict you surely *will* succeed as a fisher of men. (See Matthew 4:19.)

Facing Opposition

As we learn to "be real," we'll greatly increase our effectiveness in reaching the world for Christ. But that doesn't mean everyone will like us or accept our message. We have to get it through our head that we *will* face opposition from time to time if we speak the truth and challenge the status quo and political correctness.

Jesus made this very clear:

Blessed are you when they revile and persecute you, and say all kinds of evil against you falsely for My sake. Rejoice and be exceedingly glad, for great is your reward in heaven, for so they persecuted the prophets who were before you.
                                                    (Matthew 5:11–12)

If the world hates you, you know that it hated Me before it hated you. (John 15:18)

Jesus went on to *warn us* that our spirituality may be questionable if *everyone* loves us: **"Woe to you when all men speak well of you,** for so did their fathers to the false prophets" (Luke 6:26).

Catherine Booth, cofounder of the Salvation Army sounded this same warning about lukewarm Christianity that creates no stir or opposition:

> It is a bad sign for the Christianity of this day that it provokes so little opposition. If there were no other evidence of it being wrong, I should know from that. When the church and the world can jog along together comfortably, you may be sure there is something wrong. The world has not altered. Its spirit is exactly the same as it ever was, and if Christians were equally faithful and devoted to the Lord and separated from the world, living so that their lives were a reproof to all ungodliness, the world would hate them as much as it ever did. It is the church that has altered, not the world.

Quite a statement, don't you think? By ignoring the issues of our day, we run the risk of "jogging along comfortably" with the world, not realizing that the world is changing us much more than we are changing the world. Let's not settle for that kind of comfortable compromised Christianity.

4

EMBRACING THE
FOUR FACES OF JESUS

"You have heard that it was said, 'You shall love your
neighbor and hate your enemy.' But I say to you, love your
enemies, bless those who curse you, do good to those
who hate you, and pray for those who spitefully use you
and persecute you, that you may be sons of your Father
in heaven."

—*Matthew 5:43–45*

Recently, a friend and I were discussing some of the hot-button issues in our country today. We mentioned such things as gay marriage, abortion, healthcare, and income inequality, to name a few.

We all have our opinions on such things, of course. As believers, our opinions hopefully have been shaped by God's principles and wisdom found in the Scriptures. In a world filled with moral relativism, we desperately need the Word of God as a plumb line to reveals our off-kilter values and behaviors. (See Amos 7:7–8.)

But while discussing these things with my friend, I saw that being right on the issues is only half the battle. If our beliefs are right, but our attitudes are wrong, no one will be impacted in a positive way. Instead of having a platform to transform our society, we will either be ignored or ridiculed—and we'll have only ourselves to blame.

So, while some people are too timid to address the hot-button issues at all, others undercut their message because of a calloused, unloving attitude toward their audience. They may be *"speaking the truth"* (Ephesians 4:15), but they are failing to do so in *love*.

No wonder we've lost our audience and become largely irrelevant in the debates over the pressing social issues of our day. How sad.

The late author Francis Schaeffer said it this way: "Biblical orthodoxy without compassion is surely the ugliest thing in the world." You've probably met people like that. I know I have.

One of the most notorious groups is Westboro Baptist Church, whose members show up at Gay Pride events and military funerals with condemning picket signs, proclaiming "God Hates Fags," "God Is Your Enemy," "God Hates the U.S.A.," and "You're Going to Hell." This fringe group, led by the late Fred Phelps, considers homosexuality an abomination. Well, perhaps it's an even *bigger* abomination to be such condescending haters, all the while claiming to be followers of Jesus and the Bible.

The Message and the Heart

As I've pondered this unfortunate state of affairs, I've concluded that two problems must be remedied. First, our message must regain its clarity. The apostle Paul warned, *"If the trumpet makes an uncertain sound, who will prepare for battle?"* (1 Corinthians 14:8). Where are the pulpits and publications today that are trumpeting a clear message from God instead of just spiritual mumbo jumbo? Too often, we sound more like politicians than preachers, coming down on each side of every issue. No one will be moved to action by that kind of indistinct trumpet sound.

But as important as it is for our message to regain laser-like clarity, the other problem is perhaps even more urgent: We must speak our message with the heart and "face" of Jesus. This gets back to the attitude and spirit in which our message is delivered. Correct *words* become hollow and impotent unless spoken with a correct *heart*. (See 1 Corinthians 13:1.)

Perhaps you've never given it much thought but this is a crucial issue. If the body of Christ is supposed to express Jesus' "face" to today's world, what *expression* should that be? Anger? Accommodation? Confrontation? Fear? Smugness? Disinterest?

I've concluded there are actually *four* "faces of Jesus" presented in Scripture, and these provide us with a helpful glimpse of what our posture should be as we interact with our society. We see these four faces reflected in the description of the "*four living creatures*" in Ezekiel 1:10 (and mentioned again in Revelation 4:7):

> *As for the likeness of their faces, each had the face of a **man**; each of the four had the face of a **lion** on the right side, each of the four had the face of an **ox** on the left side, and each of the four had the face of an **eagle**.* (Ezekiel 1:10)

If you grew up in a church with stained-glass windows, you probably have seen these four faces depicted. And as Bible commentators have frequently pointed out, the four Gospels each emphasize one of these four characteristics of Jesus' personality and ministry:

+ **LION**: Matthew quotes the most Old Testament prophesies about Jesus, presenting Him as the King and the lion of the tribe Judah." (Regaining our "roar" and seeing a mandate to "reign in life".)

+ **OX**: Mark focuses on Jesus as the "suffering Servant," coming to obey the Father's will and serve humanity by laying down His life.

+ **MAN:** Luke, as a medical doctor, emphasizes Jesus' humanity and His concern for those who were hurting.

+ **EAGLE:** John presented an eagle's eye view of Jesus' life and ministry, revealing Him as the living Word of God who existed from eternity.

As Christians living in the twenty-first century, we are called upon to approach our world with each of these four aspects of Jesus' nature:

+ As **LIONS**, we need to regain our "roar." While we're called to be kings of the jungle—ruling and reigning with Christ (see Romans 5:17)—we've allowed ourselves to become tame and housebroken. Instead of being conquerors and victors, striking terror in evildoers, we've become more like kittens, a threat to no one.

+ As **OXEN**, we must approach our society with the heart of servants. Rather than being known for our angry denunciation of our nation's shortcomings, we need to offer our love, prayers, and service to make things better.

+ As **MEN** and **WOMEN**, we must model the *humanity* and *compassion* of Jesus for those in need. This means *weeping* over our city and our nation, even as we call them to *repentance.* (See Luke 13:34–35.)

+ As **EAGLES**, we must strive to see the big picture and view our world from God's heavenly perspective. The Lord is calling us to come to a higher place of revelation and wisdom than we've had before: *"Come up here, and I will show you things"* (Revelation 4:1). He is saying it again today. And in order to have the maximum impact, the church needs *"sons of Issachar"* (1 Chronicles 12:32)—people with prophetic insight, who understand the times and know what God's people should do.

Jesus said that anyone who saw Him would know what the Father looked like. (See John 14:9.) In the same way, a watching world should be able to know what Jesus looks like by observing the lives of His followers.

The world desperately needs to see Jesus again. But that will only happen if we once again model the face of a lion, an ox, a man, and an eagle. It's time to roar, serve, weep...and SOAR!

What Are YOU "Full Of"?

Years ago, someone jokingly said to me, "George, you're full of it!" While this guy meant his comment in a disparaging way, it really got me thinking: *Exactly what AM I "full of"?*

The Bible makes it very clear what *Jesus* was full of: *"The Word became flesh and dwelt among us, and we beheld His glory, the glory as of the only begotten of the Father, full of grace and truth"* (John 1:14). Do you see how profound this statement is? John isn't saying here that Jesus was full or grace *or* truth, but rather grace *and* truth.

Few of us who are Jesus' followers are really displaying *both* of these vital qualities. Some of us tend to be "grace" people. When we observe a person living in sin of some kind, it's our immediate impulse to forgive them, accept them, and nurture them. "Jesus loves everyone!" is our constant mantra.

Others take delight in being truth-tellers above all else. They don't evidence any grace at all, but they sure are full of *truth!* They love to confront, expose, and challenge, with a goal of provoking repentance in everyone they meet.

What about you, my friend? Do you tend to embrace just one of these qualities, or are you like Jesus, full of *both* grace and truth?

John goes on to say that *"the law was given through Moses, but grace and truth came through Jesus Christ"* (John 1:17). The Law was the *truth*, of course, and Jesus was the truth as well. (See John

14:6.) But while the Law only pointed out people's transgressions, Jesus came to bring forgiveness, restoration, and transformation through His grace—so we don't have to *continue* in a life of sin.

That's the beauty of the gospel message. Instead of offering some kind of "hyper-grace," detached from any truth or consequences, the gospel can be summarized as *"the grace of God in truth"* (Colossians 1:5–6). That's the kind of message God's people should be preaching again today. Not a condemning message focused on law and legalism, nor a "greasy grace" that refuses to confront sin and require repentance. Instead, let us lift up Jesus, the perfect embodiment of both grace and truth.

5

HATERS OR TRUTH-TELLERS?
HOW TO TELL THE DIFFERENCE

"I believe that unarmed truth and unconditional love will
have the final word in reality. This is why right, tempo-
rarily defeated, is stronger than evil triumphant."

—*Martin Luther King Jr.*

We live in days when it can be hazardous to tell the truth. In
some countries, you can be executed or thrown into prison
for speaking the truth, but in America you merely will be ridiculed
or ostracized. This is true even when you speak the truth with a
humble, loving heart, reflecting Jesus in both your message and
your demeanor.

It has become fashionable to brand truth-tellers as "haters."
This is a great way to shut down a debate or conversation, for if
someone truly is a hater, you can safely discredit and disregard
their message. If you question whether taxpayers should fund
abortions and birth control...you must be a *hater!* And you definitely are a *hater* if you openly wonder if gay marriage should be
sanctioned, when marriage has been limited to unions of one man
and one woman for *thousands of years* before our present day.

However, let's be honest: There *are* haters in our world today.
And as I've learned the hard way, some of them are even in the

church. This is scandalous, because Christians are called to be *lovers* rather than *haters*. The Bible clearly commands us to...

+ Love other believers. (See John 13:34–35.)

+ Love our neighbors. (See Luke 10:25–37.)

+ Live peacefully with people of all viewpoints, as much as we can. (See Romans 12:18..

+ Do good toward everyone we meet, not just other Christians. (See Galatians 6:10.)

+ Pray for and respect government leaders, even when we disagree with their policies. (See 1 Timothy 2:1–3; Titus 3:1–3; Romans 13:1–10.)

+ Extend honor to everyone, including our national leaders and our employers. (See 1 Peter 2:13–18.)

So there is no room for Christians to be haters. Even when we must challenge people's viewpoints or policies, we need to do so with humility and respect.

Aveda King, niece of Dr. Martin Luther King Jr., says it well: "There is too much accusing and too little truth and mercy abroad in this present [cultural] battle. Let us consider our frail humanity and approach each other with fear of judgment, pleading for mercy." She goes on to quote the powerful observation contained in James 2:13: *"Judgment is without mercy to the one who has shown no mercy. Mercy triumphs over judgment."*

Don't you love that last statement, about mercy triumphing over judgment? The truth is that we *all* need God's mercy. And if we are to be God's instruments of healing and restoration in this fallen world, we need to practice extending that mercy to others.

However, if we see God as a judgmental, hateful God, we will inevitably become judgmental and hateful ourselves. Only those who have deeply experienced the grace and mercy of God can be in a place speak truth and correction without becoming hateful in the process.

What's the Difference?

It's important to be able to tell the difference between a truth-teller and a hater, but it's not always easy. We can't just go by media labels when they brand a person as a hater or celebrate someone else for courageous speaking up for the truth.

Even on a personal level, our ability to discern the difference will be crucial to our future growth and success. If we give too much credence to people who truly are haters and naysayers, we will end up discouraged or confused as they tear down our identity and undercut our mission. However, if we reject the input of genuine truth-tellers, we're likely to end up full of pride, with dangerous blind spots as to our true condition.

Although it sure would be easier if the haters wore black hats and the truth-tellers wore white hats, it's seldom so clear. I've never met a hater who doesn't claim to simply be "telling it like it is."

Haters are on the rise today, and we want to make sure we aren't among them. At the same time, truth-tellers seem to be increasingly rare, because the *truth* is not politically correct or socially acceptable these days. Today's culture considers being tolerant and nonjudgmental to be the paramount human virtues, and this is problematic for truth-telling. *Anyone* who has a strong opinion is considered a hater, whether they are one or not.

So how do we distinguish between speaking the truth and being a hater? Here are six telltale differences:

1. Truth-tellers are interested in dialogue and relationship, but haters typically "fire bomb" their opponents in hit-and-run style.

2. Truth-tellers have an ultimate objective of help and

healing, but haters want to silence and destroy their adversaries.

3. Truth-tellers have hope that people will acknowledge the truth and repent, but haters are convinced people will never change.

4. Truth-tellers are humble enough to admit they're not always right about things, but haters have a smug, know-it-all attitude.

5. Truth-tellers have a track record of making positive contributions, but haters leave a trail of devastation wherever they go.

6. Truth-tellers demonstrate an ability to find the good in things whenever possible (see Philippians 4:8), but haters usually are negative about *everything*.

Handling a Hater

One day, King David was approached by a hater named Shimei. (See 2 Samuel 16:5–13.) This bitter man from Saul's clan cursed at David, threw stones at him, and called him names like "murderer," "scoundrel," and "worthless man." David's men were outraged, and they wanted to cut off Shimei's head. But to their shock, David said to let Shimei alone, for perhaps the Lord had *told him* to say those things!

David's humility enabled him to realize a vital truth: Just because someone is a hater, that doesn't mean they're not *also* speaking the truth at times. However, rather than following Shimei's example, Ephesians 4:15 says we're to *speak the truth in love.*

If you're a leader, you need to be careful how you handle haters and truth-tellers. Beware of the tendency to surround yourself with people who flatter you as if you can do no wrong. Make sure you have some people in your life who love you enough to tell you the truth—even when it hurts.

When you are criticized, don't automatically conclude that the person is a hater. Take their critique to the Lord and ask Him to show you if any part of it is true.

When Nathan the prophet confronted David about his sin with Bathsheba and Uriah (see 2 Samuel 12), can you imagine what would have happened if David had branded Nathan as a *hater* and rejected his input? We need to make sure we *love the truth* enough to find and embrace the truth-tellers around us. Paul warns in 2 Thessalonians 2:9–11 that those who fail to *"receive the love of the truth"* will be sent a *"strong delusion."* That's not a good outcome.

So, what about you? Have you been too concerned about what the haters and naysayers think about you? Do you have a few faithful friends who can tell you the truth when you've been too blind to see it?

If we're ever going to confront the sins and difficult issues in our society, we must first learn to embrace God's truth in our own lives and relationships.

A New Reformation

Haters sometimes sparkrevolutions, but only the kind of revolutions based on anger, resentment, or class warfare. Truth-tellers can spark revolutions too, bringing about radical solutions that actually make the world a better place.

And sometimes a truth-teller will set off a tidal wave of change that brings about a complete reformation...

In 1517, a common Catholic monk named Martin Luther started a tidal wave in Christendom by nailing his ninety-five theses to the door of Wittenberg Church. Initially he got very little response to this bold challenge to ecclesiastical abuses, but within a year he was put on trial for being a heretic.

The door of the Wittenberg Church was sort of a bulletin board for the university, a place where people could post their events and expound on their views. It's not too much of a stretch to say it was similar to today's blog, Twitter, or Facebook posts, giving people an interactive way to express their concerns or share words of encouragement.

Luther's message on the Wittenberg door challenged the status quo—and, of course, the status quo challenged Luther right back. But when asked to recant his message, he replied:

> Unless I am convicted by scripture and plain reason, I do not accept the authority of the popes and councils, for they have contradicted each other. My conscience is captive to the Word of God. I cannot and I will not recant anything, for to go against conscience is neither right nor safe. God help me. Amen.

According to legend, Luther also said the famous words: "Here I stand. I cannot do otherwise. God help me. Amen!"

We desperately need some "Wittenberg doors" today. The church and the secular culture are again in need of major reformation. People need safe places to ask honest questions about whether the status quo is truly representative of God's highest will for humankind.

Thanks to new technology and the rise of social networks, we have unparalleled opportunities for communication. But hopefully the truly prophetic messages of our day won't be drowned out in the sea of personal trivia and chatter that social networking sometimes represents.

Today, as in Luther's day, we need safe places to deliver "dangerous" messages. Of course, Wittenberg doors present an inevitable risk. There is nothing godly or "prophetic" about personal vendettas or doctrinal axes to grind. The writer of Hebrews warns us not to allow a *"root of bitterness"* (Hebrews 12:15), which will defile many. Yes, we are commanded to be *"speaking the truth"* (Ephesians 4:15) to one another, but Paul makes it clear that the motivation must always be *"in love".*

This call for more truth-speaking will no doubt attract some disillusioned and disgruntled believers who simply want to firebomb the church. But that is a perversion of what the Wittenberg door is all about. Even though we are called to challenge the status quo at times, it must be with a constant realization that the church—warts and all—is the beloved bride that Jesus died to create.

In the Jewish Talmud, the rabbinic teachers forbade people from mocking or jeering at anyone or anything except idolatry. However, idolatry in its many forms—sacred cows, to be exact—is a legitimate target for our inquiry or even our derision.

Luther saw the Reformation as something far more important than just a revolt against ecclesiastical abuses or petty doctrinal differences. He believed it was a fight for nothing less than the true gospel. In a similar way, may God raise up bold leaders today who will point the church and the nation back to God.

Let a new tidal wave of reformation begin!

6

THE PERILS OF STANDING OUT

"Be different, stand out, and work your butt off."

—*Reba McEntire*

I certainly can sympathize with Rodney King's famous question during the Los Angeles riots of 1992: "Can't we all just get along?" That should certainly be our objective, as the apostle Paul told us in Romans 12:18: "*If it is possible, as much as depends on you, live peaceably with all men.*"

But there's also another side to this coin. Many people today have adopted a philosophy of "Go along to get along." They'll do just about anything to fit in and avoid causing a stir. They've compromised their values so often that they no longer know what they believe or even who they are.

So while it's great to do what we can to get along with others, that doesn't mean we must become a conformist or a chameleon. Instead of just fitting in and being "ordinary," everyone has been given a distinct identity and calling. Just as God makes every snowflake beautifully unique, so He has a special design and purpose for each one of us.

Yet most people seem quite willing to blend into the crowd, to be politically correct and commonplace. Especially in today's youth culture, peer pressure promotes mediocrity rather than brilliance. People who want to do something truly magnificent are ridiculed.

The safest posture is to have the same grades, pay grade, or accomplishments as everyone else, because excelling might make others feel bad.

Innovation has always required a rare breed. Only a few people are willing to think outside the box of conventional wisdom. It has never been easy to be a Galileo, Edison, Einstein, or Steve Jobs. And today it seems harder than ever to be a groundbreaker, as the culture tries to push us toward conformity and mediocrity. Who dares to have the audacity to be above average?

Author Warren G. Bennis writes of the boring life of those who refuse to stand out and find their true selves in the midst of a conformist world: "People who cannot invent and reinvent themselves must be content with borrowed postures, secondhand ideas, fitting in instead of standing out." What a drab and empty life!

In case you haven't noticed, a socialistic spirit has been unleashed in our nation in recent years. It's a badge of honor to say you're in the "middle class," but you're certain to be vilified if you are part of the "1%"—meaning those in the upper 1 percentile of income. The Occupy Wall Street protesters proudly declared, "We are the 99%!"

What an abomination. Instead of achieving something extraordinary and uncommon, many peoplewould rather fit in with the 99 percent—the undistinguished masses of humanity.

Biblical Standouts

In contrast, one of the key traits of biblical heroes was their willingness to stand out from the crowd...to be different...to be exceptional. Noah didn't have any competitors in the ark-building industry. He stood alone, and he was mocked for it.

Joshua and Caleb stood alone among the spies who surveyed the Promised Land. Ten other spies said the land was impossible to conquer, and over a million Israelites sided with them against Joshua and Caleb. Yet these two brave men refused to back down.

David stood out as the only man in all of Israel who had the courage to fight Goliath. Despite the ridicule of his brothers and the skepticism of King Saul, David stepped out from the crowd and won a stunning victory.

On another occasion, David was mocked by his own wife, Michal, for "distinguishing" himself from the crowd and worshiping more passionately than anyone else. As the ark of the covenant was being brought into the city, Michal *"saw King David leaping and dancing before the* LORD; *and she despised him in her heart"* (2 Samuel 6:16 NIV).

When Michal later saw David, she mockingly said, *"How the king of Israel has distinguished himself today!"* (2 Samuel 6:20 NIV).

Many people, like Michal, don't want you to distinguish yourself and stand out from the crowd. They will ridicule your passion and criticize your success. Like Michal, their own lives are barren, and they are threatened by your uninhibited creativity and freedom.

But if you're going to be a world-changer, you must be willing to be different from your peers and distinguished from the crowd. You can't be wrapped up in yourself, nor can you let the world squeeze you into its mold. (See Romans 12:2.) And you'll have to accept scorn as the inevitable lot in life of those who challenge the status quo and set a higher standard.

Like David, Daniel was willing to stand out. We're told he *"began distinguishing himself...because he possessed an extraordinary spirit"* (Daniel 6:3 NASB). Faced with tremendous pressure to conform, he and his friends—Shadrach, Meshach, and Abed-nego— refused to bend or bow.

Where are the heroes today? Where are the standouts—men and women courageous enough to rise up and distinguish themselves with an extraordinary life? The future hangs in the balance. Conformists may become popular, but they will never change the world.

Domesticated Lions

It seems most of us Christians in the United States today have become like domesticated lions. While we're called to be kings of the jungle—ruling and reigning with Christ (see Romans 5:17)—we've allowed ourselves to become tame and housebroken. Instead of being predators, striking terror in the princes of darkness, we've become mere pussycats, a threat to no one.

Is anyone afraid of the church in America today? Does the devil quake when the saints of God gather? Are those who pollute our society with moral filth concerned about a holy uprising of the Lord's people in response?

And what about the TV preachers who happily go on secular talk shows to promote their books—yet refuse to take a stand on the moral issues of our day? Rather than represent the true Prince of Peace—the One who angrily cast moneychangers out of the temple—many have become mere pacifists, opting for peace at any price. Instead of challenging the world, we've taken the easy road and accommodated the world.

Meanwhile, God continues to beckon us to *"the ancient paths"* (Jeremiah 6:16 NIV) where we can find true rest for our souls.

Abraham's nephew Lot became a domesticated lion. He thought he had it made when Abraham told him he could choose the most lucrative place to live. But he became soft...spiritually dull...compromised. It's not easy to maintain your spiritual edge when you're living in the lap of luxury.

Yet Lot seemed to think all was well until two angels of the Lord came to visit him one evening. (See Genesis 19.) After all, he was on good terms with the wicked inhabitants of Sodom—or so he thought.

How tragic. But we who are domesticated lions have taken a similar path. Just as Lot thought he could placate the men of Sodom, we smugly think the world actually accepts us. Lot found out too late that the people of Sodom were never fooled by his compromised life.

We who seek to follow Jesus need to remember how He prayed to the Father for us: *"I have given them Your word; and the world has **hated** them because they are not of the world, just as I am not of the world"* (John 17:14).

We all want to be liked and accepted, don't we? That's human nature. But sometimes the call to follow Christ will put us at odds with the world. What will we do then? Will we allow the world to emasculate us and turn us into kittens instead of lions? Or will be willing to die to ourselves and let the Lion of the tribe of Judah rise up big within us?

God wants to replace our pitiful meows with the *roar* of champions again. Are you ready?

The Choice: Be Liked or Respected?

If you were given the choice between being *liked* or being *respected* by people, which one would you choose? Of course, the clever answer is to say we want *both*. We want people to like us and respect us too.

But what if I told you it's not always possible to be both liked and respected? And what if I pointed out that, too often, we tend to do things in order to be liked, even if those things cause us to lose people's respect.

For example, it's understandable if you want your kids to like you. But it's far more important to do what it takes to gain their respect. Insecure parents often try to "buy" the affection of their kids, but that approach always backfires in the end.

Insecure bosses try to be the life of the party and everybody's pal, even though sometimes a good boss has to hurt people's feelings and make decisions that are unpopular.

Many of the Bible's greatest leaders were highly unpopular at times. Moses faced major rebellions, Jeremiah was thrown into a cistern, and the crowd told Pilate to crucify Jesus, the Son of God.

Nevertheless, most of us are people-pleasers at heart. That's why it's so hard to be a good leader, or even a good disciple of Jesus.

Paul explained it this way: *"Am I now seeking the favor of men, or of God? Or am I striving to please men? If I were still trying to please men, I would not be a bond-servant of Christ"* (Galatians 1:10 NASB).

Paul understood that at times we all come to the uncomfortable place where we must choose: Will we seek people's favor or God's favor? Will we be authentic servants of Christ or mere people-pleasers?

A quote attributed to Ed Sheeran says, "I can't tell you the key to success, but the key to failure is trying to please everyone." Well said.

I hope you are a person who is both likeable and respectable. But if you have to choose, I encourage you to do the right thing, even if it's not the popular thing. Put respect above likeability. You'll be glad you did.

Shape-Shifting

Sadly, however, most people have chosen respectability over honorability. I don't want to alarm you, but you're surrounded by a culture of *shape-shifters*—and there's a good chance you may be one too.

Shape-shifters have been a part of literature and folklore in nearly every human culture throughout history. Whether it's a handsome prince who's turned into a frog or a scary alien who's masquerading as a human, shape-shifting always keeps a story interesting.

But I hope you're not offended when I suggest you may be a shape-shifter. I've concluded that we're *all* shape-shifters in one way or another, and that's not always a bad thing.

There's even shape-shifting in the Bible.

Romans 12:2 says, *"Do not be **conformed** to this world, but be **transformed** by the renewing of your mind"* (NASB). Two important Greek words here illustrate the shape-shifting principle. The first is *syschēmatizō,* which means "to be conformed to someone else's pattern or mold." It's not a good thing to allow your "shape" to be determined by external circumstances, events, fads, or relationships. God hasn't called you to be a chameleon, simply blending into whatever your surroundings happen to be at the moment.

The second word is *metamorphoō,* which means "to be transformed, transfigured, or changed into another form or appearance." This is a *good* kind of shape-shifting, for it means we are increasingly becoming on the *outside* of what we already are on the *inside.* Instead of allowing external forces to determine our identity, we have an internal revelation of who God has created us to be.

Paul explains in Romans 12:2 that positive transformation on the outside is impossible unless there has first been a *"renewing of your mind"*—transforming your thinking and nature on the inside.

Jesus, a Shape-Shifter?

It may startle you to discover that even Jesus was a Shape-shifter. Although He existed in eternity *"in the form [morphē] of*

God," He "*made Himself of no reputation, taking the form of a bond-servant, and coming in the likeness of men. And being found in appearance [schema] as a man*" (Philippians 2:6–8).

Jesus' style of shape-shifting was the exact opposite of most people you meet today. While we generally try to put our "best foot forward" and appear to others as someone *greater* than we really are, Jesus humbled Himself and took on a form that *hid* His divine majesty from people's view.

However, three of His disciples were given a brief glimpse of Jesus' inner radiance when He was transfigured [*metamorphoō*] before them one day. (See Matthew 17:1–8.) His appearance on the outside took the form of the brilliant glory He already possessed on the inside.

The devil, of course, is a diabolical kind of shape-shifter. Paul warns in 2 Corinthians 11:14 that Satan disguises himself [*metaschēmatizō*] as an angel of light. Instead of allowing his inner nature to be transformed, Satan merely puts on an outer facade.

So we certainly don't want to be Satan's kind of shape-shifter, trying to fool people by an outward appearance that is different from our true nature. Instead, we want to be changed from the inside out—increasingly transformed into the image of Christ in our daily conduct and relationships.

Our hope of reflecting the glory of God is not in putting on a religious mask or disguise, as so many still do. Since Christ already lives in us (see Colossians 1:27; Galatians 2:20), we must simply allow Him to express Himself—"shifting our shape" more and more into the shape of His image and likeness.

In the end, that's the only way to make a positive impact on the world. "Fitting in" and "getting along" may be applauded in the short run. But ultimately we must be willing to stand out and hold to our convictions if we're going to make a difference.

7

WANTED: *TRUE* RADICALS

"Even now the ax is laid to the root of the trees."

—*Matthew 3:10*

Jesus was a radical preacher, and we need some radical followers of Jesus today. However, the word *radical* has often been misunderstood today. We apply it to people who are haters or lunatics, but this misses the true meaning.

Within hours of the identification of the Boston Marathon bombing suspects, terrorism experts were barraged with an intriguing but misguided question: How did these young men become "radicalized"? After spending several years in the United States, why would they hate us—to such a degree that they would carry out horrific acts against innocent bystanders?

Well, I'm sorry, but this question totally misrepresents what it means to be *radicalized*. There's nothing "radical" about hatred or violence. Those are *easy* traits to adopt, certainly not radical ones. Nor is there anything radical about *envy*—a prominent feature of humankind ever since the sad tale of Cain and Abel.

You see, *radical* means "going to the root or origin" of a problem. Hatred, violence, and class warfare certainly aren't radical by this definition. Why? Because such things only deal with symptoms and external issues, not the root causes.

The Boston bombers weren't true radicals. They were simply angry, envious, and perhaps demonic young men. Their radicalization was counterfeit, for it failed to address the heart of the matter—which is always a matter of the *heart*.

Jesus was a true radical, for He warned people they would never enter into His kingdom as long as they held on to hatred, jealously, or unforgiveness. He rejected the Zealots' call for violence, but He said the answer wasn't in being *religious* either—you must be spiritually reborn. Your proud, hard, self-centered heart must be replaced!

Profile of a Radical

What does it look like to be a true radical? Jesus said you must love your enemies and those who persecute you. Instead of killing people who disagree with you, you must lay down your life in serving them and showing them the truth.

We need some true followers of Jesus today—people radicalized through and through by a gospel message that transforms lives and brings a touch of heaven to earth. We need genuine disciples of a Savior who offers the world healing balm instead of bombs of destruction.

We need leaders who understand what it means to go from comfortable Christianity to radicalization for Christ. May God raise up a new generation of radicals like William and Catherine Booth, who mobilized an army of love and salvation that brought transformation to hell-holes around the world.

May we have more leaders like Martin Luther King Jr., who preached that people should be judged by the content of their character instead of the color of their skin. That message was far more radical than those who prescribed violence as a solution to radical prejudice.

So, are you willing to be radicalized by the lordship of Jesus Christ? Or will you be swayed by counterfeits or an easy believe-ism that requires nothing but verbal assent to the claims of the gospel?

Lukewarm Christians will neither change the world, nor persuade misguided souls like the Boston bombers to abandon their foolish thinking. The only way to defeat counterfeit radicals like the Boston bombers is to become true radicals for Jesus, the Lamb of God and friend of sinners.

Radical Solutions

Those who are true radicals will not settle for superficial, ineffectual solutions to our nation's problems. They recognize that government handouts are temporary solutions at best, and often they make the long-term problems even worse.

True radicals don't engage in demagoguery. Instead of setting up straw men to attack, they go after the core issues and matters of the heart.

True radicals refuse to sway people's emotions by engaging in blame-shifting, unforgiveness, bitterness, or revenge. They speak the truth, resisting the temptation to be people-pleasers and tell folks what they want to hear.

According to these definitions, many would-be radicals are mere imposters, promoting themselves rather than transforming hearts and restoring communities. The list of counterfeit radicals is long. Osama bin Laden wasn't a true radical, for his message had no power to redeem people from sin, death, or hatred. Neither have Malcolm X or Louis Farrakhan been genuine radicals, because their diagnosis of the problem is mistaken or incomplete.

All along, preachers of the gospel of Jesus Christ have had the answer—yet, too often, we've squandered it. Jesus told us to pray,

"*Your kingdom come. Your will be done on earth as it is in heaven*" (Matthew 6:10). But is this the message we've preached? No, often the message of evangelicals has been, "Give your heart to Jesus and you'll go to a better place when you die."

While it's certainly good to know we can have a heavenly home when we leave this life, the true, radical gospel is even better than that. Before we enter the portals of heaven, we have the privilege of participating in the most radical, liberating commission ever presented to humankind:

> *The Spirit of the LORD is upon Me, because He has anointed Me to preach the gospel to the poor; He has sent Me to heal the brokenhearted, to proclaim liberty to the captives and recovery of sight to the blind, to set at liberty those who are oppressed; to proclaim the acceptable year of the LORD.* (LUKE 4:18–19)

You see, God not only wants to bring people to heaven, He wants to bring heaven to people while they're on the earth. But somehow we've often missed this. Either we're so focused on heaven that we're of little earthly good. Or else, we've adopted a well-meaning, humanistic worldview that tries to relieve people's suffering without any assistance from God.

True radicals recognize that they are ambassadors of a heavenly kingdom, and they tap into those resources to make the world a better place.

The Real Cause of Black Poverty

Demagogues would have us think that racism is the main cause of poverty in the black community. And since racism persists, there's little hope of remedying poverty anytime soon.

But if the diagnosis is incorrect, the proposed cures will be misguided too. No wonder poverty rates are virtually unchanged fifty years after President Lyndon Johnson launched his famed War on Poverty.

So what are the true causes of the persistent poverty we see? William Galston, a former advisor to President Clinton, has found that in order to avoid being poor you basically have to do three things: (1) graduate from high school, (2) wait until getting married to have children, and (3) wait until age twenty to have children. Only 8 percent of people who do those three things are poor, compared to 79 percent for those who do not.

Yes, racism still exists, and it means that blacks really do have fewer opportunities than whites. Nevertheless, racism is only a minor cause of black poverty in comparison to other causes, such as out-of-wedlock births and the breakdown of the family.

Racism does not completely explain the higher incidence of crime and drug addiction in the black community. Nor is it the main cause of the three conditions laid out by William Galston. As Bill Cosby said in one of his famous speeches, "What white man made you write a record calling women bitches and hoes?"

In his book, *Civil Rights: Rhetoric or Reality*, economist Thomas Sowell points out the amazing fact that married black couples with college educations and dual incomes actually make slightly *more* than whites. And college-educated black women earn a little more than college-educated white women.

So poverty is not truly a matter of skin color or race after all. At least not as the primary cause. But the race hustlers will never tell you this. Their position and prominence—not to mention their income—are dependent on blaming whites for the plight of those still languishing in poverty.

All along, the answers are much simpler and closer to home. Those who graduate from high school, wait until getting married before they have children, and don't have children until age twenty have a very good chance of avoiding poverty. Of course, there are other factors, too, like the avoidance of illegal drugs or criminal activities. But these are matters of personal responsibility rather than racism or discrimination.

Where Are the Elder Statesmen?

What voices are young black men and women listening to today? With the breakdown of the family, this question becomes even more important. Without adequate parental involvement and discipline, young people will search for wisdom in other places. This may be gang leaders or foul-mouthed rappers, but the influence is not leading the young people to the Promised Land.

So where are the African-American statesmen who can speak words of wisdom and truth to the coming generation? Hardly any of them have even heard of William Galston or Thomas Sowell.

Bill Cosby has spoken out on many of the pertinent issues too, such as his speech in 2004 critical of African Americans who put higher priorities on sports, fashion, and "acting hard" than on education, self-respect, and self-improvement. Instead of blaming the plight of black families on racism, he pleaded with African-American parents to teach their children better morals at a younger age.

But many black leaders criticized rather than applauded Cosby. Michael Eric Dyson, author of *Is Bill Cosby Right?*, wrote in the *New York Times* a few days after the speech, declaring that Cosby's comments "betray classist, elitist viewpoints rooted in generational warfare." He said Cosby was "ill-informed on the critical and complex issues that shape people's lives," and that his words only "reinforce suspicions about black humanity."

And regardless of the truth of Cosby's tough-love message to the black community, it's likely that leverage has diminished these days. Even though he may have some lingering respect and influence among baby boomers, young blacks today are unlikely to be familiar with "Dr. Cliff Huxtable" and his highly acclaimed *The Cosby Show*.

Another voice of sanity and reason today is Bishop T. D. Jakes, pastor of The Potter's House in Dallas, Texas. In an August 2013 interview with Jonathan Merritt of the Religion News Service, Jakes pointed out the lack of strong father figures in the African-American community:

> Fatherhood is seldom modeled to men. And it is hard to be what you cannot see. You and I can walk down to any department store and find a figurine of a mother holding a baby, but we'd have to work hard to find a picture of a man holding one. We're not modeling fatherhood in art or film or in our own homes.

> The fact that we are male enough to produce a child does not make us man enough to raise a child, especially when we are asking men to play a role for which they have no script. My solution is to show men that it is not as much about showing the bad job some have done but lifting up men who do a good job, so we can see what we're trying to be. Until fatherhood is modeled, our men will continue to shrink away from it and the stats will continue to worsen.

> When single parents raise children alone, especially in lower income families, the children are left at home for long periods of time. If children are left to raise themselves in inner-city areas, then gangs become families and gang leaders become daddies and drug dealers become mommas and the person who could've been the second black president of the United States becomes a major drug dealer.

How will we respond to voices of wisdom and reason like this? Will we act like helpless victims who have no control over or responsibility for our circumstances? Or will we take the prescription offered by people like Sowell, Cosby, and Jakes, taking action to restore the black family and avoid out-of-wedlock births?

The answer to these questions will not only affect our own lives but several generations to come. The decisions we make today can help transform generational poverty into a rebirth of generational blessings and prosperity. Yes it's an uphill road, but it's time we get started.

8

WWJD AND THE
RADICAL MIDDLE

"Jesus didn't come to take sides but to take over!"

—*Kirk Franklin*

Years ago, it seemed that *everyone* was wearing a WWJD bracelet. The idea was to remind people to ask "What Would Jesus Do?" as the criterion for every choice and decision.

The WWJD concept wasn't actually anything new. For centuries, theologians had written about the passion Christians should have for *imitatiodei*, the imitation of God. Paul wrote about this in Ephesians 5:1–2: *"Be imitators of God as dear children. And walk in love, as Christ also has loved us and given Himself for us, an offering and a sacrifice to God for a sweet-smelling aroma."* And Peter said Christ had left us an example as His disciples, *"that you should follow His steps"* (1 Peter 2:21).

In 1897, Charles M. Sheldon picked up on this theme in his famous book, *In His Steps: What Would Jesus Do?* Remarkably, the book has sold more than 30 million copies over the years, making it one of the best-selling books of all time.

From the popularity of Sheldon's book and the WWJD bracelets, it would seem like lots of people have been interested in finding out what Jesus would do in various situations. That's a very positive sign, for if we call Him "Lord," we should want to do what He tells us to do. (See Luke 6:46–49; Matthew 7:21–23.)

However, shouldn't we be a little troubled by the huge divides among those who profess to be following Christ? Consider this: Barack Obama, Jeremiah Wright, Jim Wallis, Jesse Jackson, and Al Sharpton all claim to be followers of Jesus. But so do many people on the opposite end of the political spectrum: Rush Limbaugh, Glenn Beck, Bill O'Reilly, Sean Hannity, Sarah Palin, and others.

What's wrong with this picture? Jesus said the world would know He was sent by the Father because of the unity among His followers. (See John 17:21–23.) Yet, day after day, political pundits who say they love Jesus are openly derisive of each other.

Making *Everyone* Squirm

Not only should we be troubled by the disrespectful conduct of professing Christians toward each other, but it's also disconcerting to see how divided they often are on the issues. Does Jesus have a position on the political issues of our day? Does He have a favorite political party, best representing the values of His kingdom?

Sorry to break your bubble, but your political party, candidate, or movement doesn't have a corner on the truth. The kingdom message of Jesus cuts both ways, exposing hypocrisy and inconsistency on the conservative, liberal, and libertarian sides of the political spectrum.

Although Jesus loved everybody, He also made everybody squirm at one point or another. He challenged His disciples when they argued about who among them was the greatest. (See Luke 22:24–26.) He told a respected Pharisee, Nicodemus, that his good works would never get him into the kingdom of God—he had to be born from above. (See John 3:1–10.) He showed the

Sadducees that they were mistaken in their denial of life after death. (See Mark 12:18–27.) He irritated His mother and brothers when He said His true family consisted of anyone who did the will of God. (See Mark 3:31–35.) And He famously made a whip and drove the corrupt moneychangers from the temple. (See John 2:13–17.)

No one "owned" Jesus, not even His family members. He didn't align Himself with any political faction or special interest group. He confronted sin and injustice wherever He found it, not sparing religious leaders, Roman soldiers, or politicians.

Although He made the religious folks uncomfortable, Jesus was criticized for being a "*friend of tax collectors and sinners*" (Matthew 11:19). But notice that He didn't befriend sinners by lowering God's standards in order to court their favor and accommodate their sins. He somehow displayed the amazing love and compassion of a holy God, even while calling on people to repent. (See Matthew 4:17.) And rather than compromising the divine standards, He told people they needed to live by an even *higher* standard of righteous than the Pharisees did. (See Matthew 5:17–20.)

Jesus and the Poor

Can you imagine how disastrous it would be for Jesus to have run for political office in a country like America? Politicians excel at obscuring what they really think. Jesus excelled at speaking the truth. Politicians strive to win votes and make people happy. Jesus strove to transform people's hearts, no matter how unpopular and uncomfortable that might be.

Was Jesus a liberal, a conservative, or a libertarian? If we are going to be like Him (remember WWJD?), it would be good to know His approach on the issues of our day.

The fact is, you can make a case that Jesus would embrace, and rebuke, aspects of each side of the spectrum. No wonder professing believers are so adamant that Jesus is on their side of the debate.

Liberals can rightfully point to Jesus' concern for the poor and the needy. Right from the beginning of His ministry, after all, He declared His passion to bring good news to the poor, the brokenhearted, the captives, the blind, and the oppressed. (See Luke 4:18–19.) While a politician typically favors his or her wealthy donors, Jesus said His constituency was made up of people who were *"poor in spirit"* and *"persecuted for righteousness' sake"* (Matthew 5:3–10).

And don't you love the fact that Jesus interrupted His evangelistic crusade in order to take time out to feed thousands of hungry people? (See Matthew 14:13–21.) What a great example of how "preaching the Word" and "social action" can provide powerful synergy for the advancement of God's kingdom. Yet evangelicals, too, often have neglected the poor, while mainline denominations have sometimes neglected to preach the gospel of salvation.

Conservatives sometimes quote Jesus' words about *"the poor being with us always"* (Mark 14:7), as if that's an excuse for doing nothing to help them. To conservatives, the main solution to poverty lies in trusting the "free market." However, Jesus would likely reply to that argument by pointing out that today's market place is anything but free. Crony capitalism and special interests have tilted the playing field, making it harder than ever for average folks to get ahead.

Pacifists for Jesus?

Entire books could be written to speculate on how Jesus would stand on the other current political issues. For example, what would He say about gun control or involvement in the military?

Again, people can cite His words to promote different sides of the debate.

On the one hand, Jesus clearly favored a nonviolent approach to the settlement of disputes: *"You have heard that it was said, 'An eye for an eye and a tooth for a tooth.' But I tell you not to resist an evil person. But whoever slaps you on your right cheek, turn the other to him also"* (Matthew 5:38–39).

When Peter cut off the ear of the high priest's servant, Jesus rebuked him, saying, *"Put your sword in its place, for all who take the sword will perishby the sword"* (Matthew 26:50–52). Does this mean we should be total pacifists, refusing to participate in our nation's military or even in our own self-defense?

Not so fast. As with many principles of Scripture, there are two sides. While Jesus warned about the dangers of living by the sword, on another occasion He told the disciples to make sure they were armed: *"He who has no sword, let him sell his garment and buy one"* (Luke 22:36).

Does that mean Jesus would advise us to have a gun on hand to defend ourselves or protect our family today? I'll let you decide, but it sure looks that way to me.

Nevertheless, I'm not sure Jesus would defend people's right to own assault weapons, would He? And although He seems to have gotten along well with a Roman centurion in Luke 7:2–10, I think there's a good chance that Jesus would caution believers today about giving unconditional support to the military of a nation that has become the world's policeman.

Regaining the Radical Middle

I've always been a little wary of those who consider themselves political moderates. Too often, this kind of "moderation" seems akin to compromise and people-pleasing. It can become a mushy gushy philosophy that is devoid of any core values or any willingness to take a stand on the issues.

Yet a growing number of people today are embracing a more independent and pragmatic approach to politics. Some of these have branded themselves as "radical centrists," willing to borrow good ideas from the left, the right, or wherever else they may be found. Yes, there is compromise at times, because one of the mottos of radical centrism is "idealism without illusions." In other words, we don't need more ivory tower or ideological proposals—we need solutions that work in the *real world*. This means being both visionary and realistic, passionate and patient.

Radical centrists look for pragmatic, common sense, and common ground answers. Often these are keys that have been in plain sight all along, but partisanship blinded our leaders from recognizing the possibilities.

Some people have sought the radical middle in the context of one of the major political parties, while others have supported independent or third-party movements. Either way, these courageous folks have helped to catalyze needed dialogue and fresh thinking instead of continued polarization.

The people of God are perfectly positioned to bring a kingdom perspective to the debates of our day. Instead of blind loyalty to the right or the left, we are called to be ambassadors of heaven. (See Philippians 3:20; 2 Corinthians 5:20.) Rather than just adding to the overheated rhetoric of our day, we can offer the wisdom of God for the difficult problems we face.

9

WHAT'S WRONG WITH WASHINGTON?

"Insanity: doing the same thing over and over again and expecting different results."

—Albert Einstein

A political revolution is underway in our country. President Obama came to office promising to end "politics as usual," and he received overwhelming support from the African-American community. But after just a few years, disillusionment with our political processes rose to an all-time high.

So what's the solution? A swing to the right? A continued veering to the left? Or should we strive for good old, middle-of-the-road, wishy-washy neutrality?

As a preacher of the gospel, it has troubled me that the church typically (1) avoids political issues altogether, leaving a spiritual vacuum in matters of governmental policy, or (2) chooses sides based on blind partisanship, as if their preferred political party can do no wrong.

So what should we conclude, when most Americans have lost confidence in *both* of the major parties, and when scandals based on money, sex, and influence-peddling have discredited all sides of the political spectrum?

There are basically two things wrong with Washington, D.C.—people and money. People are inevitably flawed, and when folks get too much power or money, those flaws get magnified.

Of course, no organization, organism, family, or social system functions perfectly. But as people throughout the world can now see in vivid display, our current government in Washington, D.C. is more dysfunctional than it has been for many years.

Campaigning or Governing?

One of the problems is that many politicians find it a lot easier to *campaign* than to *govern*. Although we may not have a teleprompter like the President, we *all* tend to be long on rhetoric but short on reality. We can paint an impressive picture of our future intentions, but it's quite another thing to actually bring our vision into fruition.

As a pastor and motivational speaker, I'm very familiar with the enormous gap between campaigning and governing. I *love* to preach (the "campaign" mode), but it's a lot harder to pastor. I find it exciting to inspire large crowds with my pearls of wisdom, but it's rarely as much fun to deal with the day-to-day governance of the church: budgets, board meetings, staff issues, and endless decisions needing my attention.

Like the president, my messages are designed to bring people "hope and change." I want everyone to go away with a new optimism that God can transform their difficult situations into a life of blessing and abundance. Ah, but this is merely the *campaign* mode of ministry. The hard part comes next: people using the truths I've shared to properly govern their lives.

Even though I've never met you, there's something I can confidently predict: Just like the politicians in Washington, your *talk* is probably a lot more impressive than your *walk*. You probably speak glowingly about your intention to lose weight, get your finances in order, help the less fortunate, or spend more time with your family. Yet make sure you don't fall into the "hot air" syndrome—campaigning to impress others with your noble goals but failing to govern your life accordingly.

Just like you and me, our politicians are badly in need of a reality check. It's time to bridge the chasm between rhetoric and reality—to do the hard work of governing, not just the easier work of campaigning.

Traits of Governmental Dysfunction

There are three major causes for the stunning level of relational dysfunction among Washington politicians:

1. *Dys-function starts with dis-respect.* No one likes to be "dissed," but the players in the Washington drama clearly have no respect for each other anymore, nor are they respected by the American people. Leaders of the past, like Ronald Reagan and Tipp O'Neil, were able to disagree without being disagreeable, but that is no longer the case.

2. *Dysfunction happens when labels don't match their accurate definitions.* What comes to mind when you think of the label "Republican"? There are many possibilities. The party of "go along to get along"? The RINOs (Republicans in Name Only)? The party of Lincoln and liberty? The conservatives...libertarians...or Tea Party?

   You see, pinning down the label is more complicated than it sounds, because even this one party has become dysfunctional in some ways. Time will tell whether the Republicans can regain any sense of equilibrium and unity.

   But this doesn't let the Democrats off the hook. The word *democratic* implies *listening to the will of the people*, but have the Democrats been *doing* that the past five years? Not in the least.

Democrats didn't seem to care that a majority of Americans were opposed to Obamacare or wanted it delayed until the bugs could be worked out. They didn't seem to hear the cries of people who are losing their jobs or being reduced to part-time because of the healthcare law's unintended consequences. Instead of living up to their name, "Democrat," they have been dissing the American people.

3. *Dysfunction happens when no one leads.* Perhaps it would be more accurate to say that dysfunction happens when the person who is *supposed* to be leading *refuses* to lead. Coining a phrase to describe President Obama's leadership style, pundits have said he "leads from behind." Instead of getting involved, taking charge, and building a consensus, he more often has been like a parent who sits on the sidelines and watches the children fight.

Sounds like a dysfunctional family doesn't it? No one is in charge, so *everyone* is in charge.

One terrible reality of most dysfunctional families is that they periodically try to patch up their differences and project a "happy family" facade to the world once again. They create some kind of short-term compromise that ignores all of the underlying issues. It's only a temporary fix until the next fight or breakdown. It's playacting, and in the church world we would call it hypocrisy.

It takes a miracle to repair a highly dysfunctional family. Disrespect has to be replaced with respect. People have to fulfill their proper roles. And there needs to be good leadership. Yes, these three things often require a *miracle*—something that only can happen with God's help in changing people's hearts.

In order for our "family" in Washington to become truly functional again, there will need to be some major heart-change as well. But how can that happen when our nation has increasingly disrespected the Lord and left Him out of the picture? It's no wonder that kids fight out of control when their heavenly Father has been banished from the scene.

Using God as Part of Our "Brand"

Washington is also suffering from the tendency we all have to put God and truth in our own "box." It's as if we want to take Him captive as an exclusive part of our own "team" or "brand." But it ends up as a perverse means of control—putting God in our corner and then feeling like *we* have a corner on the truth.

Peter certainly meant well when he offered to put Jesus in a box. (See Matthew 17:1–8.) His proposal wasn't meant as any kind of disrespect. In fact, he thought it would *honor* the Lord to build Him a proper memorial.

When Peter saw Moses and Elijah with Jesus, he got so excited that he thought it would be a great idea to put them in boxes too. He assumed Jesus would be quite pleased to have equal billing with such dignitaries.

It took a voice from heaven to show Peter the error of his ways. Along with James and John, he fell face down to the ground, and *"they only saw Jesus"* (verse 8) when they got up.

Only Jesus. That's the kind of revelation we need as well—a revelation that rids us of all the religious clutter, so Jesus is no longer eclipsed. Wouldn't it provoke an incredible spiritual awakening in Washington if we no longer saw Democrats or Republicans, liberals or conservatives—*only Jesus?*

But throughout human history, people have tried to put God in their boxes. Sometimes this is overt, and several cultures today openly build "spirit houses" to house their myriads of gods.

For those of us who are Christians, the effort to confine and control the Almighty is much more subtle. We put Him in a Sunday morning box, a denominational box, or try to confine Him to the four walls of our church building. We forget that the kingdom of God is much bigger than any church meetings or programs. It's a 24/7/365 sort of thing, after all.

Over and over, we must be reminded that *the Most High doesn't live in temples made by human hands*" (Acts 7:48 NLT). Even when the Israelites had the ark of covenant in sight, God's presence wasn't confined within the box. His glory continually filled the holy of holies and often filled the entire tabernacle or temple. It led the Israelites by a cloud during the day and a pillar of fire by night.

It's the height of arrogance to think we can keep God tucked away in our boxes. Whenever we try to do that, if we're courageous enough to open the box and look inside, we find that He's *gone!*

I'm wondering if this is what happened to the church in Laodicea, described by Jesus in Revelation 3:14–22. They had become lukewarm and spiritually blind, but that wasn't the worst part. Things were so bad that Jesus was on the *outside*, knocking on the door for permission to come back in.

Perhaps the Laodiceans thought they had successfully confined Jesus to their tidy box of religious rituals and programs. Yet all the while, He had *escaped*—as He always does when we attempt to confine Him. Fortunately, there was still time to hear His voice and have fellowship with Him again. Do you hear Him knocking today?

Jesus is knocking on your door and the door of your church. He's also knocking on the door of our nation, patiently waiting for people to invite Him back to the place of reverence and honor He once was given.

Getting the Favor Back

I can't tell you for sure whether America's Founding Fathers were influenced by the New Age or infiltrated by the Illuminati. But some of the Latin phrases they used are pretty intriguing.

Recently I took a look at *Annuit Coeptis,* a motto found on the back of the Great Seal of the United States and on the back of our one-dollar-bills. This Latin phrase can be translated "He (or Providence) favors our undertakings" or "He has prospered our endeavors."

Wow. Our Founders somehow realized they never would have succeeded without divine favor. This recognition of the need for God's favor should be *our* testimony as well.

A psalm attributed to Moses reflects this passion very well: *"May the favor of the LORD our God rest on us; establish the work of our hands for us—yes, establish the work of our hands"* (Psalm 90:17 NIV).

Of course, there are two sides of this "favor" issue. In one sense, if we are positioned *in Christ,* we already have as much of God's favor as we could ever have. (See Romans 8:31–32.) It's surely not a commodity we can *earn.*

Yet we're also given examples in Scripture of people—including Jesus Himself—who *"grew in wisdom and stature, and in favor with God and man"* (Luke 2:52 NIV). Isn't it good to know you can have *more* of God's favor tomorrow than you have today?

So my prayer for you and me—and for our nation—is that we will recognize the incredible favor God offers through a position in His beloved Son. (See Matthew 3:17.) And then may we *grow* in His wisdom, experiencing an ever-increasing outpouring of His favor on your endeavors.

Friend, *Annuit Coeptis* can be the testimony of our lives! And once that happens, there will be a ripple effect throughout our family, our community, and perhaps all the way to Washington, D.C.

10

THE BLIND MEN AND
THE ELEPHANT

"Every truth has two sides; it is as well to look at both,
before we commit ourselves to either."

—*Aesop*

R*adicals*, by definition, have a passionate commitment to
"truth." They know what they believe and are zealous about
sharing that truth with others.

But what happens if the "truth" we see is incomplete—only a
partial glimpse at something that is much bigger than our present
comprehension? You've probably heard the oath courtroom witnesses
often take to tell "the truth, the whole truth, and nothing but the
truth." Although that is a noble objective, can any one of us really say
that we possess "the *whole* truth"? And even in our finest moments,
can we legitimately claim that our message is "*nothing* but the truth"?

There's a lot we can learn about this from the famous poem by
John Godfrey Saxe (1816-1887):

It was six men of Indostan
To learning much inclined,
Who went to see the Elephant
(Though all of them were blind),
That each by observation

Might satisfy his mind.
The *First* approached the Elephant,
And happening to fall
Against his broad and sturdy side,
At once began to bawl:
Is very like a WALL!"

The *Second*, feeling of the tusk,
Cried, "Ho, what have we here,
So very round and smooth and sharp?
To me 'tis mighty clear
This wonder of an Elephant
Is very like a SPEAR!"

The *Third* approached the animal,
And happening to take
The squirming trunk within his hands
Thus boldly up and spake:
"I see," quoth he, "the Elephant
Is very like a SNAKE!"

The *Fourth* reached out an eager hand,
And felt about the knee
"What most this wondrous beast is like
Is mighty plain," quoth he:
"'Tis clear enough the Elephant
Is very like a TREE!"

The *Fifth*, who chanced to touch the ear,
Said: "E'en the blindest man
Can tell what this resembles most;
Deny the fact who can,
This marvel of an Elephant
Is very like a FAN!"

The *Sixth* no sooner had begun
About the beast to grope,

Than seizing on the swinging tail
That fell within his scope,
"I see," quoth he, "the Elephant
Is very like a ROPE!"

And so these men of Indostan
Disputed loud and long,
Each in his own opinion
Exceeding stiff and strong,
Though each was partly in the right,
And all were in the wrong!

I love this story, which has spread across the world in various versions. It's fascinating that each of these men could be both right and wrong at the same time. They were correct about what they perceived, yet each of them had perceptions that were *incomplete*.

I see this principle at work all the time, both in politics and in the church. People tend to feel very certain about what they have *experienced*, and rightfully so. Those of us from minority groups are more likely to have experienced racial prejudice, and that is very real to us. Meanwhile, those in the white majority often have a hard time believing that racial discrimination is still much of a problem a full century and a half after the Emancipation Proclamation.

We all have a limited view of the "elephants" in the room, don't we? Smug about what we think we "know," we don't recognize that we can be right and wrong at the same. As a result, we tend to adopt *half-truths*, not realizing that the *other* half may be in error.

God is the only One who sees the whole picture. Yes, we can experience more and more of the Lord as we read His Word and draw near to Him in prayer. But nevertheless, the Bible says, *"we know in part and we prophecy in part"* (1 Corinthians 13:9). In eternity, we will have a much fuller view of the elephant, but *"now we see in a mirror, dimly"* (verse 12).

So if you ever have to take the witness stand in a court of law, you may want to think twice when they ask if you swear to "tell the truth, the whole truth, and nothing but the truth." When it gets right down to it, you're only qualified to testify about the part of the elephant you've actually *experienced*. Even then, your perceptions may be clouded in some way. And don't dare try to promote hearsay or secondhand theories as credible evidence.

Acting Like Adolescents

Have you ever met someone who thinks they "know it all," with no need for the advice or input of anyone else? That's a common characteristic of adolescence. Young children usually are humble enough to recognize their need for the wisdom of their parents. Likewise, as people enter their twilight years, they often are struck by how much they still don't know about life.

In contrast, teens frequently think they've got it all figured out. They can't believe how *ignorant* and narrow-minded their parents and teachers are. Who do the old fogies think they are?

But here's the sad thing: Every day, we can see politicians and preachers who *still* are acting like adolescents. They've only touched a portion of the elephant, yet they arrogantly act like they are experts on everything. It's humbling to face the fact that you only know *"in part,"* but that's *reality.*

The sad thing about the six blind men is *not* that they couldn't fathom what the whole elephant was like. Even if they had their eyesight, they're perceptions would be incomplete, just as our knowledge of God will inevitably be: *"Oh, the depth of the riches both of the wisdom and knowledge of God! How unsearchable are His judgments and His ways past finding out!"* (Romans 11:33)

The trouble with the blind men is that they didn't *listen to* or *respect* the perceptions of the others. If they would have quit arguing for a second, they could have *learned something* from each other. Even though they only knew in part, think of how much more they would have known if they had the humility and wisdom to put their "parts" together.

Abraham Lincoln once said, "I don't like that man. I must get to know him better." This principle has profound implications. What if the Democrats, Republicans, and independents actually *listened* to each other? What if fundamentalists, mainline denominations, charismatics, and Pentecostals could acknowledge and appreciate the value of each other's experiences and beliefs? And what if rich and poor, black and white, young and old could all join hands to celebrate their unique perspectives and personalities?

In Ephesians 3:18–19, Paul says it is only *"with all the saints"* that we will experience *"what is the width and length and depth and height—to know the love of Christ which passes knowledge; that you may be filled with all the fullness of God."* Without each other, we will never be complete—yet, too often, we have remained isolated and detached from other parts of the body politic or the church.

Spiritual Inbreeding

You may think it's a disgusting word picture, but I'm going to say it anyway: There's a whole lot of spiritual and political inbreeding going on in today's world. Let me explain why this is a big problem.

The Old Testament laws against incest are related to laws of genetics that are now well known. When those in a family or a small group only engage in marriage or sexual relations within their group, the eventual result tends to be sterility, retardation, and other malformations in their offspring. The more generations the process continues, the more severe the results will become.

Do you see the parallels with the political world and the church? Many groups are suffering from political or spiritual inbreeding. Decades of interaction mostly within their own group has left them sterile, malformed, and retarded from their full potential.

At times the body of Christ looks like a jigsaw puzzle that has been poured out and scattered all over the floor. If the pieces would ever come together in proper alignment, the world would see a beautiful picture of Jesus instead of fragmentation or even animosity and distrust.

Jesus said our love and unity would be a sign to a watching world. (See John 13:34–35, John 17:20–23.) And the psalmist described the outbreak of God's blessings when Christians "*dwell together in unity*" (Psalm 133:1–3). Do you see why the devil fights our unity so tenaciously?

Unity without Uniformity

Unity doesn't necessarily require uniformity. We shouldn't have to have perfect agreement on all points of doctrine. In fact, just as with the blind men, we actually can benefit from rubbing shoulders with people who come from different backgrounds.

Of course, there are some basic truths that every Christian should acknowledge. And, in the same way, there are some central precepts of liberty that every American should embrace.

But I love the old maxim that puts our unity in perspective:

In essentials, unity.
In non-essentials, liberty.
In everything, charity [love].

But often I run into people who think it's the *other* group who doesn't want unity. Republicans say the disunity in Washington is because of the Democrats, and vice versa. Pastors tell me they would *love* to have more unity among churches in their city—but the *other* pastors just don't seem interested.

We need each other! The problems facing America won't be solved by Democrats or Republicans operating alone. The Great Commission will never be fulfilled by just one denomination or movement.

I've discovered over the years that I even need people who are much different than me. I've come to appreciate the *diversity* of the body of Christ as each member and every group expresses their unique spiritual gifts and callings. (See 1 Corinthians 12:20–27; 1 Peter 4:10–11.)

But what if someone is intent on discrediting you and tearing down everything you believe in? This is how many of us felt when John MacArthur promoted his vitriolic book and conference, called *Strange Fire: The Danger of Offending the Holy Spirit with Counterfeit Worship*. How would *you* like your worship style and beliefs to be branded as "counterfeit" and offensive to the Holy Spirit?

However, at times like that, it's good to remember Edwin Markham's famous poem entitled "Outwitted." Markham wrote the poem after he was defrauded by a business partner, but finally was able to forgive the man after much struggle:

> He drew a circle that shut me out,
> Heretic, rebel, a thing to flout.
> But love and I had the wit to win,
> For we drew a circle that took him in!

Some of us need to reexamine the circles we've drawn in the past. Instead of shutting people out, our heart should be to include all who are sincerely following Christ. Yes, they may not have a "revelation" of the entire elephant—but neither do you.

I love this quote from British author C.S. Lewis:

> There is someone I love, even though I don't approve of
> what he does.
> There is someone I accept, though some of his thoughts
> and actions revolt me.
> There is someone I forgive, though he hurts the people I
> love most.
> That person is me.

This is a good reminder to stay humble in our opinion of ourselves and our dealings with others. When it comes right down to it, we rarely have as much trouble with the other guy than we with ourselves—the man (or woman) in the mirror.

Whose Side Is God On?

If you listen to preachers debate theological issues, they generally imply that *they* are the true guardians of sound doctrine, while their opponents are the heretics. We see the same principle at work in the political world, where Democrats and Republicans all love to promote the idea that God supports them on the issues. And I guess if you were a blind man trying to describe an elephant, you surely would want people to know that God endorsed your conclusion.

So whose side is God *really* on?

There's a great story in Joshua 5:13–15 that should give us cause for concern on this subject. The scene takes place shortly before Joshua is planning to lead the Israelites against the formidable city of Jericho. This was the first step in his campaign to take possession of the Promised Land, and Joshua was facing some anxiety.

As he was gazing at Jericho in preparation for the coming events, Joshua was suddenly confronted with a mighty angel of the Lord, with his sword drawn for battle. The angel clearly would be a formidable warrior, and Joshua certainly hoped he had come to fight on the side of the Israelites.

"Are You for us or for our adversaries?" (Joshua 5;13) was his logical question for the angel.

However, the angel didn't frame his answer the way Joshua might have hoped: *"No,"* the angel replied, *"but as Commander of the army of the Lord I have now come"* (verse 14).

Do you see the irony here? Joshua hadn't asked a yes or no question. He wanted to know—as we *all* do—whether God was going to fight on his side or on his enemy's side.

But God never comes to *take sides;* He comes to *take over!* The angel's reply let Joshua see an important insight about spiritual warfare: Instead of trying to get God to fight on *our* side, we had better humble ourselves to make sure we are aligning ourselves with *His* side.

Joshua got the message loud and clear. Falling on his face to the earth, he worshiped God and said, *"What does my Lord say to His servant?"* (verse 14). Liking this response, the Commander of the Lord's army told Joshua to take off his sandals, for he was standing on holy ground. (See verses 14–15.)

What a great model for us, as well. The Bible tells us, *"If God is for us, who can be against us?"* (Romans 8:31). But the surest way to know that God is truly *"for us"* is to make sure our highest objective is to seek His kingdom and accomplish His will. When we're willing to do that, Jericho will be no match for us.

11

THE HUMILITY OF TRUTH-TELLERS

"Do you wish to rise? Begin by descending. You plan a tower that will pierce the clouds? Lay first the foundation of humility."

—*Saint Augustine*

As we've already seen, being a truth-teller is a hazardous proposition. Nevertheless, God wants to raise up a prophetic generation of people willing to boldly declare the truth.

Why are we willing to take the risk of speaking the truth? Paul tells us in 2 Corinthians 3:12: "*Since we have such a hope, we are very bold*" (ESV). You see, we speak out boldly on the issues of our day because we have *hope* that people will receive our message and take corrective action. We believe that the truth will make the world a better place.

But I've learned that it's vitally important to speak the truth in *humility*, in addition to hope and boldness. Yes, it's a high calling to be God's spokespeople, but we must never forget the other side of the coin: "*We have this treasure in jars of clay to show that this all-surpassing power is from God and not from us*" (2 Corinthians 4:7 NIV). Hubris is an occupational hazard of radicals and truth-tellers, for we tend to forget where our strength comes from.

Yes, God wants to use us to shake the world for Jesus, but an old story helps to put this in perspective:

An elephant and a mouse were crossing a rickety wooden bridge. As they set foot on the bridge, it rumbled and shook at the impact. Once they had safely reached the other side, the mouse proudly remarked, "We really shook that bridge, didn't we?"

When we walk with the Lord, the "bridges" we cross may shake at times. We are called to make an impact in our communities…our cities…our nations. If we aren't careful, though, we will make the same mistake as the mouse—taking *credit* for the impact, as if we were the star of the show.

Paul made a number of statements to the Corinthians that showed his deep awareness that he would accomplish nothing of substance without the power of God (the elephant!). He rejoiced at the wonderful treasure that the Lord had deposited in his life, but he also realized that he himself was merely an earthen vessel—a "*jar of clay*" as the *New International Version* translates it.

Paul said his role with the Corinthians was as a servant. (See 2 Corinthians 4:5 niv.) Doesn't that seem ironic in a way? One of the greatest men of God who ever lived changed the world not only through his boldness—but also through being a servant to others.

What Humility Is and Isn't

When the subject of humility comes up, many believers picture some sort of self-flagellation, or a mindset of constantly putting themselves down. That is not true humility at all. Rather than being genuine humility, which comes from seeing the holiness and awesomeness of our God, this is a pseudo humility, spawned by a "religious spirit" rather than by the Holy Spirit.

You see, instead of thinking *bad* about ourselves, true humility is not thinking much about *ourselves* at all! Samuel Wilberforce recommended, "Think as little as possible about yourself. Turn your eyes resolutely from any view of your influence, your success, your following. Above all, speak as little as possible about yourself."

Humility is basically the grace to accept God's evaluation of us. It means recognizing that we are merely "jars of clay" that have been honored to hold the priceless treasure of the Spirit of God. It means having an awareness that if the bridge shakes, we can't take the credit. Paul said it this way:

> He who boasts is to boast in the Lord. For it is not he who commends himself that is approved, but he whom the Lord commends. (2 Corinthians 10:17–18 NASB)

> By the grace of God I am what I am. (1 Corinthians 15:10)

There is a vast difference between true humility and false humility. Those who project false humility are often some of the proudest people around! When someone gives them a compliment, they get a "holy" look in their eyes and reverently point to heaven, saying, "It really wasn't *me*; it was the Lord." While their words may sound quite religious and modest, they are in effect putting on airs—they are *boasting* in their "humility." D. Martyn Lloyd-Jones pointed this out:

> If our humility is not unconscious, it is exhibitionism. We can be proud of our humility, and indeed I think we always are if we try to give the impression of humility.

Far from trying to give the impression of humility, some of Paul's statements may sound to us as the epitome of conceit:

> I am not in the least inferior to the 'super-apostles,' even though I am nothing. (2 Corinthians 12:11 NIV)

> I know that when I come to you, I will come in the full measure of the blessing of Christ. (Romans 15:29 NIV)

Would you consider someone humble if he told you he ranked right up there with Peter, John, and the other top apostles in church history? Wouldn't you think it a bit presumptuous if he promised that on his next visit he would doubtlessly come in *"the full measure of the blessing of Christ"*?

Though we might well be put off by such apparent boasting, this was actually a display of true humility! Paul was accurately communicating *God's* view of him! Indeed, he wasn't inferior to the most eminent apostles. And his confidence that the full blessing of Christ would work through him was not meant as a reflection on his personal merit—it was a declaration of his trust in God's faithfulness. Paul admitted to the Corinthians that having to boast about such credentials was a foolish thing to do, but he insisted that their obstinacy drove him to do it. (See 2 Corinthians 12:11.)

False Humility Doesn't Please God

Many Christians hold the mistaken view that God is pleased when we put ourselves down. How could that be, when *"we are His workmanship"* (Ephesians 2:10 NASV)? To criticize ourselves is to criticize the workmanship of God. As the saying goes, "God doesn't make junk!"

Many of the great men and women in the Bible initially tried to use false humility to excuse themselves from the commission God had for them. Each time, the Lord rebuked them. For example, God wasn't impressed with Moses' "humility" when he claimed he wasn't eloquent enough to lead the Israelites:

Then Moses said to the LORD, "O my Lord, I am not eloquent, neither before nor since You have spoken to Your servant; but I am slow of speech and slow of tongue." So the LORD said to him, "Who has made man's mouth? Or who makes the mute, the deaf, the seeing, or the blind? Have not I, the LORD? Now therefore go, and I will be with your mouth and teach you what you shall say." But he said, "O my Lord, please send by the hand of whomever else You may send." So the anger of the LORD was kindled against Moses.

(Exodus 4:10–14)

From our perspective, Moses was just being humble. From God's perspective, Moses was actually doing the very opposite of true humility—he was placing his own evaluation of himself above God's. While hiding under the guise of modesty, nothing could be more proud and presumptuous. Rather than being pleased by Moses' excuses, *"the anger of the LORD was kindled against Moses."*

When God called Jeremiah, a similar conversation took place:

Then the word of the LORD came to me saying: "Before I formed you in the womb I knew you; before you were born I sanctified you; I ordained you a prophet to the nations." Then said I: "Ah, Lord GOD! Behold, I cannot speak, for I am a youth." But the LORD said to me: "Do not say, 'I am a youth,' for you shall go to all to whom I send you, and whatever I command you, you shall speak. Do not be afraid of their faces, For I am with you to deliver you," says the LORD. Then the LORD put forth His hand and touched my mouth, and the LORD said to me: "Behold, I have put My words in your mouth. See, I have this day set you over the nations and over the kingdoms, to root out and to pull down, to destroy and to throw down, to build and to plant....Therefore prepare yourself and arise, and speak to them all that I command you. Do not be dismayed before their faces, lest I dismay you before them. For behold, I have made you this day a fortified city and an iron pillar, and bronze walls against the whole land—against the kings of Judah, against its princes, against its priests, and against the people of the land. They will fight against you, but they shall

not prevail against you. For I am with you," says the LORD,
"to deliver you." (Jeremiah 1:4–10; 17–19)

Like Moses, Jeremiah had an excuse for why he could not possibly fulfill the awesome call of God on his life. But as He had done in response to Moses' pleas of inadequacy, God told Jeremiah to quit sucking his thumb: "Prepare yourself and arise!"

Contrary to what we might expect, the Lord never seems very impressed when we tell Him how inadequate we are. Paul made it clear that he had learned this very lesson: *"Not that we are adequate in ourselves to consider anything as coming from ourselves, but our adequacy is from God, who also made us adequate as servants of a new covenant"* (2 Corinthians 3:5–6 NASB).

Aren't I Humble!

One of the most amazing Bible verses on humility is found in Numbers 12:3: *"Now the man Moses was very humble, more than all men who were on the face of the earth."* What's incredible is that Moses himself was the one who wrote this glowing account of his humility! It's like the old joke about the guy who said, "I used to be proud, but then I recognized that pride was a sin. So I repented, and now I'm humble."

Moses' statement that he was the most humble man on earth made its way into Scripture—because it was God's assessment too. If you are "too humble" to ever say anything good about yourself, you are merely the victim of false modesty, which may be the greatest hubris of all.

David, like Moses, was not afraid to declare his humility:

O LORD, my heart is not proud, nor my eyes haughty, nor do
I involve myself in great matters, or in things too difficult for
me. (Psalm 131:1 NASB)

Can you say, as David did, "My heart is not proud"? If not, it is probably either because you are in fact full of pride and need to humble yourself, or because you have been gripped by false humility and need to learn to tell the truth about yourself, even if it sounds "proud."

An Indispensable Leadership Trait

Most true leaders throughout history have come across as cocky or arrogant at times. That is because confidence is an indispensable quality of every successful leader. One such leader was General George Patton, of whom it was said by one of his biographers, Porter B. Williamson, in *General Patton's Principles for Life and Leadership*:

> Several Patton authors called the General arrogant, foolhardy and flamboyant. No writer caught the importance of the pistols, the arrogant lectures, and the flamboyant actions as the carefully rehearsed and planned actions of a man who knew how to lead men into combat with the enemy and with death. No writer who called General Patton foolhardy caught the importance of immediate pursuit of the retreating enemy. No writer caught the humility andthe religion of General Patton.

What is remarkable about this observation concerning Patton is that Williamson could at the same time point out his outward arrogance and flamboyance, yet his actual humility of heart. As inconsistent as this might seem to us, leaders throughout history could have been described in similar terms. Churchill, MacArthur, and Teddy Roosevelt are just a few of those who could be named in the twentieth century alone. Likewise, some of the most effective church leaders in history—people such as Luther, Wesley, Finney, and the apostle Paul—all had a confidence that at times appeared to be arrogance.

Is this cockiness to be considered a godly quality? Before going on to address the very real dangers of spiritual pride, we need to recognize the tragedy of leaders who have jettisoned all confidence, in fear of being seen as arrogant. Hebrews 10:35–39 warns:

> *Therefore do not cast away your confidence, which has great reward. For you have need of endurance, so that after you have done the will of God, you may receive the promise: "For yet a little while, and He who is coming will come and will not tarry. Now the just shall live by faith; but if anyone draws back, My soul has no pleasure in him." But we are not of those who draw back to perdition, but of those who believe to the saving of the soul.*

As many other Scripture passages make clear, this confidence is not to be based on our own ability or merit, but on the faithfulness of God. Our English word *confidence* comes from two Latin words, *com*, meaning "with", and *fidere*, meaning "trust" or "faith". Genuine confidence simply means that we are able to move forward *"with faith."*

Not only is this confidence indispensable to a leader's *survival*, it is also an indispensable quality for *motivating anyone to follow us.* Listen to the way Patton would motivate his troops: "I want the enemy to know they are fighting the toughest fighting men in the world! We are the best, and don't ever forget it. Don't let anyone forget that we are the best!"

Church leaders can learn a lot from the leadership principles modeled by great military generals such as Patton. We too are in a war! The church needs leaders full of the same confidence and boldness that were displayed by Patton. God is not pleased when we exchange our confidence for the false humility of a "Caspar Milquetoast."

The Other Side of the Coin

There is another side to all of this, of course. Solomon says it bluntly: *"Pride goes before destruction, and a haughty spirit before a fall"* (Proverbs 16:18). As Vance Havner once remarked, "If we learned *humility*, it might spare us *humiliation."*

While false humility is a worthless sham, we desperately need true humility. *"God is opposed to the proud, but gives grace to the humble"* (James 4:6 NASB). If you think it's bad having the devil oppose you, try facing the opposition of God!

Paul repeatedly warns the Corinthians about the dangers of spiritual pride, describing it as the exact opposite of God's character, which is love: *"Knowledge puffs up, while love builds up"* (1 Corinthians 8:1 NIV); *"Love...does not boast, it is not proud"* (1 Corinthians 13:4 NIV). Ironically, both pride and false humility have the same effects—keeping us from obeying God and loving people.

This is no minor issue. Paul compares the arrogance of the Corinthians to the leaven that had to be purged every year by the Jews at the Feast of Unleavened Bread:

> *Your boasting is not good. Do you not know that a little leaven leavens the whole lump of dough? Clean out the old leaven, that you may be a new lump, just as you are in fact unleavened. For Christ our Passover also has been sacrificed. Therefore let us celebrate the feast, not with old leaven, nor with the leaven of malice and wickedness, but with the unleavened bread of sincerity and truth."* (1 Corinthians 5:6–8 NASB)

By definition, a leader is one who exercises authority. Power has an inherent tendency to produce a sense of arrogance, which makes it all the more essential that those in leadership continually humble themselves before the Lord. *"Humble yourselves under the mighty hand of God, that He may exalt you in due time"* (1 Peter 5:6),

Peter says—in a context particularly focusing on the role of leaders. (See 1 Peter 5:1–11.)

As already stated, the goal of humility is not to produce self-abasement, but rather to help us see ourselves accurately. Paul tells the Romans, *"I say, through the grace given to me, to everyone who is among you, **not to think of himself more highly than he ought to think**, but to think soberly"* (Romans 12:3). True humility enables us to see ourselves as God sees us—not more highly *or* more lowly than we really are.

Jesus Himself set the ultimate example of a leader's humility:

> *Let this mind be in you which was also in Christ Jesus, who, being in the form of God, did not consider it robbery to be equal with God, but made Himself of no reputation, taking the form of a bondservant, and coming in the likeness of men. And being found in appearance as a man, He humbled Himself and became obedient to the point of death, even the death of the cross. Therefore God also has highly exalted Him and given Him the name which is above every name, that at the name of Jesus every knee should bow, of those in heaven, and of those on earth, and of those under the earth, and that every tongue should confess that Jesus Christ is Lord, to the glory of God the Father.* (Philippians 2:5–11)

For those who would follow Jesus' model of leadership, *the way up is down!* As He instructed His disciples, *"Whoever desires to become great among you shall be your servant. And whoever of you desires to be first shall be slave of all. For even the Son of Man did not come to be served, but to serve, and to give His life a ransom for many"* (Mark 10:43–45).

The Humility Test

The ultimate humility test is simply going into the presence of God and asking Him what He thinks of you. In His presence, our arrogance is shattered and our areas of inferiority are healed. This is described in Isaiah 40:3–8, a passage foreshadowing the ministry of John the Baptist:

> *The voice of one crying in the wilderness: "Prepare the way of the LORD; make straight in the desert a highway for our God. Every valley shall be exalted and every mountain and hill brought low; the crooked places shall be made straight and the rough places smooth; the glory of the LORD shall be revealed, and all flesh shall see it together; for the mouth of the LORD has spoken." The voice said, "Cry out!" And he said, "What shall I cry?" "All flesh is grass, and all its loveliness is like the flower of the field. The grass withers, the flower fades, because the breath of the LORD blows upon it; surely the people are grass. The grass withers, the flower fades, but the word of our God stands forever."*

God makes it clear that He wants to not only level the *"mountains"* of pride in our lives, He also wants to raise up the *"valleys"* of inferiority and negative self-talk. Only then will He have a highway upon which to move in our lives and reveal His glory.

In order to be effective, truth-tellers must be confident without being cocky, bold without being bombastic. This kind of posture is only possible with God's help. Some of us have a natural tendency toward arrogance, while others struggle with feelings of inferiority and shame. Fortunately, the Lord can heal *either* of these conditions if we let Him.

Whose Applause?

Billy Graham told a fanciful story about the young donkey that carried Jesus down the Mount of Olives into Jerusalem during His triumphal entry. (See Luke 19:28–40.) Later that day, the colt is talking to one of his fellow donkeys:

"You'll never guess what happened to me today."

"What?" his friend inquired.

"As I was coming into town, everyone bowed down and laid palm branches and garments in the road to greet me!" the donkey exclaimed. "They all shouted, 'Hosanna! Blessed is he who comes in the name of the Lord!'"

"That is incredible," marveled his friend. "I've been down that road many a time, and no one ever gave me that kind of reception. How do you merit such treatment?"

"Well, I always knew I would be famous someday," the young donkey explained. "It's about time I got the respect I deserve!"

Silly as this story may seem, many leaders have made precisely the same mistake as the donkey that carried Jesus. When Jesus is "riding us," there will indeed be applause at times. But we must never forget that the *hosannas* are not for us, but for the One who accompanies us. True humility knows Who the applause is for, and true humility will ultimately cast all its crowns and accomplishments at His feet:

The twenty-four elders fall down before Him who sits on the throne and worship Him who lives forever and ever, and cast their crowns before the throne, saying: "You are worthy, O Lord, to receive glory and honor and power; for You created all things, and by Your will they exist and were created."
(Revelation 4:10–11)

A Hedge Against Temptation

One of the most important traits of humble people is the ability to admit their mistakes and repent when they recognized when they've been wrong. Along this line, conservative broadcaster Glenn Beck made a very interesting statement as he reflected back on his days as a host on Fox News:

> I made an awful lot of mistakes, and I wish I could go back and be more uniting in my language. I think I played a role, unfortunately, in helping tear the country apart. I didn't realize how really fragile the people were. I thought we all knew we were in it together.

You may or may not agree with Glenn Beck on the issues. But you have to admire this kind of willingness to humble himself and admit his mistakes and the effect they've had on others. Hopefully, you can acknowledge your errors as well. In the end, this kind of introspection and humility will cause people to respect you more and be more willing to accept your message.

Keep humility in mind when we take a look at the temptations of a leader in the next chapter. Because *"pride goes before destruction"* (Proverbs 16:18), there is no better hedge against temptation than humility. As *The Pilgrim's Progress* author John Bunyan once observed, "He that is down needs fear no fall."

Yet pride is an occupational hazard of many truth-tellers. Hey, if we are "right," it's easy to get puffed up and full of ourselves, isn't it? This means we must be *intentional* about humbling ourselves—first before the Lord, and then as servants of humanity.

But arrogance is a dangerous and unacceptable path for those who want to accurately represent God's kingdom in a broken world. Saint Augustine rightly said, "It was pride that changed angels into devils; it is humility that makes men as angels." I don't know about you, but I still have a long way to go before people call me an angel!

12

WHY DO SO MANY
MINISTERS FALL?

*"We have renounced the hidden things of shame, not walking
in craftiness nor handling the word of God deceitfully, but
by manifestation of the truth commending ourselves to every
man's conscience in the sight of God."*

—2 Corinthians 4:2

Sometimes I'm tempted to be embarrassed to tell people I'm a minister of the gospel. Don't misunderstand me. I'm *not* saying I'm ashamed of Jesus or the gospel. But the embarrassing thing is that there are so many preachers who have fallen into one scandal or another.

Yes, the clergy is in disrepute in many people's minds these days—especially those of us who have TV ministries or large churches. What will it take to restore people's respect for preachers today? How can ministers shut the door on temptation and scandal in their lives?

Some of my ministry friends blame the media, of course. "We've got to face it, Bishop Bloomer," they tell me, "the world hates men and women of God, and they'll do whatever they can to destroy us."

How would *you* respond to a statement like that? There's clearly an element of truth in the fact that secular comedians and news executives often take delight in the mishaps of preachers. But why do we give them so much *ammunition* for their attacks and ridicule?

A reporter once asked me what is the biggest challenge facing the Black church—education, the recession, broken homes, or some other problem. While numerous social and economic issues could be cited, I'm convinced the fundamental need in the Black church (or *any* kind of church) is for integrity in the pulpit, where leaders drop their pomp and pretense and come clean before God and their flock. Only then will we become a mighty force for righteousness and restoration in our communities.

Black churches teach our parishioners to respect, honor, and cover their leaders. But the church also needs a relentless pursuit of truth and holiness, holding pastors accountable to their high calling. As the prophet Amos declared long ago, *"Let justice roll down like waters and righteousness like an ever-flowing stream!"* (Amos 5:24 NASB). And instead of just blaming our critics, we need to make sure *justice* and *righteousness* are beginning with *us*.

Peter makes an important distinction between being *"reproached for the name of Christ"* or simply suffering because of our own foolish behavior:

> *If you are reproached for the name of Christ, blessed are you, for the Spirit of glory and of God rests upon you. On their part He is blasphemed, but on your part He is glorified. But let none of you suffer as a murderer, a thief, an evildoer, or as a busybody in other people's matters. Yet if anyone suffers as a Christian, let him not be ashamed, but let him glorify God in this matter. For the time has come for judgment to begin at the house of God; and if it begins with us first, what will be the end of those who do not obey the gospel of God? Now "If the righteous one is scarcely saved, where will the ungodly and the sinner appear?"* (1 Peter 4:14–18)

So, if you are being criticized by the news media or by your unbelieving coworkers, don't automatically assume they just "hate Jesus." Take an honest look at your life and make sure your actions and attitudes are a good representation of Christ. If not, it's time to repent!

Be Wary of Pedestals

Part of the problem is that preachers have too often allowed themselves to be put on pedestals by their followers. We strut around like proud peacocks, as if we're so close to God that we can never be tempted.

However, the truth is this: Although we may have God's anointing and heavenly halos, we also have feet of clay. We are subject to the full range of human temptations, and in many ways, our circumstances make us a special target for Satan's snares.

The most frequent scandals among ministers involve one of three broad areas of temptation: money, sex, and power. Or as one old preacher used to say, "The devil has no new tricks. He is still trying to tempt men of God with the gold, the gals, and the glory."

Many ministers and churches have discovered the hard way that it is important to have precautions in place to guard against financial wrongdoing. No temptation other than sexual sin has resulted in more disgrace to the body of Christ. Whether it is the deacon who steals money from the offerings or the pastor who controls the church finances and pays himself an exorbitant salary, integrity in financial issues is crucial for regaining the church's credibility in our society.

The key financial safeguard is accountability. Each aspect of the finances of a church or ministry should have checks and balances. Much of this is simply common sense:

+ It is unwise to have just one person count the offerings.

+ Someone should be reviewing the bank deposits, checks written, and other cash-flow matters.

+ Instead of pastors setting their own salaries, this should be done by a financial council within the church and/or an impartial group of leaders outside the local congregation.

+ Ministers normally should be prohibited from receiving salaries or bonuses in the form of cash or items of property that make verification and accountability impossible.

+ Churches and ministries should have clear written guidelines about how preachers should be compensated from such things as the sale of their books, music, teaching series, or other products.

+ Church members or supporters of a ministry should have the right to see the budget and know how the money is being spent.

Will these kinds of financial safeguards prevent all abuses? Unfortunately not. However, abuses can be minimized if wise precautions are put into effect. A church or ministry that enacts such safeguards will increase its credibility and foster a sense of trust and security among the people.

Influence-Peddling

While many Christian leaders express disgust when our nation's political leaders pander to the biggest donors, perhaps we should also look in the mirror. Do we grant more authority or prominence to people in the church who have the big bucks?

No honest pastor can look you in the eyes and say they haven't faced this temptation, if not actually succumbed to it. Churches need money, and those with money often expect power—do you see the potential for an unholy matrimony?

The Bible makes it clear that the selection of those given authority in the church must be on the basis of spiritual maturity and character. (See Acts 6:3; 1 Timothy 3:1–13; Titus 1:5–9.) Instead, the church has often given special favor to the proud and courted the involvement of those who have the most to give financially.

Godliness is often made secondary when selecting church officers, and in many churches it seems to be scarcely considered at all. Church boards have been stocked with those who have succeeded in business rather than those who have succeeded in shepherding their family or fulfilling the Great Commission.

Yet this is not a new problem. James saw the same danger in the churches of his day:

> My brethren, do not hold the faith of our Lord Jesus Christ, the Lord of glory, with partiality. For if there should come into your assembly a man with gold rings, in fine apparel, and there should also come in a poor man in filthy clothes, and you pay attention to the one wearing the fine clothes and say to him, "You sit here in a good place," and say to the poor man, "You stand there," or "Sit here at my footstool," **have you not shown partiality among yourselves**, and become judges with evil thoughts? (James 2:1–4)

If James were writing today, what would he say to pastors who deny giving preferential treatment to major financial contributors? "Take a look at your appointment books," he might challenge them. "Have your lunch appointments been only with the rich and powerful members of your church? Has your time been spent pouring your life into those who have the most spiritual hunger, or merely wooing those most able to advance the church bank account and image?"

This is certainly not to advocate that we favor the poor and reject people just because they are wealthy. God forbid. That, too, is an ungodly form of partiality. There is only one form of partiality that is proper, and it has nothing to do with a person's financial assets. Paul tells Timothy to give priority to the discipleship of *"faithful men"* (2 Timothy 2:2 NASB). We may—in fact, we *should*—give ourselves disproportionately to those who are truly hungry for the things of God.

The Devil's Playground

You've probably heard the old maxim, "Idle time is the devil's playground." Although many preachers have little "idle time" at all, few occupations present more opportunities for sin—especially sin of a sexual nature.

Consider these risk factors:

- *Ministers frequently have unstructured and unsupervised time.* Even though ministers may be extremely hard working and busy, their work usually isn't the same as those who punch a time clock. Those in ministry often can set their own hours, enabling them to disappear from the church office for hours at a time, without anyone really knowing where they've gone.

- *Many ministers are involved in counseling their parishioners.* This sometimes includes hearing rather intimate details about marital problems, emotional needs, and temptations.

- *In some churches, it is considered permissible, if not expected, for the pastor to make house calls.* Few other professions have this built-in vulnerability to temptation.

- *In the process of caring for the needs of others, those in the ministry often become drained and lonely themselves.* Constantly giving out to others, ministers often feel a deep need for affirmation and affection. If we don't learn to get our needs met from our relationship with God and our spouse, this yearning for warmth and intimacy can lead to disastrous results.

- *All too often, ministers neglect their own marriages.* When those in ministry are not enjoying their relationship with their spouses, they are putting themselves in a position of great vulnerability. This frequently is compounded when the neglected spouse becomes a nag, and then the minister then has even *less* of a desire to spend time at home. After "fighting the good fight" on the church "battlefield" all day, it isn't much fun to come home to an unhappy, unfulfilled spouse. In the meantime, the devil is more than willing to send you some adoring church member of the opposite sex who thinks you are terrific.

- *Members of the opposite sex are often particularly attracted to those in ministry, regardless of the minister's outward appearance.* Even a bald, wrinkled minister with a potbelly may be appealing if he exudes the love of God and a concern for others. There is something "sexy" about a man or woman of God who is filled with the Spirit and who speaks with a sense of confidence and authority.

- *Members of the opposite sex (and most people, in general) tend to have a higher regard of a minister than his or her own spouse does.* The spouse knows what the minister is like when dead tired or irritated at unruly church members. Most parishioners, on the other hand, see the minister only when behind the pulpit and full of faith and power. What a trap this is, for an affection-starved minister can be very susceptible to positive, seductive feedback that is too seldom received at home.

- *After constantly giving out to others, ministers can feel a twisted sense of "deserving" someone else to minister to them.* The fact is, we all do need others to encourage and minister

115

to us, but if this need is not being met in proper ways, there will be a great temptation to meet it in illicit ways.

* *Those in authority often have a unique ability to rationalize their sins away.* A dangerous arrogance often comes with "power." How could a man of God like David fallinto adultery with Bathsheba? One likely factor was arrogance—feeling that because he was king, he had a *right* to do whatever was necessary to get his "needs" met. (See 2 Samuel 11.) Another aspect of this pride is the delusion that because we're in authority we will be able to *get away with* sin. The Word of God is clear that leaders should not expect to get away with anything, for their judgment will actually be even *more severe* than non-leaders face. (See James 3:1.)

* *Those under extreme stress (whether in the ministry or a secular leadership position) have a greater tendency to fall into sexual sin as an attempt to relieve the pressure.* Successfully handling the pressures of ministry is an important part of minimizing sexual temptation. Many ministers have taken on burdens that God never intended them to shoulder, not realizing how susceptible that makes them to the enemy's schemes.

* *Ministers often have a particularly difficult struggle with being transparent and accountable.* While a person who wants to be delivered from sexual addiction might go to his pastor for confession, counsel, and accountability, who are the pastors to go to if *they* get caught in some sin? It's crucial for those in the ministry to have genuine and "safe" friends—people with whom they can share their struggles without fear of rejection or betrayal. However, since such relationships among leaders are rare, areas of temptation often do not get addressed until the leaders have already fallen and been found out.

• *Ministers are a prime target of the enemy.* This may seem like a lame excuse, akin to the comedian's famous line "The devil made me do it!" But this explanation isn't totally off the mark. The devil is real, and leaders are his favorite target.

Precautions for Purity

Although the ministry has many built-in "risk factors," that shouldn't be a cause of fatalism or despair. Each of the danger points listed above can be counteracted, at least to some degree, by prayerful, positive action on the part of ministers. Paul spoke of *"taking precaution so that no one will discredit us"* (2 Corinthians 8:20 NASB). If we are wise, we will take some precautions too.

In November 1948, toward the beginning of his ministry, Billy Graham held a rather unfruitful crusade in Modesto, California. Graham and his team sought God for why the community response was so poor, asking themselves the probing question, "Why do people tend not to trust Christian ministries, especially evangelists?"

This honest self-examination by Billy Graham's team brought six areas of preventative concern into focus: money, sexual immorality, sensationalism, hyper-emotionalism, digressions into temporary emphases or issues other than the gospel, and insensitivity to the entire body of Christ. After identifying these areas of vulnerability, Graham's team wrote up a "Modesto Manifesto," which provided specific precautions they would adhere to. This was a strategic point in their ministry, laying a firm foundation for the integrity that would characterize the organization ever since.

In a similar way, Rick Warren, senior pastor of Saddleback Valley Community Church in Foothill Rancho, California, has taken a proactive approach to guarding himself and his staff from sexual temptation. As a safeguard against moral lapse—or even the *appearance* of evil—he has presented his staff with these "Ten Commandments":

1. Thou shalt not visit the opposite sex alone at home.
2. Thou shalt not counsel the opposite sex alone at the office.
3. Thou shalt not counsel the opposite sex more than once without the person's mate being present.
4. Thou shalt not go to lunch alone with the opposite sex.
5. Thou shalt not kiss any attender of the opposite sex or show affection that could be perceived as improper.
6. Thou shalt not discuss detailed sexual problems with the opposite sex in counseling situations.
7. Thou shalt not discuss *your* marriage problems with an attender of the opposite sex.
8. Thou shalt be careful in answering cards and letters from the opposite sex.
9. Thou shalt make your secretary your protective ally.
10. Thou shalt regularly pray for the integrity of other staff members.

Some may quibble about the details of Rick Warren's proposal, thinking him too strict in some areas. But the question remains: What precautions are *you* taking to avoid falling into sexual sin?

A pastor friend of mine was helped by a Christian "recovery group" to gain some insights into the sexual addiction he had fallen into. One of his discoveries was that there are four conditions that heighten someone's susceptibility to temptation, which spell the acronym H-A-L-T:

+ **H**unger
+ **A**nger
+ **L**oneliness
+ **T**iredness

When you are hungry, angry, lonely, or tired, you need to take *extra* precautions that you don't fall prey to Satan's traps. A good example of this is Elijah in 1 Kings 19, where it seems that each one of the four H-A-L-T conditions was present. These conditions combined to make the normally courageous man of God much more vulnerable to Jezebel's verbal arrows than he otherwise would have been.

The Power Trip

Lord Acton, the British historian, once said, "Power corrupts, and absolute power corrupts absolutely." Of course, this statement is not always true. God has absolute power and obviously isn't corrupted by it. The Lord wants to empower His people too, not to corrupt us but to make us His witnesses. (See Acts 1:8.)

Yet it is true that power and influence often *do* appeal to our tendency to become proud and seek our own glory. Paul warned the Corinthians that knowledge often *"puffs up"* (1 Corinthians 8:1.), or makes people arrogant. And John described the *"pride of life"* as one of the three ways the world would tempt us, along with *"the lust of flesh"* and *"the lust of the eyes"* (1 John 2:16 NASB).

Are there precautions we can take to avoid the trap of pride? Yes, indeed. The first is simply to regularly and consciously humble ourselves. It was in the context of addressing leaders that Peter gave one of the Bible's clearest warnings about pride:

> *All of you be **submissive to one another**, and be clothed with humility, for "God resists the proud, but gives grace to the humble." Therefore **humble yourselves under the mighty hand of God, that He may exalt you** in due time.*
>
> (1 Peter 5:5–6)

Peter's exhortation contains two parts, challenging us to both *humble ourselves before God* and ***also** submit to other people* the Lord has put over us. How are you doing in these two areas? Are you regularly humbling yourself under God's mighty hand? And are you receiving the input, correction, and accountability provided by other believers God has put in your life?

However, God is not limited to these two methods of bringing us to humility. The apostle Paul discovered that along with the tremendous revelations he received, he also was given a *"thorn in the flesh"* (2 Corinthians 12:7 KJV). Though Paul clearly describes this as a *"messenger of Satan"* (not God), he nevertheless recognized that God permitted the thorn to continue *"lest I should be exalted above measure through the abundance of the revelations."*

If we don't humble ourselves, or allow ourselves to be humbled by the input of other believers, God may choose to take matters into His own hands and *help* us humble ourselves!

Eradicating Dishonesty

Although the Bible gives plenty of warnings to leaders about sexual immorality, financial wrongdoing, and the arrogance of power, there is another danger that Paul frequently mentions. In fact, this sin—dishonesty—is at the root of almost every other temptation.

Paul made it a point to tell the Corinthians that he had *"renounced the **things hidden** because of shame, not walking in **craftiness** or adultering the word of God, but by the **manifestation of the truth** commending ourselves to every man's conscience in the sight of God"* (2 Corinthians 4:2 NASB). At their very roots, sexual or financial sins are based on dishonesty. They are *"things hidden,"* the result of walking in darkness instead of the light. Unless we have a sincere love for the truth, we will find ourselves drifting into craftiness and deceitfulness.

Paul spoke the truth, and the truth brought conviction to people's consciences. He told the Corinthians, *"By setting forth the truth plainly we commend ourselves to everyone's conscience in the sight of God"* (2 Corinthians 4:2 NIV). But Paul realized that before he could impact the conscience of others, he first needed to take pains to maintain a clear conscience himself:

> Now this is our boast: **Our conscience testifies** that we have conducted ourselves in the world, and especially in our relations with you, with integrity and godly sincerity.
> (2 Corinthians 1:12 NIV)

> So **I strive always to keep my conscience clear** before God and man. (Acts 24:16 NIV)

Paul likewise warned his apprentice Timothy to keep his conscience pure, saying that some other leaders had suffered shipwreck because of failing to do so:

> Timothy, my son, I am giving you this command in keeping with the prophecies once made about you, so that by recalling them you may fight the battle well, holding on to faith and a **good conscience** which some have rejected and so have suffered shipwreckwith regard to their faith.
> (1 Timothy 1:18–19 NIV)

Too often, those of us in ministry allow ourselves to indulge in small acts of dishonesty. We don't see the exaggerations in our fund-raising letters, conference ads, and brochures as *lying*, yet often they come pretty close. We may even jokingly refer to such falsehoods as "evangelistically speaking," somewhat akin to fishermen who "harmlessly" embellish their tales about the fish they've caught.

But such dishonesty grieves the Holy Spirit. Although it typically starts small and seems relatively harmless, it will ultimately destroy our ministry unless we repent. More than anything else, *Satan's* leaders are characterized by deceit and disguise. (See 2 Corinthians 11:13–15.) When we participate in exaggeration or deception, we put ourselves in league with that same spirit. (See John 8:44; Revelation 21:8.)

Have you, like Paul, *"renounced the hidden things of shame"*—or are there still secret areas of your life that you would be ashamed to have your friends and family see? If a tabloid like the *National Enquirer* investigated your life, what kind of story would they write? Would you be embarrassed if people knew the books and magazines you read, and the movies and TV shows you watch?

Even though such concerns about our reputation may validly serve to keep us from sin at times, there is a much more important reason to flee from temptation. When Paul told the Corinthians he had renounced deceitfulness, he explained that it was *"in the sight of God"* (2 Corinthians 4:2). That is the ultimate key to overcoming temptation—the realization that *God* is constantly watching.

Although Paul wanted to do what was right *"not only in the eyes of the Lord but **also in the eyes of man"*** (2 Corinthians 8:21 NIV), his main concern was pleasing the Lord. (See 2 Corinthians 5:9.) He understood that the coming judgment would delve into matters invisible to those around us—not just our actions but the hidden motives of our hearts.

> *My conscience is clear, but that does not make me innocent. It is the Lord who judges me. Therefore judge nothing before the appointed time; wait till the Lord comes. **He will bring to light what is hidden in darkness and will expose the motives of the heart.** At that time each will receive his praise from God.*   (1 Corinthians 4:4–5 NIV)

We should not wait to address our secret sins until we stand before the judgment seat. Unresolved sin is a perilous matter that will ultimately affect our family, our flock, and our testimony among unbelievers. If we don't repent, we might even become another tragic ministry casualty on the public stage. And it's always a devastating outcome when truth-tellers who have faithfully preached to others end up stumbling in their own lives.

13

BACK TO THE OLD-TIME RELIGION?

"Oh, that You would rend the heavens! That You would come down! That the mountains might shake at Your presence."

—Isaiah 64:1

I'll admit, I have mixed feelings when I hear people talk about getting back to the "old-time religion." You see, I've met some "religious" folks who don't look much like Jesus. They seem more like old-time *legalists* than old-time saints.

I know what I'm talking about. I grew up in a legalistic church where the women all wore long dresses and had their hair put up in buns. They weren't allowed to wear jewelry, wear pants, or use makeup. And they always kept their head covered in church.

To tell you the truth, they all looked *miserable* most of the time. And I was miserable too. If this was what it was like to truly follow Jesus, I decided I wanted no part of it.

Fortunately, I eventually met the real Jesus. I was relieved to discover that He was nothing like the legalists who were so proud of their religiosity and so condescending toward others who didn't dress like them or share their views.

Jesus made it clear that *love* and *unity* would be the earmarks of His followers (see John 13:34–35; 17:20–23), and we just don't see enough of that in the church today. The church needs an awakening today, making us lovers rather than haters, problem-solvers rather than mere critics. As Abraham Lincoln once said, "He has a right to criticize, who has a heart to help."

And when it comes to true religion, we're sorely misguided if we think that means carrying a big Bible, attending church with all our Christian friends, and saying "Praise the Lord!" all the time. Instead, we're told, *"Pure and genuine religion in the sight of God the Father means caring for orphans and widows in their distress and refusing to let the world corrupt you"* (James 1:27 NLT).

So I'm totally in favor of going back to the old-time religion if it means loving Jesus enough to care for orphans, widows, and other people in distress. Any other kind of spirituality is *false* religion, putting people in bondage rather than setting them free.

You've probably run into smug religious people like this. Like the Pharisees Jesus scolded, *"They crush people with unbearable religious demands and never lift a finger to ease the burden....Like whitewashed tombs—beautiful on the outside but filled on the inside with dead people's bones and all sorts of impurity....Hypocrisy and lawlessness"* (Matthew 23:4; 27–28 NLT).

If we are going to successfully challenge our society on the moral issues of our day, we must do some housecleaning at home. We must regain true spirituality—to make us more like Jesus— and discard religious hypocrisy that has made us too much like the Pharisees.

Although I consider myself an evangelical, I'm not always on board with how things are done in some evangelical churches. We've done a pretty good job of preaching on John 3:16 and the need for an individual to be born again, and that is a crucial starting point. But if our religion is genuine, it will bear fruit not only in changing our own lives, but also our families and our communities. Transformation starts with the salvation of a "soul," but God then wants to save families, churches, communities, and even nations.

Jesus' Keynote Address

In Jesus' first recorded teaching, He chose Isaiah 61 as His text. (See Luke 4:16–22.) He could have selected many other excellent passages from the Old Testament, so why was His keynote address based on Isaiah 61? For one thing, it was widely acknowledged as a messianic prophecy, and Jesus was beginning to reveal Himself as the Messiah. But it also provided a fitting preamble to His anointed earthly ministry *"to bring good news to the poor... comfort the brokenhearted...proclaim that captives will be released and prisoners will be freed"* (Isaiah 61:1 NLT). He was telling *"those who mourn that the time of the LORD's favor has come"* (verse 2).

Isn't that wonderful news, even today? There are *still* countless people who are poor, brokenhearted, and in need of comfort. There are *still* multitudes of people imprisoned by sin, addictions, toxic relationships, fear, and depression, desperately in need of deliverance.

Jesus came to help people like this—people like you and me. Instead of allowing us to languish on the ash heap, He offers us *"a crown of beauty"* and *"a joyous blessing."* He wants to replace our anxiety and despair with *"festive praise."* And instead of leaving us like hapless trees blown over by the circumstances of life, He wants to make *"great oaks...planted for his own glory"* (verse 3).

Isaiah 61 is a beautiful passage, and I have heard many excellent sermons on how God can transform a person's life through the "great exchange" described there. However, it's important not to forget the rest of the chapter. The good news presented in Isaiah 61 extends past individual salvation to the transformation of entire communities and cities.

Those whose lives are changed by God's grace are given a powerful mission to fulfill: *"They will rebuild the ancient ruins, repairing cities destroyed long ago. They will revive them, though they have been deserted for many generations"* (Isaiah 61:4).

Read that again and let it really sink in. If you are a child of God, He has commissioned you to *"rebuild the ancient ruins, repairing cities."* Do you know any cities that need to be rebuilt and repaired today? Of course you do. Places like Detroit and Oakland are in the news, but it's a good bet that *your* city needs some repairs as well.

It's time for the urban churches to lead a turnaround in their communities. We need to throw off our feelings of defeat and victimhood, instead embracing what God's Word says about us:

> *Instead of shame and dishonor, you will enjoy a double share of honor. You will possess a double portion of prosperity in your land, and everlasting joy will be yours....I will faithfully reward my people for their suffering and make an everlasting covenant with them. Their descendants will be recognized and honored among the nations. Everyone will realize that they are a people the* Lord *has blessed.*
>
> (Isaiah 61:7–9 NLT)

You are called to be a victor instead of a victim. Instead of being bullied by the world and squeezed into its mold, you are called to be salt and light, bringing hope and transformation in the name of Jesus.

How to Change the World

Just as *religion* is a word often misunderstood in our society, so is the word *revival*. You've no doubt driven by churches that proudly display a sign that says: REVIVAL TONIGHT! Often, the sign includes the name of some evangelist, pastor, or bishop who is conducting a series of meetings to win people to Christ and fire up the church.

I'm certainly not against holding a special series of meetings like this, but we need a different kind of revival today.

Years ago, there was a pastors meeting where two different pastors shared radically different paradigms of how the church can change a city or a nation. Edward and Richard were both sincere men of God, and their churches were roughly equal in size at that point. Even though they served churches in the same city, they had never met each other.

As the pastors ate breakfast and shared their visions for ministry, Edward spoke of his passion for a revival in his church. He believed that Christ would return in a short time, and the best way to gain a harvest was to fervently pray for a mighty spiritual awakening that would sweep thousands into the kingdom. For Edward, this wasn't mere talk—he and the intercessors of his church were holding regular prayer meetings to ask God for a fresh outpouring of the Holy Spirit. They had not seen any dramatic changes yet, but they were full of anticipation.

As Edward shared his vision, Richard listened patiently, but you could tell he didn't share Ed's zeal for revival. When his turn came, Richard revealed that he wasn't expecting Christ to return anytime soon. He made it clear that he believed in the second coming, but he said he didn't want his church to use that as an excuse for failing to lay a strong foundation for future generations. To him, revival would be fine if it came, but his focus was on faithfully discipling Christians, day by day—whether revival ever came or not.

Like Edward, Richard carried out his ministry in a way that was consistent with his paradigm. His church had a persistent outreach to the local college campus, and several hundred students had been converted over a period of years. Many of these students had gone through Richard's lengthy discipleship and leadership training program, and several of these young people were now on his staff.

So what's the point to this story? you may be wondering. Actually there are several points. First of all, we need to realize how our entire ministry will be shaped by the basic assumptions and paradigms that we hold. In the case of Edward and Richard, their ministries were simply a reflection of their understanding of Bible prophecy and their paradigm for how the harvest could best be reaped.

Second, the story of Edward and Richard should cause us to ask several questions about our own ministry priorities. Should we put all our eggs in the "revival" basket, or focus more on building a careful infrastructure where evangelism, discipleship, leadership training, and church planting can occur? Is this really an either/or question, or can we successfully pursue both at the same time?

Let's take a closer look at these issues.

Do We Need a Revival?

Any fair and thoughtful observer of church history would have to acknowledge that God has, from time to time, brought powerful moves of His Spirit to bear upon the church. Nearly always, these have come in response to the desperate prayers of His people, at a time when the church was in general decline. It is hard to imagine the low level that Christianity would have sunk to by today if it had not been for these periodic spiritual awakenings.

Famed revivalist Jonathan Edwards spoke of the importance of these "special seasons" of God's powerful intervention:

> God hath had it much on His heart, from all eternity, to glorify His dear and only begotten Son; and there are some

special seasons that He appoints to that end, wherein He comes forth with omnipotent power to fulfill His promise and oath to Him; and these times are times of remarkable pouring out of His Spirit, to advance His kingdom; such is a day of His power.

Although Edwards was wary of emotionalism, he knew that genuine revival was a matter of the heart, not just the mind. "The heart of true religion is holy affection," Edwards wrote. "Our people do not so much need to have their heads stored, as to have their hearts touched." As someone has observed more recently, the key to revival is not *theology* but "*knee-ology.*"

The word *revival* comes from a Latin word meaning "to bring back to life." Jesus could rightly challenge many American churches in the same strong terms He used to address the church at Sardis in Revelation 3:1: "*You have a name that you are alive, but you are dead*" (NASB). At such times, it is fitting to cry out as the psalmist did, "*Will You not revive us again, that Your people may rejoice in You?*" (Psalm 85:6).

Arthur Wallis' classic book, *In the Day of Thy Power*, provides evidence that even a brief revival can often accomplish more than would otherwise be achieved by fifty years of ordinary ministry. That being true, Wallis points out, the questions are inescapable:

> If God can achieve such mighty things in times of revival, and if the spiritual labors of 50 years can be surpassed in so many days when the Spirit is poured out, why is the church today so satisfied with the results of normal evangelism? Why are we not more concerned that there should be another great revival? Why do we not pray for it day and night?

If we could catch a glimpse of the amazing way God worked in past revivals, we would surely have more hunger for one today. The revivals of the past shook nations. Bars shut down. Prostitution became unprofitable. The jails were nearly empty because crime practically stopped. The very foundations of the church and the surrounding society were shaken.

The revivals around Rochester, New York, in the early 1830s resulted in between fifty thousand and one hundred thousand conversions in a little more than a year. From 1830 to 1835, approximately two hundred thousand people were saved in that area. Many of these conversions were the result of Charles Finney's ministry, and 80 percent of his converts remained true to the Lord and a part of a church.

In 1904, the Welsh Revival broke out, and more than seventy thousand converts were reported in just two months. Evan Roberts, the most notable figure in the revival, was only in his mid-twenties when it started, and most of the others used in the revival were even younger. With scarcely any organization, advertising, or human leadership, a flame was lit that visitors carried with them around the world.

The Azusa Street Revival began at a little house at 312 Azusa Street in Los Angeles, with seats for only about thirty people. The seats consisted of wooden planks on empty nail kegs. The leader was an uneducated Black man named William J. Seymour, who was blind in one eye. Despite these humble beginnings, the whole world has been impacted by what God began there!

What about Now?

As stirring as these revival stories might be, we still have to ask the question: What about today? Should we be as Pastor Edward, who centered his entire church life around the quest for revival, or can we learn something from Pastor Richard too?

At least part of the answer can be seen in the results of an informal survey taken by youth evangelist Winkie Pratney, and reported in his book, *Revival: Principles to Change the World.* When he speaks on the subject of revival, Pratney often asks his audience four questions:

+ **How many of you know we *need* a revival?** Almost every hand goes up here, for this sounds like the most spiritual answer.

+ **How many of you *want* a revival?** Again, the vast majority of professing Christians vote in the affirmative, and a Gallup survey even reported the astonishing fact that 80 percent of the people in America claim to desire a revival!

+ **How many of you know what a revival *is?*** Pratney reports that here the number drops incredibly low. From this, he concludes that although we are sure we need and want a revival, most of us have no idea what a revival is!

+ **How many of you have ever *experienced* a true revival?** On this final question, very few, if any, ever respond.

Several lessons can be gleaned from Pratney's survey. First of all, it is clear that we have often "romanticized" the concept of revival, even though we don't have an understanding of what it is or what it will require from us. If we are truly serious about revival, we will have to make a commitment far beyond our present lip service.

The second observation is perhaps even more significant: As much as we might long for a revival, most of us have never seen one. Yes, we have been in some powerful meetings at times, but it is hard to claim that true "revival" occurred. This is particularly true in light of the fact that after all was said and done, our dynamic meetings seldom translated into a significant impact on the lost world around us.

Does this mean we should abandon the quest for revival? Is it just a quixotic fantasy that distracts us from day-to-day Christian living? No, it is obvious that the church needs revival fire to burn away our apathy and "jump start" our passion for the Lord. As Arthur Wallis contends, more can be accomplished in fifty *days* of true revival than in fifty *years* without one.

One day, when I was studying about past revivals, I came across an illustrative statistic about the United States stock market: over the past thirty years, 95 percent of the gains in the stock market occurred on 1.2 percent of the days the stock market has been in session. In a similar way, many of the gains of the church throughout history have come during short periods of spiritual awakening.

However, whether you are investing in the stock market or seeking revival, you never know for sure when the major gains will occur. For that reason, we cannot afford to idly wait around for revival. We must be faithful to pray and plant gospel seeds, whether we are in a time of revival or not. When revival comes, it will be like a rainfall that penetrates dry ground and brings to life the seeds we have been faithfully sowing.

Reformation Too

Remember Edward and Richard, the pastors with radically different views on the proper priorities of the church? Edward's passion for revival was noble, but also shortsighted. By putting all his emphasis on the need for revival, he neglected to build an infrastructure that could handle the revival if it came. He passionately sought the new wine of the Spirit, but forgot that the new wine must have suitable wineskins to fill.

Edward's perspective was also shortsighted because of his view of the end-times. He might end up being correct—Jesus may come back tonight! However, even though we must have an urgency as if Jesus is coming back soon, we also need to build strong foundations as if He won't return for another thousand years.

If you became a Christian in 1960s or 1970s, you probably were told that Jesus would return in just a few years. Some participants in the Jesus Movement dropped out of college and lived as if the world would end at any time. Hopefully you didn't follow in their steps.

Some Christians are like people who quit their jobs and head to Las Vegas to win their fortunes at the slot machines. They realize that if they hit upon a true revival they will "strike it rich," and they are willing to put all their eggs in that basket. Admittedly, a regular job is boring by contrast. Nevertheless, some aspects of the kingdom of God are based on the patient implementation of a vision for harvest, not on some kind of sensational divine intervention.

Richard was a master at creating an infrastructure for his church. He wasn't all that concerned about having a dramatic breakthrough that would qualify as a "revival," but his focus was on the daily implementation of his vision. Perhaps he would never see thousands saved in one day, but his church was at least winning a few new people every month. Not only that, but the converts were being effectively discipled and trained for ministry.

Edward and Richard each had something of value to share with the body of Christ. While Ed's emphasis was on *revival*, Richard's approach was geared more toward *reformation*. If Edward's quest is successful, the Lord will honor his hunger and pour out the new wine of revival. Richard, in the meantime, will be methodically working to bring a spiritual reformation to the church, preparing a wineskin equipped to handle the new wine.

The last time I saw Richard, his church was thriving. Yet I envision a day when he will pay a visit to Edward, asking for some input on how the flame of renewal can be ignited in his church.

And if the Lord answers Edward's cry for revival, he could really use Richard's help in forming an infrastructure to contain and process the resultant harvest.

I guess we need each other after all. And perhaps our lack of awareness of that fact is one of the reasons revival tarries.

14

STRANGERS IN A STRANGE LAND

"Earth changes, but thy soul and God stand sure."

—*Robert Browning*

My ministry takes me all across America, and I frequently hear Christians voice their frustration with the present political and cultural climate of our country. Many from the older generations openly ask whether America will ever be the same as the great and godly nation they grew up in. They see the cultural winds increasingly blowing against biblical values, and they are appalled that today's political correctness is clearly at odds with God's view of correctness.

As much as I understand these concerns, I think our frustration largely stems from forgetting that there's an inherent difference between God's kingdom and the kingdoms of this world—even the American kingdom. Having been seduced by the myth of cultural Christianity, we forget that we are "*foreigners and exiles*" (1 Peter 2:11 NIV) in this world. Other translations say we're sojourners, pilgrims, aliens, or temporary residents.

Is it possible that God will use the election results to remind us that, as His Word has always taught, we are basically called to be strangers in a strange land? Could it be that we had grown too comfortable living in America?

If you're like me, Jeremiah 29:11 is one of your favorite promises in God's Word: *"'I know the plans I have for you,' declares the* Lord, *'plans to prosper you and not to harm you, plans to give you hope and a future.'"*

However, as I recently pondered our current cultural situation, the Lord reminded me that we usually take this great promise totally out of context. No wonder we're often caught off guard when His plans for us seem unexpectedly difficult.

Picture yourself in this frightening scene, which is the backdrop of Jeremiah 29:11: Your city is invaded by a fierce enemy army. You, your family, and your those you love are taken captive and forcibly removed to the capital city of the invading nation. But you are proud and independent-minded people, not willing to accept this fate without a struggle. Should you join together to try and overthrow the government that is oppressing you? Should you devise a plan to escape one night, either returning to your homes or finding some faraway land where you will be safe?

Who Has Heard from God?

God has plans for His people, even at such times as this. But not everyone who claims to speak for the Lord has truly heard from Him. In Jeremiah's day, and throughout history, pied pipers and false prophets have led their gullible followers toward destruction.

In the distressing situation Jeremiah described, various people claimed to have a word from God. Most advocated some form of rebellion or escape, but Jeremiah was the lone prophetic voice who offered this unthinkable advice:

Build houses and settle down; plant gardens and eat what they produce. Marry and have sons and daughters; find wives for your sons and give your daughters in marriage, so that they too may have sons and daughters. Increase in number there;

*do not decrease. Also, seek the peace and prosperity of the city
to which I have carried you into exile. Pray to the* LORD *for it,
because if it prospers, you too will prosper.*

(Jeremiah 29:5–7 NIV)

At such advice, you might have protested, "What!? Are you
saying we should just accept our captivity? And why in the world
would we want to ask God to grant peace and blessing to our
captors?"

Sensing that your complaints are getting you nowhere, you
make one final argument: "But what about all the prophetic people
who are urging us to overthrow this evil civilization we find ourselves in? They certainly seem to be in the majority!"

Again, God speaks through the lone prophet: "*Do not let the
prophets and diviners among you deceive you. Do not listen to the
dreams you encourage them to have. They are prophesying lies to you
in my name. I have not sent them*" (verses 8–9 NIV). God went on
to say that His people might as well *enjoy* their time in the foreign
land—for they were destined to remain there seventy years.

Living in Foreign Territory

You see, we live our lives—our *"seventy years"* (Psalm 90:10)—
in a foreign land. Of all the nations on earth, I'm surely glad to live
in America, but I need to be reminded that this country is not my
true home. I'm a citizen of heaven and one of heaven's ambassadors
to a world that desperately needs to be reconciled to God. (See
Philippians 3:20; 2 Corinthians 5:20.)

So, what should be our attitude toward our leaders and the
country where God has placed us to live? Will we be smugly aloof,
trying to keep ourselves unstained by the evil values we perceive
in our society? Will we be angry and condescending, projecting
an air of superiority to unbelievers? Or will we just give up and

surrender, trying so hard to be accepted by the world that we end up imitating its values?

Hopefully we'll display the same attitude as Jesus displayed during His days on earth. Instead of staying aloof from unbelievers, He was known as *"a friend of tax-gatherers and sinners"* (Luke 7:34 NIV). He was able to be in the world without becoming absorbed by it. That's why He prayed for His followers, *"I do not pray that You should take them out of the world, but that You should keep them from the evil one"* (John 17:15).

Like the Israelites who were in exile in Babylon, we are living in a foreign land. But that should not be grounds for rebellion, escape, or anger. Rather, we are called, as Jesus did, to take the posture of a servant. Laying aside our garments of superiority, we are to pour water into a basin and *"wash the feet"* (John 13:1–5 MSG) of our society. And let's not forget to pray for our nation's political leaders—whether or not we voted for them. (See 1 Timothy 2:1–4.)

Changing the Temperature

Fortunately, God's people aren't helpless victims amid the cultural wars. Called to be salt, light, and intercessors, we can make a difference. Even though our nation may never fully reflect God's heavenly kingdom, at least we can play a significant role in changing the cultural climate.

You've probably heard the old song, "Baby, It's Cold Outside." In case you haven't noticed, the spiritual weather in our country is becoming increasingly "chilly" for true believers. Multiculturalism has turned into pantheism, paganism, and relativism for many people—not exactly a welcome environment for those of us who still believe that Jesus is the only way to heaven.

But this situation gives us an opportunity to learn a very important lesson:

In life, you will either be a THERMOMETER or a THERMOSTAT.

You see, thermometers merely reflect the temperatures around them. If it's cold outside, a thermometer will let you know. It's not hard to be a thermometer. You just have to report and reflect the conditions around you. Lots of people are like that. When you ask them how things are going, they simply give you a weather report concerning their present circumstances. Allowing themselves to be controlled by external situations, their mood goes up and down according to what's happening around them.

However, some people have learned to be a thermostat instead. Rather than just accepting and reflecting the temperature around them, they have a way of changing the temperature in every situation they are in. When it's cold outside, they warm things up. When conflicts arise and relationships get uncomfortably hot, they know how to generate cooling breezes.

Jesus was a thermostat. Although He continually faced icy reactions from the religious establishment, He never allowed His heart to become cold. Yes, Jesus sometimes gave a weather report about the conditions He saw around Him. But He never left things like He found them. Instead of reflecting the animosity and unbelief He encountered, He brought compassion, faith, and healing.

But Jesus warned about the temptation we would face to become mere thermometers, reflecting the surrounding culture rather than transforming it. *"Because lawlessness will abound, the love of many will grow cold"* (Matthew 24:12).

What a tragic outcome Jesus described. In a day of lawlessness, many people will become calloused and cynical. Surrounded by growing narcissism and self-centeredness, many will allow their love to become cold. Instead of being change agents, people will be like thermometers, swayed up and down by the changing world around them.

Jesus used the Greek word *agape* for love, so there's a good chance He had believers in doing so. He was warning that we'll surely face times when it's "cold outside," but we can't let that change our disposition or ruin our day. Instead, we must be filled with the Holy Spirit, bringing His kindness and warmth into even the harshest weather around us. Consumed with the holy fire of God, we can be a positive force in *setting* the temperature, not just reflecting it.

Don't Sleep Through the Revolution

We live in perilous times (see 2 Timothy 3:1)—probably even more perilous than we realize. And events in Washington are generally part of the problem rather than part of the answer.

As I watched a cable news show recently, I found myself wondering if our country is experiencing a new Civil War. Or maybe *Un-civil* War would be a better description, based on the behavior of some of the participants. Anger is high, nerves are frayed, and polls say only 20 percent of the American people trust their government.

Sometimes a Civil War is necessary to free slaves—and there are *lots* of slaves today. They may not be bought and sold to work on plantations, but they're chained to things like addictions, debt, immorality, poverty, gangs, and the consequences of broken homes and out-of-wedlock births. Many are enslaved by a welfare mentality, trusting government as their ultimate savior and provider.

As a preacher, I feel one of my responsibilities is to issue an Emancipation Proclamation. It's time to liberate the oppressed and free the slaves—even those who don't yet realize their state of bondage.

But when I told a friend my theory that a new Civil War is underway, he replied, "George, this is no Civil War—it's a

Revolutionary War!" He went on to draw parallels like "taxation without representation," tone-deaf governmental leaders, and even modern-day Tea Parties.

The strange thing about this new revolution is that most people are sleeping through it. No shots have been fired, the military draft hasn't been reinstated yet, and, for most of us, life goes on as it did before.

People sometimes tell me it's wrong for preachers to get involved in politics. I understand what they mean, for how can representatives of the King of Kings and Lord of Lords lower themselves to become mere Democrats, Republicans, independents, or Tea Partiers? The leader of our "party" needs no one to vote Him into office, and His kingdom transcends America and every other nation on earth.

So don't expect me to put a bumper sticker for your political party on the back of my car. I'm too busy liberating the slaves—no matter what the color of their skin or their political affiliation may be. When Jesus returns, I want to be found doing My heavenly Father's business rather than serving the political agenda of one party or another. However, He may have a different calling for *you*. We need kingdom-minded believers to infiltrate every area of life, including the world of politics.

However, my point is this: I don't want to sleep through the revolution—nor should you. And we need to recognize that the most *important* revolution is what happens when a human heart is set free to follow in the steps of the greatest Revolutionary who ever lived. We can't settle for anything less.

15

DO YOU HAVE SKIN IN THE GAME?

"The hottest place in hell is reserved for those who remain neutral in times of great moral conflict."

—*Martin Luther King Jr.*

We will never transform our communities by sitting at a distance and shouting out our opinions through a bullhorn. No, we have to roll up our sleeves and get involved—to "put skin in the game."

Attributed to renowned investor Warren Buffet, "skin in the game" is a term describing the willingness of a company's top executives to invest some of their own money in a project. It's a sign of good faith and their confidence in the outcome.

The concept makes a lot of sense, if you think about it. Why should you or I want to invest in a company or a project if the insiders don't believe in it enough to risk their *own* money?

But the skin-in-the-game principle actually started long before the days of Warren Buffet.

Perhaps you've heard the story of three-year-old Jenny, who was terrified by a fierce thunderstorm one night. With each flash of lightning or clap of thunder, she screamed in fear, pulling the covers over her head for protection. And when the covers proved inadequate to comfort her, she ran downstairs, where her mom was still working in the kitchen.

"I'm scared, Mommy!" she said, firmly wrapping her little arms around her mother's legs.

"Go back to your room, Jenny," her mom told her. "God will take care of you."

"OK, mommy," she reluctantly agreed.

But no sooner was she back in bed than another roar of thunder shook her room, once again sending Jenny back to the kitchen, where she wept as she clung to mom.

"What did I tell you, Jenny? God will take care of you," the mother said, getting somewhat irritated.

"But mommy, God doesn't have any *skin* on Him!" the little girl protested.

Well, even though we surely can sympathize with Jenny's point, the good news is that God did, in fact, come to us with skin on. We're told in John 1:14 that *"the Word became flesh and dwelt among us."* Not content to remain hidden away somewhere in the heavenlies, our Lord became Immanuel, *"God with us"* (Matthew 1:23).

Yes, God put skin in the game. Real skin. You see, He believed enough in His "redemption project" to become personally involved—fully invested, we might say.

Notice that He didn't just send His Word through prophets, angels, stone tablets, or handwriting on the wall. He came *Himself* and lived among us.

However, this doesn't totally negate Jenny's point. People today still are looking for "God with skin on." They need something more than a pat answer or an encouraging Bible tweet. They're longing to see and interact with other human beings who are filled with the presence and power of Christ. (See Colossians 1:27.)

So the next time you send a tweet, post a blog, or put something on your Facebook wall, remember this sobering statement by the apostle Paul: *"We were well pleased to impart to you not only the gospel of God, but also **our own lives**, because you had become dear to us"* (1 Thessalonians 2:8).

If Paul was still around today, I'm sure he would be using Twitter, Facebook, YouTube, LinkedIn, and every other possible means of sending out the gospel. Yet, even more importantly, he would be modeling an "incarnational" faith and *investing his life* into people he loved.

For Paul, presenting our bodies as *"a living sacrifice"* (Romans 12:1) wasn't just theology or theory. It meant putting our skin in the game.

As you interact with people through social media on your computer or smart phone today, don't forget to also put some of your "skin" in the game. Your friends and followers may need to see you *in person* from time to time. Like Jenny, they may even need a hug.

Somebody Cares About Your City

Hopefully our attitude toward our community is the same as Jesus displayed during His days on earth. He didn't stay aloof from unbelievers, but was known as *"a friend of tax-gatherers and sinners"* (Luke 7:34). He was able to be in the world without becoming absorbed by it. He prayed for His followers, *"I do not pray that You should take them out of the world, but that You should keep them from the evil one"* (John 17:15).

For more than two decades now, my friend Doug Stringer has passionately spread the gospel on the streets of Houston, Texas. One of his strategies involves the use of a simple business card with the following words:

Somebody Cares.

Because of what Jesus Christ has done for us, area churches and ministries want you to know we care. Call 24 hours a day.

"A true witness rescues lives" (Proverbs 14:25).

Doug's card communicates several important things. First, it let people know that our primary message is not "turn or burn," but we genuinely care about their situation. Second, it points not to our own virtue, but to what Christ has done for us. Third, instead of directing people just to our own ministry, it sends a message that we are related to a network of other "area churches and ministries." Fourth, it offers help on a 24-hour basis, letting people know that we care enough to be available day or night.

Over the years, Doug has developed a Somebody Cares Houston network of churches and ministries, all dedicated to winning their city to Christ. Now the Somebody Cares concept is spreading to other cities as well. In addition to the business cards, the word is spread through billboards, door hangers, and other ads that let people know help is available from this network of compassionate Christians.

Somebody Cares is not just a motto or a theory—it has become a reality. There have been tangible results as Houston area churches have networked together:

- Prayer coverage is provided on a daily basis for 70 percent of the populated area of Houston's twenty seven hundred square miles.

- Adopt-a-Gang prayer coverage has started for three hundred Houston-area gangs.

- More than one hundred fifty thousand Somebody Cares New Testaments have been distributed. Somebody Cares

Spanish Bibles are being distributed through Algien Se Interesa, the local Hispanic chapter of Somebody Cares.

+ In 1997, Action Ministries coordinated an effort to distribute 102 million pounds of food. They were so effective and efficient in their efforts to feed the poor that government leaders from Washington, D.C., came to study how they did it!

+ Through joint ventures with national ministries, Houston Christians distributed eighty thousand pounds of food in *one day*. At another event, food was provided for five thousand families.

In these and many other practical ways, Doug Stringer and other Houston Christians have shown their city that Somebody Cares. Their strategy is not a modern invention, but simply a rediscovery of Jesus' example. As the apostle John instructs, *"My little children, let us not love in word or in tongue, but in deed and in truth"* (1 John 3:18).

Servant Evangelism

Steve Sjogren, pastor of Vineyard Community Church in Cincinnati, Ohio, has initiated similar evangelism methods in his city. Sjogren has found that many people are closed to the gospel because of their perception that Christians are uncaring and judgmental. Instead of preaching on the streets or promoting the ministries of his church, Sjogren has trained his people in "servant evangelism."

Critics might ask whether servant evangelism is truly "evangelism" at all. Sjogren's church sponsors free car washes, where they refuse to take any money for their services. They also shovel snow for neighbors, clean toilets at area businesses, give out cold water to people on hot summer days, and even put money into expired parking meters. All of these services are provided absolutely free—expecting nothing in return. This is *agape* love in one of its purest forms, sharing God's grace with people, without regard for their merit or godliness.

But is this really evangelism? Isn't it just a time-consuming distraction? Good works for no good purpose? When people ask the "servant evangelists" what is motivating them, the response is usually, "We just want to show the love of God to our community in practical ways." Is this truly the gospel?

Sjogren would admit that much of his approach is not strictly evangelism, but *pre*-evangelism. In other words, he is not expecting to win a lot of converts at the free car washes, but he is hoping that seeds will be planted so that people want to know more. For many unbelievers, their preconception of church people is that our main mission in life is to make them feel guilty or to ask them for money. Sjogren's approach breaks down all these stereotypes, making people more open to eventually receive our gospel message. He quotes a statement commonly attributed to Saint Francis of Assisi: "Witness for Christ each day, and, if necessary, use words."

Let's face it: There are countless theories about sharing the gospel, but many of them don't produce much fruit. However, servant evangelism has proven extremely effective if practiced over the long haul. The church Sjogren planted now has thousands of people, most of whom were completely unchurched before meeting Christ through the church's various ministries. Not only that, but the church now has planted numerous other branches, where servant evangelism is also practiced. All this is the result of approaching the surrounding culture with *agape* instead of having an aloof or angry attitude.

Are You a False Witness?

Jesus says in Acts 1:8 that when the Holy Spirit comes upon us, we will receive power to be His witnesses. Yet the question is this: Are we true witnesses or false ones? When people see us, do they catch a better glimpse of the nature of God? Can we say, as Jesus did, *"He who has seen Me has seen the Father"* (John 14:9)?

This is a serious matter. One the Ten Commandments is, *"You shall not bear false witness against your neighbor"* (Exodus 20:16). If it is so important not to be a false witness against people, how much more serious is it to be a false representative of the Lord?

Somebody loves your city. He not only *says* He loves it, He *demonstrated* His love by laying down His life for every man, woman, and child in your community. If we are truly His followers, we will lay down our lives too.

16

TURNING THE BITTER WATERS
SWEET

"Let all bitterness, wrath, anger, clamor, and evil speaking be put away from you, with all malice."

—Ephesians 4:31

If you forgive my crude language, let me make something clear: Sometimes the circumstances in this world simply *suck*. You know what I mean.

Circumstances among nations…circumstances in your country's economy…circumstances in the culture wars…or circumstances in your church, family, health, and finances—sometimes they all seem to *suck*.

I'm not just being a pessimist here. The Bible gives numerous examples of men and women of God who faced days like this—but it also describes how they found encouragement and victory:

- David *"encouraged himself in the LORD his God"* (1 Samuel 30:6 KJV) after the Amalekites attacked Ziklag and took the women captive.

- Jeremiah had to remember God's incredible faithfulness as he was watching his beloved city of Jerusalem being invaded by the Babylonians. (See Lamentations 3:1–26.)

✦ Even Jesus Himself found it necessary to withdraw *"to a secluded place by Himself"* (Matthew 14:13 NASB) after He received news that John the Baptist had been beheaded by Herod.

But my favorite story about reversing life's difficult circumstances is found in Exodus 15:22–25, 27:

> *Moses brought Israel from the Red Sea; then they went out into the Wilderness of Shur. And they went three days in the wilderness and found no water. Now when they came to Marah, they could not drink the waters of Marah, for they were* **bitter.** *Therefore the name of it was called Marah. And the people complained against Moses, saying, "What shall we drink?" So he cried out to the LORD, and the LORD showed him a* **tree.** *When he cast it into the waters,* **the waters were made sweet....** *Then they came to Elim, where there were twelve wells of water and seventy palm trees; so they camped there by the waters."*

What a fascinating story. God's people had escaped from captivity in Egypt and had seen the Lord part the Red Sea and miraculously deliver them from Pharaoh's army. But then they found themselves in a desolate wilderness, where there was no water. Finally, they discovered abundant water at Marah—but the water was bitter.

Maybe you've found yourself in a similar place. You've sincerely tried to follow God's leading, and yet you've found yourself in a barren spiritual desert. And right when you think there's some hope, the water turns out to be bitter.

We can encounter many different kinds of bitter waters in life. Divorces, church splits, career downsizing, rebellious kids, financial setbacks, persecution—all of these can create bitter, frustrating situations. And when the water turns into a toxic cesspool, you drink it at your own peril!

Reversing a Bitter Situation

Fortunately, there's good news in this remarkable story. Bitter waters can be turned sweet, whether in our personal lives, in our career or ministry, or in the surrounding culture.

How can this be? When you are facing bitter waters, it can be tempting to feel hopeless about the situation.

But the story in Exodus 15 provides a beautiful picture of the solution: *You can detoxify the bitter waters we face by applying the cross (the tree) to the situation!*

The cross of Jesus Christ provides *everything you need* to reverse toxicity in your community, your church, or your family. Through the cross...

+ You receive forgiveness from God.

+ You're reconciled into an intimate relationship with Him.

+ You forgive others, as He has forgiven you.

+ The dividing walls between you and your enemies can be shattered.

+ You die to yourself, making it possible to love and serve others.

Perhaps you're saying in your heart at this point, "But Bishop Bloomer, what if I'm the *only one* trying to apply the cross to a toxic situation I face? How can it possibly work, if everyone else isn't on board?"

Well, you are partially correct. But although you won't be able to transform the whole world into an oasis of sweet waters through your own efforts, when you touch the nearby bitter waters with the power of the cross, your *own* attitudes will change...and gradually you'll see transformation come to *others* around you as well.

Are you willing to take the first step? Don't wait for someone else to initiate the healing process. The change you are looking for begins with *you*. When you embrace the cross and die to yourself, you'll soon find yourself transported from the barren desert to *"Elim, where there were twelve wells of water and seventy palm trees."*

Happy Endings

When you see so much conflict and negativity around you, it's easy to become discouraged. You can wonder if your bitter waters will ever change and whether you'll ever find victory over your difficult circumstances.

The culture wars can certainly be discouraging as well. The devil wants us to believe we're on the losing side, but that's simply not true.

There's an old saying that tells us, "All's well that end well." Although I'm not sure this is absolutely true, the Bible clearly says there will be a "happy ending" for the people of God when the final chapter of history is written. And I'm convinced God wants us to experience breakthroughs and turnarounds in our lives *today*, not just when Jesus comes back.

But sometimes we face the bitter waters first. Consider these examples:

+ There would have been nothing "good" about Good Friday if it weren't for Resurrection Sunday. The seemingly tragic and unjust story of the cross ended in complete triumph. Resurrection changes everything.

+ The final word in the Old Testament (Malachi 4:6) is **curse** (Hebrew *cherem*), quite a sobering reminder if we're ever tempted to live under the Law again. But fortunately the story of redemption isn't over yet. The New Testament ends on a completely different note: *"The **grace** of our Lord Jesus Christ be with you all. Amen"* (Revelation 22:21). Praise God for His grace. It changes everything.

✦ If you would have met Job midway through his story, you would have declared him a quite pathetic fellow. But his story certainly ended well *"The* LORD *restored his fortunes and gave him twice as much as he had before"* and *"The* LORD *blessed the latter part of Job's life more than the former part"* (Job 42:10–12 NIV). Don't you love happy endings like this? Happy endings can change just about anything.

Friend, I'm believing God for happy endings in your life and in our nations. As the old hymn says, you and I may have to pass through "many dangers, toils, and snares," but grace has brought me safe thus far, and grace will lead me home."

Yes, we may even have to pass through the Valley of Tears at some point. But through God's grace we will *"make it a spring"*as we *"go from strength to strength"*(Psalm 84:5–7).

So let's encourage one another, believing God for the happy endings He has promised.

17

THE EARTH IS THE LORD'S!

*"Every place that the sole of your foot will tread upon
I have given you."*

—*Joshua 1:3*

I get irritated when I hear some preachers paint a doom and gloom picture of the church's prophetic destiny. The Bible's snapshot of the people of God is not a picture of huddled victims waiting for a rescue mission to save them from the Antichrist. No, we are to be more than conquerors. (See Romans 8:37.)

Instead of having us live in fear and defeat, God wants His people to be so victorious and blessed that desperate unbelievers stream to us, looking for answers. They will cry out for us to teach them the ways of the Lord, and God's law will once more go out from us to shape the surrounding culture. (See Isaiah 2:3.)

I'm convinced we've often given the devil more credit than he deserves. Yes, he's a wily foe, but he must *flee* from us when we submit ourselves to God and learn to resist him. (See James 4:7.)

If you ask most Christians who owns the earth, they are likely to say, "The devil!" But while it's true that Satan is referred to as *"the god of this age"* (2 Corinthians 4:4), that does not negate the revolutionary truth of Psalm 24:1: *"The earth is the LORD's, and all it contains, the world, and those who dwell in it"* (NASB).

You see, God is the rightful owner of the whole earth and every person in it. The devil's claim is, at best, that of a squatter.

If our worldview is firmly rooted in this amazing fact, it will revolutionize our lives. Instead of timidly or apologetically walking the earth, we'll confidently know that every square inch of it belongs to our Lord. We will be able to declare that everywhere the sole of our foot treads, He has given it to us. (See Joshua 1:3.) And instead of sheepishly begging people to give their hearts to Jesus, we will boldly warn them that one day they, and every other human, will bow their knees and acknowledge that Jesus Christ is Lord. (See Philippians 2:9–11.)

In his book, *City Reaching: On the Road to Community Transformation*, Jack Dennison puts it this way: "The neighborhoods of your city belong to God. The cities of America belong to God. The nations of the world belong to God. He wants them, and He will have them—every one of them!"

He Bought the Whole Field!

I was shocked when I finally understood the meaning of Jesus' story in Matthew 13:44 about the treasure in the field: "Again, the kingdom of heaven is like treasure hidden in a field, which a man found and hid; and for joy over it he goes and sells all that he has and buys that field."

When I first considered this passage, I misread it, assuming that the man sold all he had in order to buy the treasure. That's not what it says! The man not only bought the treasure, he bought the whole field!

Do you see the distinction? While I understood that Jesus "sold all that He had" by laying down His life for our salvation, I didn't see the full scope of what He was purchasing. I realized that

He died to purchase precious men and women—the treasure—for God. However, I didn't see that He also bought the entire field.

There are two reasons why the earth—including your city— belong to the Lord. First, the Lord has a right based on creation. He created the earth and each person on it, and for that reason He has a just claim to rule over them. Second, the Lord owns the earth and its inhabitants because He purchased them on the cross. He created them, and then He redeemed them. When we approach people with the gospel, we can boldly challenge them that God not only created them, He has also purchased them with the blood of Christ. He thus has a rightful claim to their allegiance.

The story of treasure hidden in the field reveals another important paradigm often missed by Christians today. Instead of just reaching individuals, we should have a vision to impact our entire culture. Why? Because Jesus didn't just purchase the church. He is the rightful Lord over every sphere of life: families, music, arts, sports, education, science, government, publishing, business, recreation, and everything else. He wants to manifest His sweet fragrance "in every place" (2 Corinthians 2:14), not just in religious places.

Jesus died to save individuals and give birth to the church, but He also purchased the entire cultural "field" that we find ourselves in. Our mandate as believers is to fill the whole earth with God's glory—not just every Christian or every church. Yet too often we have allowed ourselves to be boxed in to a "stained glass ghetto." We have patted ourselves on the back when the glory of the Lord appeared in our church services. Yet, all the while, God's purpose was to fill the entire earth—the whole field—with His glory.

A Message of Hope

I've sometimes heard the doom and gloom preachers quote Isaiah's prediction that *"darkness shall cover the earth, and deep darkness the people*" (Isaiah 60:2). But that's not the end of the story! The passage goes on to state: "*The LORD will arise over you, and His glory will be seen upon you....Then you shall see and become radiant, and your heart shall swell with joy....And I will glorify the house of My glory*" (verses 2, 5, 7).

It sure helps to read the entire passage, doesn't it? You see, we have reason for optimism today. No matter how bad things may look like around us, we can respond to God's powerful word of prophetic encouragement: "*Arise, shine; for your light has come! And the glory of the LORD is risen upon you*" (verse 1).

When we "*arise*" and "*shine*" with the glory of the Lord, we can boldly take His light into every area of life. We won't shy away from expressing God's kingdom in the marketplace, the education system, the sports world, or the entertainment media.

Scottish preacher George MacLeod describes our "marketplace mandate" this way:

> I simply argue that the cross should be raised in the center of the marketplace as well as on the steeple of the church. I am recovering the claim that Jesus was not crucified between two candles, but on a cross between two thieves; on the town's garbage heap; at a crossroads, so cosmopolitan they had to write his title in Hebrew, in Latin, and in Greek. At the kind of place where cynics talk smut, and thieves curse, and soldiers gamble. Because that is where He died. That is what He died for. And that is what He died about. And that is where church people ought to be, and what church people ought to be about.

Instead of huddling in defensive posture amid the culture wars our nation faces, we must go on the offensive. It's time to boldly take the kingdom of God into the marketplaces of our society, penetrating every sphere of human endeavor.

Jesus or Jonah?

We face a fork in the road. We are sent to bring salvation to our city, and we will respond in one of two ways: like Jesus or like Jonah. When Jesus approached Jerusalem in the final days of His ministry, He wept. (See Luke 19:41–42.) His heart broke with compassion as He saw the needs of the people who would soon cry out for Pilate to crucify Him.

Jonah, likewise, was sent to proclaim repentance to a city, Nineveh. Not only did he fail to weep over the condition of the lost people, he tried running away the other direction! As much as we might ridicule Jonah's decision, haven't we often done the very same thing? When the needs of our inner cities cried out for divine solutions, we ran to the suburbs. When unreached people groups around the world languished for want of the gospel, we clung to our comfortable American lifestyles.

Even after the Lord rescued Jonah from his escapism, Jonah still didn't have a change of heart toward the people he was sent to warn. Instead of feeling compassion, he separated himself and sulked: *"So Jonah went out of the city and sat on the east side of the city. There he made himself a shelter and sat under it in the shade, till he might see what would become of the city"* (Jonah 4:5).

As the church has so often done, Jonah became aloof and withdrew from the city. Instead of becoming a participant in the revival he reluctantly sparked, he simply became an observer, watching to see what would happen.

Jonah knew better. Although he was displeased and angry when he saw the repentance of the Ninevites, Jonah still could proclaim with his lips that the Lord is *"a gracious and merciful God, slow to anger and abundant in lovingkindness, One who relents from doing harm"* (Jonah 4:2).

What a tragic contrast between God and the one who represented Him! Yet that same contrast is too often still found between the Lord and His people today.

Remember: The earth is the Lord's. Jerusalem and Nineveh are the Lord's. Your city is the Lord's. May we heed God's mandate to love our cities with His love, turning the world upside down with bold proclamation of King Jesus as Lord of all. (See Acts 17:6–7.)

PART II:

A Recent History of Christian Activism in America——
the Good, the Bad, and the Ugly

1

WHO HIJACKED MLK'S DREAM?

"I know this, that after my departure savage wolves will come in among you, not sparing the flock. Also from among yourselves men will rise up, speaking perverse things, to draw away the disciples after themselves."

—*The Apostle Paul (Acts 20:29–30)*

Every time I hear the famous *I Have a Dream* speech by Dr. Martin Luther King Jr., I get inspired—and angry. I get inspired by Dr. King's powerful and lofty vision of a better world, where racial harmony is the norm rather than the exception. Yet I get angry because we're still a long way from the fulfillment of that dream.

Think of how ironic this is. People on all sides of the political spectrum claim to agree with King's stirring vision—conservatives, liberals, and independents alike. Who could be against racial harmony? In theory, no one is.

Unfortunately, Dr. King's dream has been hijacked. Countless examples could be cited, from the trumped up rape case against the Duke lacrosse team to the George Zimmerman trial for the killing Trayvon Martin. Just when you think you can breathe a sigh of relief and declare that peace and brotherhood reign supreme, some ugly incident proves otherwise.

And even Barack Obama's two electoral victories haven't created a harmonious, colorblind nation. Perhaps we've even taken a few steps backward.

There's plenty of blame to go around, of course. Politicians, preachers, activists, educators, rappers, media executives, and self-described "civil rights leaders"—we've all fallen short of our responsibility to further the cause of racial harmony.

But it's troubling that some of the primary culprits have been those who most piously claim to be the guardians of Dr. King's dream. Yes, you know who I mean. Some race-baiters have gotten rich by stirring up the cauldron of prejudice and bigotry.

Many of these race hustlers have gladly used the title of "Reverend," even when their ministerial credentials are dubious. Rather than *"contend earnestly for the faith which was once for all delivered to the saints"* (Jude 1:3), they're quick to sell out to the highest bidder or lobbyist.

Instead of bowing to the Word of the Lord and the infallible Scriptures, these opportunists insert their own opinions and bend to every cultural fad. Just as the Bible predicted, they *"pervert the grace of our God into a license for immorality"* (Jude 1:4 NIV).

Are these the kinds of leaders who should be the guardians of MLK's noble dream?

Beyond the Blame Game

However, before we assign blame for the hijacking of Dr. King's dream, let's first look at what he said in that majestic speech in front of a crowd of over two hundred fifty thousand people at the Lincoln Memorial on August 28, 1963. King did not pull any punches when he contrasted the continuing plight of many black Americans in his day with the American dream envisioned in lofty documents such as our Declaration of Independence, Constitution, and Emancipation Proclamation. MLK referenced such things as poverty, discrimination, segregation, and police brutality as ongoing problems, even a hundred years after emancipation.

While Dr. King didn't shy away from honestly addressing the issues, his message that day was also filled with abounding hope:

> Let us not wallow in the valley of despair. I say to you today, my friends, that in spite of the difficulties and frustrations of the moment, I still have a dream. It is a dream deeply rooted in the American dream.

It's important to notice that Martin Luther King Jr. saw his dream as being "deeply rooted in the American dream." It could be argued that, like Barack Obama, King wanted to "fundamentally change America." However, I think there is a difference between the two.

Dr. King wanted to see America transformed into the shining city on a hill that its founders proclaimed. In a nutshell, he was calling the nation to live up to its own dream and potential—to "walk its talk" and reflect its highest values. "I have a dream," he said, "that one day this nation will rise up and live out the true meaning of its creed: 'We hold these truths to be self-evident: that all men are created equal.'"

There's evidence that Barack Obama, in contrast, had his foundational worldview shaped by anticolonial philosophies that focus more on America's flaws than its sublime and noble vision. His 2008 campaign famously preached "hope and change." But instead of being rooted in America's original promises not yet fulfilled, President Obama's message seemed to imply that he alone could bring the country into the Promised Land. In contrast, just a few days before MLK's death, he sensed that although he saw a vision of a Promised Land filled with racial harmony and justice, he admitted, "I may not get there with you." He fully understood that his dream was dependent on a higher power than human personalities.

MLK's Hope-Filled Crescendo

Dr. King's closing crescendo painted an awesome portrait of what race relations could look like in our nation:

> I have a dream that one day on the red hills of Georgia the sons of former slaves and the sons of former slave-owners will be able to sit down together at a table of brotherhood....
>
> I have a dream that my four little children will one day live in a nation where they will not be judged by the color of their skin but by the content of their character.
>
> I have a dream today!
>
> I have a dream that one day, down in Alabama...little black boys and little black girls will be able to join hands with little white boys and white girls as sisters and brothers.
>
> I have a dream today!
>
> I have a dream that one day every valley shall be exalted, every hill and mountain shall be made low, the rough places will be made plain, and the crooked places will be made straight, and the glory of the Lord shall be revealed, and all flesh shall see it together.
>
> This is our hope. This is the faith that I will go back to the South with. With this faith we will be able to hew out of the mountain of despair a stone of hope. With this faith we will be able to transform the jangling discords of our nation into a beautiful symphony of brotherhood. With this faith we will be able to work together, to pray together, to struggle together, to go to jail together, to stand up for freedom together, knowing that we will be free one day.

This will be the day, this will be the day when all of God's children will be able to sing with a new meaning: "My country, 'tis of thee, sweet land of liberty, of thee I sing. Land where my fathers died, land of the pilgrim's pride, from every mountainside, let freedom ring."

And if America is to be a great nation, this must become true. So let freedom ring from the prodigious hilltops of New Hampshire. Let freedom ring from the mighty mountains of New York. Let freedom ring from the heightening Alleghenies of Pennsylvania! Let freedom ring from the snow-capped Rockies of Colorado. Let freedom ring from the curvaceous peaks of California.

But not only that; let freedom ring from Stone Mountain of Georgia. Let freedom ring from Lookout Mountain of Tennessee. Let freedom ring from every hill and every molehill of Mississippi, from every mountainside, let freedom ring!

And when this happens, when we allow freedom to ring, when we let it ring from every village and every hamlet, from every state and every city, we will be able to speed up that day when all of God's children, black men and white men, Jews and Gentiles, Protestants and Catholics, will be able to join hands and sing in the words of the old Negro spiritual: "Free at last! Free at last! Thank God Almighty, we are free at last!"

The Ultimate Liberator

Notice that Dr. King's dream was not *only* rooted in the American dream. He was also a preacher of the gospel, and his message of hope and change was tied to his scriptural perspective that God is the ultimate Liberator. Why should people of all racial groups be treated equally? Because God is their Creator, and they all have a right to be His children.

Many people today claim to share Dr. King's objective. Yet often there's something missing. While their mission typically is fueled merely by well-meaning humanism, King's was energized by holy zeal and a sense of divine purpose. Nothing less will get the job done.

But, as I describe in the next chapter, sometimes MLK's dream has been hijacked by corrupt demagogues on all sides of the political spectrum. Some of these leaders claim to be preachers of the gospel, but their actions seem more like wolves in sheep's clothing. Instead of advancing the unity and brotherhood Dr. King envisioned, they have stirred the pot of racial prejudice and distrust.

2

REJECTING THE RACE-BAITING BUSINESS

*"Stay away from mindless, pointless quarreling….That gets
you nowhere. Warn a quarrelsome person once or twice, but
then be done with him. It's obvious that such a person is
out of line, rebellious against God. By persisting in
divisiveness he cuts himself off."*

—Titus 3:9–11 (MSG)

Nothing has damaged race relations in America more than the deceitful activities of some black leaders who claim to be on the side of racial justice. While claiming a desire to advance African-American equality, these demagogues have used the plight of the urban black community to make themselves rich.

The *Random House Dictionary* defines *demagogue* as someone who "gains power and popularity by arousing the emotions, passions, fears, ignorance, and prejudices of the people." Instead of using factual, rational arguments, demagogues gain followers by vilifying their opponents and setting up "straw men" that can easily be attacked and discredited. They are skilled organizers and agitators, but rarely does their work produce any constructive outcomes.

History has had its share of demagogues on both the right and left sides of the political spectrum.

Adolf Hitler brought his Nazi party to power in Germany not by a military coup d'état but by democratic elections. How could the German people be so shortsighted and deceived? Hitler was a classic demagogue. He appealed to the ethnic pride of the German people and promoted false conspiracy theories that blamed Jews for the nation's economic woes. People were swayed by emotions rather than reason as he used his charisma and oratorical skills to lead them into a senseless war.

In the 1950s, Senator Joseph McCarthy rose to national prominence by claiming that the United States government and military had become infested with high-ranking communists. Playing upon people's fears and anger, he spearheaded a "Red Scare" that captivated the news media for many months during congressional hearings. However, his inability to provide solid proof for his accusations eventually caused him to fall from popularity and be censured by the Senate.

We still have some right wing demagogues stirring up false issues today. However, many of today's biggest demagogues are liberals, often claiming to be men of God. These self-styled "reverends" or "bishops" have a message completely different from what the Bible teaches. Instead of promoting biblical messages such as forgiveness, personal responsibility, and spiritual transformation, these leaders often promote the very things the Bible warns against—things like anger, blame shifting, and "pay back."

As a result, many people remain stuck in the grip of poverty, dependent on the welfare state instead of dependent on God and the fruit of their own labor. White people and conservatives are blamed for the lack of progress, while the demagogic leaders refuse to address root issues such as broken families, out-of-wedlock births, drug and alcohol use, gangs, and simple laziness.

Saviors or Demagogues?

Is it possible that some leaders who speak out against alleged racial injustice are just race hustlers and race-baiters, motivated by a desire for power and media attention? Could some prominent civil rights leaders actually be wolves in sheep's clothing?

As if foreseeing the rise of racial demagogues, Booker T. Washington warned many years ago of "problem profiteers" within the black community:

> There is a class of colored people who make a business of keeping the troubles, the wrongs and the hardships of the Negro race before the public. Having learned that they are able to make a living out of their troubles, they have grown into the settled habit of advertising their wrongs—partly because they want sympathy and partly because it pays. Some of these people do not want the Negro to lose his grievances, because they do not want to lose their jobs.

What a searing indictment of leaders today who "make a business" of keeping black people's grievances before the public. Using intimidation, coercion, and demagoguery against major corporations and governmental entities, they enrich themselves and steer billions of dollars of business to their friends and family. And these corrupt leaders know that if black grievances ever found real solutions, it would cause them to lose their jobs and their power base.

While some leaders specialize in shaking down Wall Street and the corporate world, others have gained a following through involvement in high profile criminal cases. But instead of truly advancing the cause of racial justice and economic prosperity, such people are merely racial arsonists, stirring up unrest, suspicion, and discontent.

Jonah Goldberg, a commentator with *National Review* online, points out that some of those who claim to be defenders of the oppressed and downtrodden are now proud members of the "1 percent." Instead of actually hanging out with the down and out, he says, the race-baiters hobnob with "power brokers and captains of industry."

Wisdom from Above

It's time to quit listening to demagogues—no matter which side of political spectrum they are on. We should be leery of any leader, no matter how eloquent, who tries to manipulate our emotions and make us feel like helpless victims. And we must reject *anyone* who fosters unforgiveness and blame-shifting rather than personal accountability.

I'll admit, sometimes it's difficult to discern who's for real and who's a fraud. But I love the guideline provided by Jesus' half-brother James:

> *Do you want to be counted wise, to build a reputation for wisdom? Here's what you do: Live well, live wisely, live humbly. It's the way you live, not the way you talk, that counts. Mean-spirited ambition isn't wisdom. Boasting that you are wise isn't wisdom. Twisting the truth to make yourselves sound wise isn't wisdom. It's the furthest thing from wisdom—it's animal cunning, devilish conniving. Whenever you're trying to look better than others or get the better of others, things fall apart and everyone ends up at the others' throats. Real wisdom, God's wisdom, begins with a holy life and is characterized by getting along with others. It is gentle and reasonable, overflowing with mercy and blessings, not hot one day and cold the next, not two-faced. You can develop a healthy, robust community that lives right with God and enjoy its results only if you do the hard work of getting along with each other, treating each other with dignity and honor.* (James 3:13–18 MSG)

I encourage you to read this again. Apply it to your own life and media voices you are listening to. Is your pastor or your favorite talk show on TV or radio promoting the wisdom from above or the wisdom from below?

James warns against boasting, mean-spirited ambition, twisting the truth, and engaging in hypocritical posturing. In contrast, he makes it clear that God's wisdom *"is characterized by getting along with others,"* and is *"not two-faced."* When we treat each other with *"dignity and honor,"* James says, the result will be *"a healthy, robust community that lives right with God."*

It's time for all us—leaders and followers alike—to remember Jesus' description of the kind of leaders who will rise to prominence in His kingdom: *"You know that the rulers of the Gentiles lord it over them, and their great men exercise authority over them. It is not this way among you, but whoever wishes to become great among you shall be your servant"* (Matthew 20:25–26 NASB).

Let's quit following the merchants of victimhood or the shrill voices of hate and division. It's time for a new generation of leaders to arise, preaching a gospel of responsibility, accountability, and spiritual transformation. Like never before, we face a desperate need for God's wisdom instead of the worldly wisdom of the self-promoters.

3

FREE AT LAST? BREAKING OUT AND BREAKING IN

"Christ has set us free to live a free life. So take your stand!
Never again let anyone put a harness of slavery on you."

—Galatians 5:1 (MSG)

I still get goose bumps every time I hear the stirring conclusion of MLK's *I Have a Dream* speech. Dr. King prophesied about a day when all God's children would "join hands and sing in the words of the old Negro spiritual: 'Free at last! Free at last! Thank God Almighty, we are free at last!'"

This is a beautiful sentiment, and I believe King was moved by the Spirit of God to declare them that day. But it breaks my heart to see so many people—more than fifty years later—who still aren't truly "free at last."

Didn't the Emancipation Proclamation and Thirteenth Amendment officially abolish slavery? What still needs to happen before we can experience the kind of freedom Dr. King spoke of so eloquently in 1963?

I believe the "Dream speech" has new relevance at this particularly time in our nation's history. While the bondage of Southern plantations may be gone, many people remain enslaved. The shackles may be different now, but the bondage is just as real.

Millions of people today are held hostage to dependence on the government as their provider and savior. This is not a new issue, for Henry Ward Beecher noted in his *Proverbs from Plymouth Pulpit* in 1887: "It is for men to choose whether they will govern themselves or be governed."

Instead of properly "governing themselves," many people are enslaved to alcohol or drug addictions. Others are held captive to pornography and sexual perversion. Many are trapped in codependent relationships, looking for love in all the wrong places.

Ironically, some of the worst types of enslavement come when folks pursue a false freedom—discarding the time-tested precepts of Scripture in favor of a hedonistic lifestyle. Peter describes this well, warning that lawlessness always results in bondage: *"While they promise them liberty, they themselves are slaves of corruption; for by whom a person is overcome, by him also he is brought into bondage"* (2 Peter 2:19).

So beware, my friend. God wants you to be *"free indeed"* (John 8:36) and stand fast in the liberty you have in Christ. (See Galatians 5:1.) But sin is not freedom. To the contrary, *"whoever commits sin is a slave of sin"* (John 8:34). The drug dealers and pimps aren't your friends—they are slave masters.

The Debt Trap

But by far the most common form of modern slavery is described in the ancient words of King Solomon: *"the borrower becomes the lender's slave"* (Proverbs 22:7 NASB). Think about it; debt creates slavery, and this isn't confined to just one ethnicity. As people of every ethnic group have discovered today, unsustainable debt *equals* slavery. You inevitable become enslaved to whoever you owe money to.

So if we're truly going to be "free at last," we must break the chains of debt in our lives. Otherwise, we will stay in never-ending bondage to the loan sharks, mortgage companies, bankers, and credit card companies.

Of course, our national leaders have set a terrible example in this, continually spending far more than the country takes in. Congress must raise the national debt ceiling with ever-greater frequency. Do we really think there will be no adverse consequences of borrowing more and more money from China and other nations?

After enslaving millions of our citizens in their personal lives, today, debt is shackling our entire national economy. Like a boa constrictor that wraps itself around its prey before squeezing out the life, debt has seductively positioned itself for our destruction.

Soon it will take our entire national revenue just to make the interest payments on our debt. Perhaps you've experienced this in your own life, when you could only make the minimum payments on your credit card bills. Whenever money comes in, it's quickly gobbled up by obligations to your lenders.

Like Dr. King, I have a dream. As a minister of the gospel, I want people to be "free at last." But as long as our debt remains, so will our shackles. On both the personal and national level, the slaveholders of today are our creditors. It's time to leave the plantation for good.

No Longer Slaves

Throughout the Bible, we are shown two sides of "free at last" theme. We must break *out* of the things that enslave us, so we can break *into* the destiny God has ordained for our lives.

The Israelites were given instructions for how to break *out* of their slavery in Egypt, so they could ultimately break *into* the Promised Land. The journey from Egypt to the Promised Land should have required less than *forty days*, but it took the Israelites *forty years*. Why? Because of their fear, unbelief, and disobedience.

You see, it's one thing for us to get out of Egypt, but it's quite another thing to get Egypt *out of us!* Forty years after the Israelites escaped from the slavery of Egypt, they were still dealing with some of the internal issues of whether they would be "free indeed" and move into their destiny as children of God.

Do you see the pattern here? No wonder it has been so difficult for many African-Americans to break into their Promised Land. Yes, slavery has been legally abolished. The Emancipation Proclamation and Thirteenth Amendment took care of that. But many people are still carrying around the mentality of captivity instead of embracing their new identity in Christ.

Even Jesus' disciples had to break free from a mentality of slavery and servitude. Jesus told them:

> *You are my friends if you do what I command. I no longer call you slaves, because a master doesn't confide in his slaves. Now you are my friends, since I have told you everything the Father told me.* (John 15:14–15 NLT)

Paul made a similar statement in Romans 8:15–17:

> *So you have not received a spirit that makes you fearful slaves. Instead, you received God's Spirit when he adopted you as his own children. Now we call him, "Abba, Father." For his Spirit joins with our spirit to affirm that we are God's children. And since we are his children, we are his heirs. In fact, together with Christ we are heirs of God's glory."* (NLT)

Isn't this good news? It's time to quit approaching life as "*fearful slaves.*" God has adopted us into His family. Now we are joint heirs with Christ, with full access to all the blessings and provisions of the kingdom of God.

So I ask you today: Do you truly see yourself as God's beloved son or daughter? Or have you allowed yourself to hang on to the old mentality of a slave?

Paul says there's "*a spirit*" that makes people feel like fearful slaves. But, praise God, we've been given a *different* Spirit—*not* "*a spirit of fear, but of power and of love and of a sound mind*" (2 Timothy 1:7).

Prison Break

If you're still plagued by a slavery mentality, it won't help to blame it on racism in society or say it's the fault of how people have treated you. You need to trade in your false ID for the new identity God wants to give you as His blood-bought child. And you may even need some *deliverance*, because there's clearly a demonic component to this battle.

On a practical level, you must study what God says about you in His Word. You must replace the lies you've believed with the truth of Scripture. And you then need to *proclaim* your new identity by testifying to what God has done in making you His *friend* instead of a slave. Like the victorious saints who overcame the Accuser through "*the word of their testimony*" (Revelation 12:11), your words have great power to change the trajectory of your life.

But what if you still find yourself enslaved or imprisoned in some way? I love the story of Paul and Silas triggering an earthquake and "prison break" in Acts 16:22–34. Many people today desperately need a similar earthquake to change their circumstances and shake things up in the *spiritual realm*—demolishing satanic strongholds that are hindering God's blessings in their finances, health, family, or peace of mind.

Paul and Silas had experienced a rough time. Through no fault of their own, they had been brutally beaten and mistreated. They were shackled to the wall of a dark, damp prison cell.

Can your relate? Perhaps you find yourself "confined" by your circumstances today. You've done your best, but life just hasn't been fair.

Paul and Silas had every reason to grumble and complain, but that would have done nothing to improve their situation. Instead, they prayed, gave thanks, and sang God's praises. And the Lord responded with *"a great earthquake"* (Acts 16:26) that completely transformed their circumstances!

What a fantastic picture of the overwhelming *victory* God will give you and me as we worship and obey Him today. In a remarkably short time, He can unleash a tidal wave of blessings to reverse every negative situation!

Just as God broke the chains of bondage in that jail in Philippi, He wants to break *your* chains today. As you draw near and worship Him with a thankful heart, you can be released from...

+ Poverty or debt

+ Sickness or depression

+ Loneliness or hopelessness

+ Addiction or family strife

+ Dependence on the government or other people

+ And so much more!

There are so many important lessons in this story. As Paul and Silas passionately worshiped the Lord during their time of distress, *"all the **doors** were opened"* (Acts 16:26). This means that, in addition to liberating us from enemy strongholds, God wants to *open doors* for us in our career, relationships, or ministry.

This story also offers good news if you are concerned about loved ones who aren't yet followers of Christ. Acts 16 says Paul and Silas started an earthquake that not only released them from their chains and brought salvation to their jailer, the ripple effect of the jailer's conversion resulted in the salvation of *"all his family"* (verse 33). Friend, God wants your *entire family* to experience His salvation and victory!

So, regardless of your present situation, I encourage you to take a minute right now to thank the Lord. Thank Him for the victory you need, for the doors you need opened, for the answers to the prayers you've been praying, and for the salvation and restoration of your loved ones. *Thank Him for His faithfulness!*

Don't Forget to Break In

As much as I love the prison break story in Acts 16, I'm also concerned about another side of the coin. Many Christians have broken out of sin or addiction in their lives, yet have never really entered *into* the abundant, impactful life God intends for them.

We learn in Mark 2:1–12 that there's a time to break *into* the Lord's purpose for our lives. Jesus was teaching in someone's home one day, and the place was so packed that no one else could enter. However, four men carried a paralytic to the meeting, hoping Jesus would heal him.

This is great picture of what so often happens in our lives. We have a vision of something God wants to do in our lives, but we run into seemingly insurmountable obstacles along the way. Most people would simply have given up at this point, concluding that there was no way to get the paralyzed man to Jesus.

Yet these men weren't about to give up. They were *radical* in their pursuit and their perseverance: *"When they could not come near Him because of the crowd, they uncovered the roof where He was. So when they had **broken through**, they let down the bed on which the paralytic was lying"* (Mark 2:4).

You see, if you want a *breakthrough* from God today, you may need to *break through* the barriers and obstacles keeping you from getting to Jesus. Instead of giving up when things don't go your way at first, you may need to dig a hole in the roof!

Jesus saw the faith of these men, and the paralytic was both forgiven and healed. In the same way, the Lord wants to *see* you exercise your faith today—both to break *out* of your negative circumstances and break *into* His calling for your life. Don't let anything, or anyone, get in your way.

4

CHILDREN OF THE WOMAN AT THE WELL

"He who sows iniquity will reap calamity and futility."

—*Proverbs 22:8 (AMP)*

Sometimes we forget that our children and grandchildren are the ones who will reap many of the consequences or rewards for the decisions we make today. The Bible says *"a good man leaves an inheritance to his children's children"* (Proverbs 13:22), but that *"inheritance"* can either be positive or negative.

However, the good news is that none of us are automatically *stuck* with the kind of situation we've inherited. I grew up in deep poverty, living in a government-subsidized housing project in Brooklyn, New York. It was a tough place to live, and my early education was a cruel joke. I went to school each day to get the free breakfast and lunch, and then left to smoke cigarettes or pot with my friends. I finally found myself in high school and unable to read—and I'm embarrassed to admit that I *still* couldn't read until I reached my mid-30s.

Perhaps you can't relate to these experiences. In fact, I hope you *can't* relate. But suffice it to say, the ghetto is a strange place to grow up. In some ways, it's not much different than a concentration camp, filled with hopelessness and despair. Blacks, whites, Latinos, and other ethnicities are locked behind fences of government entitlement, with little hope of breaking out of the prison.

My mother raised my sister and me on welfare, and I saw first-hand how difficult it is to break free from that kind of culture. My sister, and now even her daughter, are still locked in the entitlement trap—the deadly myth that someone owes you something you don't have to work for.

Perhaps a word picture will help you understand what this is like:

If you attach a baby elephant to a stake in the ground, it soon learns that it's not strong enough to break free. As the years go by and the elephant grows bigger, he is easily powerful enough to pull the stake out of the ground, yet he never does. Why? Because he has been conditioned to think he's not capable of that. How sad. But that's exactly what happens to many people growing up in the inner city today.

By God's grace and lots of hard work, I'm happy to report that I broke free from all of that—and so can you. From being unable to read even as a young adult, I've now written more than thirty books! Praise God. We truly *can* do all things through Christ who strengthens us. (See Philippians 4:13.)

Lessons from a Familiar Story

I've heard the John 4 story of Jesus' encounter with "the woman at the well" hundreds of times—and you probably have too. But it occurred to me recently that I've missed a fascinating component of the story. Actually, this point isn't mentioned in the story at all. But when we look between the lines, it's hard to miss.

First, let's review the highlights of the story. One day Jesus is weary from his travels and comes to a well at noon. No one is at the well except a Samaritan woman. Everyone else got their water before the scorching noonday heat. But this woman had a bad reputation among the local women and preferred to draw water when none of the town busybodies were around.

Most of the "proper" Jews refused to speak to women in public, *especially* if they were Samaritans. (See John 4:9). But Jesus loved to break down barriers. Why? Because He loved people—*all kinds* of people.

It turned out that this woman had a very checkered past. She had already had five husbands, and the man she was currently living with (number six!) wasn't actually her husband.

The story is packed full of great preaching material. But let me just ask you a few personal questions.

If you met a woman with this kind of "history," how would *you* treat her? Would you hold your nose in the air and feel you're too *respectable* to relate to such a person? Would you conclude that "People like that never change?"—or would you see God's intention to make her a new creation?

What about the Children?

But the question I never asked until recently is this: What became of this woman's children? Of course, the text doesn't say she *had* children. But if she was on her sixth sexual relationship (at least), it's almost certain she would have had kids. Perhaps even *lots* of kids. Hey, she was living centuries before *Roe v. Wade*, after all.

Those poor kids. This woman had become a single mom after all the relationships fizzled with the men in her life. With no man to provide for her, she had to shoulder the entire burden herself. When she was out working in the heat of the day, who was taking care of the kids? Just as she had to fend for herself, so did they.

The gossipy women in town branded her as a slut and a home-wrecker. Perhaps so. But this Samaritan woman also was a *victim*.

So many women in the African-American community have been victimized in similar ways. Men "loved" them and left them—and often left the children too. The inevitable result has been torn emotions, destroyed self-respect, financial devastation, and shattered lives.

This is more than a matter of statistics, but the statistics tell a woeful tale. In the early 1960s, only 6.4 percent of all children in America were born outside of marriage. But now unwed childbearing has jumped to more than 40 percent of all births and a whopping 73 percent among black children. And roughly 63 percent of all impoverished children reside in single-parent families.

The next time you read the story of the Samaritan woman, remember to ask yourself what happened to her children. They are the ultimate victims, just like they are in countless single-parent homes today.

As Lutheran pastor and theologian Dietrich Bonhoeffer correctly pointed out, "The ultimate test of a moral society is the kind of world that it leaves to its children." That should be a challenge to us as we see children damaged by the destruction of many families today, particularly in the urban areas.

A New Beginning

Fortunately, the story of the woman at the well doesn't end here. Isn't that good news? Jesus doesn't leave people like He finds them, as this downtrodden woman discovered.

The last we see of this woman, she has left her water pot and gone into the city to tell people about Jesus. Revival breaks out as people see her transformed life and receive her testimony about the Lord.

Just like a stone tossed into a lake, there is a ripple effect when God changes a person's life. When I get to heaven someday, I want to search out this woman and ask her what happened to her children. I hope her ripple effect of healing, hope, and salvation extended to them as well.

We desperately need some similar ripple effects today. Countless women have been used and abandoned, and they need a personal encounter with Jesus and the love of His people.

Never underestimate the impact one transformed life can have. If we are alert to the opportunities and willing to get involved, we can be God's tools to bring about those divine transformations.

But What about the Men?

The story of the Samaritan woman makes a specific reference to the men in her town. This is surely a good thing, isn't it? Too often, pastors find themselves preaching to congregations where the women greatly outnumber the men. The men are responsible for many of the problems occurring in the lives of these women and their children, but on Sunday morning, many of the men often are nowhere to be found!

It's time for a revival among the men, especially in the Black community. Women have carried more than their fair share of the responsibility for their family's spiritual well-being, and it's time for the men to step up to the plate.

Look what happened in Samaria as a result of this woman's transformation: *"The woman then left her waterpot, went her way into the city, and said to the men, 'Come, see a Man who told me all things that I ever did. Could this be the Christ?' Then they went out of the city and came to Him"* (John 4:28–30).

Don't lose heart, dear women of God. Jesus not only wants to transform you and your children. He also wants to raise up a new generation of men who will truly fulfill the biblical mandate to "*act like men*" (1 Corinthians 16:13 NASB).

However, I find that many women have a totally wrong picture of what the Bible *means* when it says men should "*act like men.*" This Scripture certainly *doesn't* mean acting like some of the deranged, violent, addicted, or egotistical men you may have encountered in the past. Instead, God wants to provide godly women with men who will love them and their children the same way Christ loved the church. (See Ephesians 5:25–33.)

Don't settle for anything less. God wants to give you His *best*.

5

WAS THE "MORAL MAJORITY" TRULY MORAL...OR A MAJORITY?

"The idea that religion and politics don't mix was invented by the devil to keep Christians from running their own country."

—*Jerry Falwell*

Martin Luther King Jr. tried to rally America to its highest virtues—and so did another preacher, Jerry Falwell. However, each of these two leaders had a different focus as to *which* values the country needed to recapture.

As a preacher of the gospel, King often spoke of the need for Americans to reclaim the country's "precious values" and "moral foundations":

If we are to go forward, we must go back and rediscover those precious values—that all reality hinges on moral foundations and that all reality has spiritual control.

Yet King's main areas of emphasis were racial injustice and poverty. He also had pacifist leanings and became an ardent opponent of the Vietnam War.

Falwell, in contrast, was primarily concerned about an entirely different spectrum of moral issues. Rather than concern himself with issues like segregation and poverty, he preached against such things as homosexual behavior and abortion.

Jerry Falwell is especially known for founding the Moral Majority. In 1976, Falwell had launched a series of "I Love America" rallies to address the nation's deteriorating morality. Falwell was a long-time Baptist pastor, and the prevalent Baptist view at that time was that religion and politics shouldn't be mixed. According to the usual approach of Baptists and other evangelicals, the answer to the nation's problems was found in preaching the gospel. The culture would be changed as a by-product, but most preachers weren't willing to address social issues head-on.

The Moral Majority was formally launched in 1979 as Falwell formed a coalition of people concerned about the nation. The national organization and state chapters grew quickly, fueled by Falwell's *Old Time Gospel Hour* mailing list. Although the core membership was composed of evangelical Christians, Falwell insisted that the Moral Majority leadership also include conservative Catholics and Jews.

At its peak, Falwell's group had more than four million members and two million donors. As the name implied, the Moral Majority touted its views as representing the common sense consensus of the majority of Americans.

By the end of Ronald Reagan's second presidential term, the Moral Majority was running its course. Falwell dissolved it in 1989, declaring victory rather than defeat: "Our goal has been achieved....The religious right is solidly in place...and religious conservatives in America are now in for the duration."

Conservative Activism

Make no mistake about it, Falwell wasn't just theoretician, he was an *activist*. His Moral Majority campaigned aggressively on a number of core conservative causes:

- Censorship of media outlets that were perceived to be promoting an "anti-family" agenda

- Enforcement of a traditional vision of family life

- Opposition to the Equal Rights Amendment

- Opposition to the Strategic Arms Limitation Talks

- Opposition to state recognition and acceptance of homosexual acts

- Promotion of laws outlawing abortion, except in cases involving incest, rape, or the life of the mother

- Targeting of Jews and other non-Christians for conversion to conservative Christianity

Taking positions like these made Falwell a hero to many and the archenemy of others. Conservatives often hailed him as a courageous and visionary man of God, but liberals despised him as an opportunistic demagogue. While the Moral Majority could claim adherents among both Republicans and Democrats, their ranks were considerably stronger among Republicans.

Whether or not you agree with Falwell on the issues, a few things should be noted about his legacy:

1. He was clear and straightforward when addressing the issues he cared about.

2. His scope was generally limited to traditional conservative causes, not subjects like racial justice and the kinds of cultural issues that someone like MLK would be passionate about.

3. His conservative worldview tended to blind him to some of dangers of America's military-industrial complex.

4. He was a fantastic grassroots organizer, mobilizing millions of people to get involved in the issues affecting their country.

Love him or hate him, at least Falwell didn't duck the issues. But were they always the *right* issues—the moral issues most important in the eyes of God?

Political Involvement

One of Falwell's lasting legacies was a change in many Christians' perspective on political involvement. Prior to the Moral Majority, most conservative Christians were content to be involved in their church activities, while leaving politics to others. Falwell promoted a new form of conservative activism that made it a moral imperative for believers to be "salt and light" in the political arena.

The Moral Majority engaged in political activity in a variety of ways. Through national media campaigns and grassroots organization, they supported particular candidates and issues in elections. They also lobbied for their views by contacting officeholders via mail and phone calls. For example, one of the Moral Majority's first political activities was to support Senator Jesse Helms' proposed legislation promoting school prayer.

Many of the Moral Majority constituents were also heavily involved in Ronald Reagan's presidential campaigns in 1980 and 1984. This was an interesting development, since Jimmy Carter's election as president in 1976 was a milestone for evangelical Christians. Carter was a self-professed evangelical who openly talked of his experience of being "born again." Yet he was more liberal on social issues and did not actively oppose his Democrat party's pro-choice position on abortion.

Later, in his book *White House Diary*, Carter wrote that Jerry Falwell and the Moral Majority were largely to blame for his defeat in the 1980 election. Why? Because they "purchased $10 million in commercials on southern radio and TV to brand me as a traitor to the South and no longer a Christian."

Falwell didn't deny Carter's claims. In fact, he openly gloated that his organization had tilted the nation in favor of Reagan. And in Reagan's 1984 reelection campaign, the Moral Majority and other Christian Right organizations had a significant impact on the Republican platform, especially on issues such as abortion and school prayer. However, a study of 1984 voters indicated that more anti-Moral Majority voters cast votes for Walter Mondale than pro-Moral Majority voters voted for Reagan. This suggests that the impact of Falwell's group was already waning by that time, and a negative backlash was arising among many voters.

By the 1988 election, the Moral Majority's influence was seriously eroding, partly because of divisions in its ranks. Evangelical minister and televangelist Pat Robertson sought the Republican nomination, and his political platform seemed to perfectly mirror the Moral Majority. However, Falwell instead gave his organization's endorsement to George H. W. Bush, Reagan's vice president.

At first glance, this seemed like a very odd development. But Falwell's decision highlighted both the personal rivalry between Falwell and Robertson as televangelists and also the deep-seated tensions between Falwell's fundamentalism and Robertson's charismatic tradition.

Lessons and Legacy

This history lesson about Jerry Falwell and the Moral Majority may seem like a strange thing to include in a book about ignoring the hot-button issues today. However, George Santayana was correct when he famously observed, "Those who do not remember the past are condemned to repeat it." There are important lessons that can be gained from a study of the Moral Majority, and we ignore them at our peril. Here are just a few of the things we can learn from Jerry Falwell's movement:

1. *When people are mobilized in a united effort, they can have*

a powerful impact. God himself confirms this principle when describing the builders of the tower of Babel. (See Genesis 11:5–6.)

2. *It's not enough to successfully mobilize and unite people, for we must also make sure our agenda is aligned with God's agenda.* The builders of Babel were "succeeding" in their project, but their plans were at odds with God's plans. Throughout history, spellbinding leaders have mobilized the masses in powerful ways—but often in ways that were misguided. Napoleon, Lenin, and Hitler are just a few examples.

3. *We must beware of the tendency to allow personal ambition and rivalries to sidetrack otherwise noble objectives.* Many movements begin with the best of intentions, only to fall prey to egotism on the part of the leader.

4. *We must avoid the tendency to have such tunnel vision about our own priorities and passions that we fail to acknowledge and respect the vision of others.* Often, conservative and liberal activists fail to see any value in the positions on the other side. Conservatives sometimes just don't "get it" when people like MLK describe the concerns of the poor. Liberals, on the other hand, often have been blinded from seeing the legitimate concerns of those who advocate for traditional values.

5. *Christian activists must follow Jesus' advice and seek first the kingdom of God instead of the agenda of their own political party* (See Matthew 6:10, Matthew 6:33.) Some of the Moral Majority objectives could be categorized as "kingdom" objectives, but others are simply one party's political bent.

6. *It's not enough to be "right" on the issues.* In addition to projecting the *truth* of God, we must also display the *heart*

of God. That's why the apostle Paul said believers should *"speak the truth in love, growing in every way more and more like Christ"* (Ephesians 4:15 NLT). Whatever our political or cultural viewpoints may be, our persuasiveness will be undercut if people don't sense true sincerity and compassion in our lives. Whether in the realm of politics or in the church, this old maxim is a good one to follow: In essentials, unity; in non-essentials, liberty; in everything, love."

Jerry Falwell never could be accused of ignoring the hot-button issues. While his Moral Majority movement was rather short-lived, it had a profound and lasting impact on the politics of our nation. Even though the organization is now gone, it's legacy lives on. The seeds it planted are springing up today in such things as conservative talk shows and the Tea Party movement.

Regardless of whether you consider the Moral Majority a success or a totally misguided failure, I hope you will consider some of the important lessons its history raises. And take a few minutes to dream with me: What if there truly *was* a "moral majority" of Americans who rose up to rescue the nation from its downward spiral? I don't mean a conservative majority or a liberal majority, but a kingdom majority—people willing to put politics and parties aside in order to seek God's will above all else.

What if the spiritual descendants of Martin Luther King Jr. could kneel down together with the spiritual descendants of Jerry Falwell, repenting of pride and disrespect, and seeking one another's forgiveness and blessing? It would surely be revival time in the U.S.A. And how sweet that would be.

6

JEREMIAH WRIGHT: RIGHT ALL ALONG?

"America is still the number one killer in the world."

—*Jeremiah Wright*

One of Barack Obama's biggest obstacles to getting elected in 2008 was the fact that he had spent many years in the pews of Jeremiah Wright, long-time pastor of Trinity United Church of Christ in Chicago. Reverend Wright had performed the wedding ceremony of the Obamas and baptized both of their children.

But during the campaign, Obama's political opponents made an issue of controversial sermon excerpts Wright had made throughout the years. In a September 16, 2001, message entitled "The Day of Jerusalem's Fall", Wright said the September 11 terrorist attacks were evidence that "America's chickens are coming home to roost":

> We bombed Hiroshima, we bombed Nagasaki, and we nuked far more than the thousands in New York and the Pentagon, and we never batted an eye....And now we are indignant, because the stuff we have done overseas is now brought back into our own front yards. America's chickens are coming home to roost. Violence begets violence. Hatred begets hatred. And terrorism begets terrorism.

Wright's defenders said his statements had been taken out of context. But many people were outraged by Wright's implication that America had brought the 9-11 attacks on itself because of its past transgressions.

Another controversial sermon, "Confusing God and Government", was delivered on April 13, 2003. Wright's theme was that governments lie, but God does not lie:

> [The United States] government lied about their belief that all men were created equal. The truth is they believed that all white men were created equal. The truth is they did not even believe that white women were created equal, in creation nor civilization. The government had to pass an amendment to the Constitution to get white women the vote. Then the government had to pass an equal rights amendment to get equal protection under the law for women. The government still thinks a woman has no rights over her own body, and between Uncle Clarence who sexually harassed Anita Hill, and a closeted Klan court, that is a throwback to the nineteenth century, handpicked by Daddy Bush, Ronald Reagan, Gerald Ford, between Clarence and that stacked court, they are about to undo Roe vs. Wade, just like they are about to undo affirmative action. The government lied in its founding documents and the government is still lying today. Governments lie.

Wright's sermon went on to give a long list of alleged examples of lying by the U.S. government: Pearl Harbor, the Gulf of Tonkin incident, Nelson Mandela, the Tuskegee experiment, HIV/AIDs, the connection between Al Qaeda and Saddam Hussein, and weapons of mass destruction in Iraq. According to Jeremiah Wright, the government lied to us about all these things.

Wright then spoke of injustices to Native Americans and African Americans, ending with his infamous crescendo of "God damn America":

> The United States of America government, when it came to treating her citizens of Indian descent fairly, she failed. She put them on reservations. When it came to treating her citizens of Japanese descent fairly, she failed. She put them in internment prison camps.
>
> When it came to treating her citizens of African descent fairly, America failed. She put them in chains, the government put them on slave quarters, put them on auction blocks, put them in cotton field, put them in inferior schools, put them in substandard housing, put them in scientific experiments, put them in the lowest paying jobs, put them outside the equal protection of the law, kept them out of their racist bastions of higher education and locked them into positions of hopelessness and helplessness.
>
> The government gives them the drugs, builds bigger prisons, passes a three-strike law and then wants us to sing "God Bless America." No, no, no, not God Bless America. God damn America—that's in the Bible—for killing innocent people. God damn America, for treating our citizens as less than human. God damn America, as long as she tries to act like she is God and she is supreme. The United States government has failed the vast majority of her citizens of African descent.

So, what do you think? Reverend Wright's accusations against America are not entirely unfounded. Yes, governments often lie—including the United States government. Does that mean every national tragedy is evidence that our chickens are coming home to roost? Does the Lord truly want to "damn" our country because of our national sins?

Before returning to those questions, let's first look at how Barack Obama responded to the critics of his involvement with Jeremiah Wright.

To Affirm or Disavow?

When his pastor's controversial statements first came to light in the national media, Obama tried both to shrug them off and to distance himself. He told Charles Gibson of ABC News, "It's as if we took the five dumbest things that I've ever said or you've ever said in our lives and compressed them and put them out there—I think that people's reaction would, understandably, be upset."

But, sensing that a little more outrage was required, Obama added: "Words that degrade individuals have no place in our public dialogue, whether it's on the campaign stump or in the pulpit. In sum, I reject outright the statements by Rev. Wright that are at issue."

Of course, the critics weren't satisfied. How could the Obamas have remained in a church for seventeen years, when such hateful preaching was taking place? Why would a man want to be president of the United States if he sympathized with such critical, anti-American sentiments?

There was only so far Obama could go in claiming ignorance of Reverend Wright's inflammatory teachings. In his book *Dreams from My Father*, Obama had quoted Wright as saying in a sermon, "It's this world, where cruise ships throw away more food in a day than most residents of Port-au-Prince see in a year, where White folks' greed runs a world in need."

Wright was originally scheduled to deliver an invocation at the February 2007 announcement of Obama's presidential candidacy, but Obama called his pastor the night before to withdraw his request. A campaign spokesperson later explained, "Senator Obama is proud of his pastor and his church, but...decided to avoid having statements and beliefs being used out of context and forcing the entire church to defend itself."

In March 2007, as the controversy threatened to derail his campaign, Obama delivered a speech entitled "A More Perfect Union" at the National Constitution Center in Philadelphia. Although the speech condemned Reverend Wright's statements, Obama sought to place them in the historical context some key events that formed Wright's views on race-related matters in America. Explaining why he could not disown Wright, whom he described as being like "an old uncle," he said that would be akin to disowning the entire black community. And, seeming to sympathize with Wright's positions, he said American had a "tragic history when it comes to race."

Hillary Clinton, who was running against him at the time, was critical of Obama's attendance at Trinity United Church of Christ: "You don't choose your family, but you choose what church you want to attend." During a press conference, Clinton described her personal preference in a pastor: "I think given all we have heard and seen, [Wright] would not have been my pastor."

The Debate Continues

Meanwhile, the Republican and conservative onslaught continued. Fox News radio and TV host Sean Hannity pointed out that Wright's church had given a lifetime achievement award to Louis Farrakhan, "a virulent, anti-Semitic racist." And Salon.com editor-in-chief Joan Walsh described additional sermon clips that captured Wright saying the Iraq war was "the same thing al-Qaida is doing under a different color flag."

But defenders of Wright sought to put his racially charged comments in context of the black struggle for equality in America.

For example, cultural critic Kelefa Sanneh traced Wright's theology and rhetoric all the way back to Frederick Douglass, analyzing his 1854 reference to antebellum American Christians as "bad, corrupt, and wicked."

In 2004, before the Wright controversy had broken out during the 2008 campaign, Anthony E. Cook, a professor of law at Georgetown University, provided a detailed comparative analysis of sermons delivered after 9-11 by Jerry Falwell, T. D. Jakes, and Jeremiah Wright. Cook contended that the intent of Falwell's and Jakes' sermons was to use the Christian religion as a justification for the War on Terror, while Wright's objective was to side against war and to get listeners to engage in introspection about their daily behavior and relationship with God.

Another defender was Georgetown University sociology professor Michael Eric Dyson, who wrote: "Patriotism is the affirmation of one's country in light of its best values, including the attempt to correct it when it's in error. Wright's words are the tough love of a war-tested patriot speaking his mind." And J. Kameron Carter, associate professor of theology and black church studies at Duke Divinity School, stated that Wright "voiced in his sermons a pain that must be interpreted inside of the tradition of black prophetic Christianity." Other commentators pointed out that Martin Luther King Jr. had also expressed very critical statements about the United States at times.

But when Wright continued to make racially charged statements, Obama attempted to further distance himself from him, expressing outrage and shock at a press conference on April 2007:

> The person that I saw yesterday was not the person that I met twenty years ago. His comments were not only divisive and destructive, but I believe that they end up giving comfort to those who prey on hate, and I believe that they do not portray accurately the perspective of the

black church. They certainly don't portray accurately my values and beliefs. And if Reverend Wright thinks that that's political posturing, as he put it, then he doesn't know me very well. And based on his remarks yesterday, well, I may not know him as well as I thought either....

What became clear to me is that he was presenting a worldview that contradicts who I am and what I stand for, and what I think particularly angered me was his suggestion somehow that my previous denunciation of his remarks were somehow political posturing. Anybody who knows me and anybody who knows what I'm about knows that I am about trying to bridge gaps and I see the commonality in all people....Whatever relationship I had with Reverend Wright has changed, as a consequence of this."

On May 31, 2008, Barack and Michelle Obama announced that they had withdrawn their membership in Trinity United Church of Christ, stating that "Our relations with Trinity have been strained by the divisive statements of Reverend Wright, which sharply conflict with our own views."

What Should We Conclude?

What should we conclude about the theology and worldview of Jeremiah Wright? And why does it matter?

Although entire books could be written on this controversy and its implications, let me just make a few observations:

- *Was Jeremiah Wright correct on the facts?* Any fair-minded analysis of Wright's statements would have to conclude that the answer to this is yes and no. Yes, the U.S. government has done plenty of lying, but not on *everything* cited by Wright. For example, although we were clearly wrong about weapons of mass destruction in Iraq, was it an intentional lie by George W. Bush and our other leaders? Many commentators believe it was an honest mistake—even though it was arguably a foolhardy one. But Wright was correct about a number of his points concerning injustices to Native Americans, blacks, and other minorities.

◂ *Was he correct on his conclusions about the consequences of America's sins?* If we acknowledge that America has often grieved God's Spirit in its national and international policies, does that mean that we can expect our "chickens to come home to roost" and the Lord to "damn" our country? Defenders of Wright have pointed out that ministers on the conservative side—such as Jerry Falwell, Pat Robertson, and John Hagee—have made somewhat similar statements about God's judgment on America. Even Billy Graham famously said many decades ago that if God doesn't judge America, He will owe an apology to Sodom and Gomorrah.

◂ *Why do preachers tend to select different sins to preach against?* Jeremiah Wright, echoing preachers like MLK, tends to focus on national sins like violence and racial and economic injustice against minorities. Many of the white preachers, in contrast, are more likely to preach against things like abortion and homosexuality as the focal points of our cultural demise.

◂ *Where's the repentance?* America has sinned—in many different ways, no doubt. The Bible says hope and forgiveness are available for individuals and nations that have sinned, so that is not a problem for God. However, this *is* a problem: Are we willing to *acknowledge* and *repent of* our sins? Are white Christians willing to face the ugly legacy of racial injustice throughout much of our history? Are liberal Christians, like Jeremiah Wright, willing to call for national repentance over issues such as abortion, out-of-wedlock births, and sexual perversion?

Before we dismiss Jeremiah Wright as a racist or a lunatic, we should at least recognize that there's a thread of biblical logic to this argument. The apostle Paul wrote,

Do not be deceived, God is not mocked; for whatever a man sows, that he will also reap. For he who sows to his flesh will of the flesh reap corruption, but he who sows to the Spirit will of the Spirit reap everlasting life. (Galatians 6:7–8)

This is a principle that applies to both individuals and nations. We all will reap what we sow.

But exactly what has America sown? If you listen to Reverend Wright, you will conclude that America's history is filled with continuous lies, unprovoked wars, and racism. But what about the other side of the story? What about the humanitarian aid we've provided again and again when natural disasters strike other countries? What about the millions of dollars we've invested to help alleviate the HIV/AIDS epidemic in Africa? What about our courage in standing up to vicious tyrants like Hitler?

Yet it probably does little good to defend ourselves against the tirades of critics like Wright. We need to acknowledge whatever sins we've committed, intentionally or unintentionally. And then we must follow the great formula God gives us for the healing of our land:

If My people who are called by My name will humble them-selves, and pray and seek My face, and turn from their wicked ways, then I will hear from heaven, and will forgive their sin and heal their land. (2 Chronicles 7:14)

Instead of living in denial or ducking the issues, are we will-ing to follow this prescription for national restoration? Will we humble ourselves, pray, seek God's face, and turn from our wicked ways? If we do, God has promised to hear from heaven, forgive our sins, and heal our nation—even if Reverend Wright was correct about all our sins.

7

BEWARE OF PIED PIPERS—OF WHICHEVER JERSEY

"Yesterday we obeyed kings and bent our necks before
emperors. But today we kneel only to truth, follow only
beauty, and obey only love."

—*Khalil Gibran*

There are lots of Pied Pipers today—both on the right and the
on the left side of the political spectrum. And most of the
pied pipers in America claim their worldview has been shaped
by Christianity and the Word of God. Nevertheless, rather than
truly contending for the faith laid out in Scripture, many of these
leaders have substituted their own opinions, just as Jude predicted:

> *I have to write insisting—begging!—that you fight with every-
> thing you have in you for this faith entrusted to us as a gift to
> guard and cherish. What has happened is that some people
> have infiltrated our ranks (our Scriptures warned us this
> would happen), who beneath their pious skin are shameless
> scoundrels. Their design is to replace the sheer grace of our
> God with sheer license.* (Jude 1:4 MSG)

The Message paraphrase is pretty graphic here, isn't it? How
could people be *"shameless scoundrels"* underneath their *"pious*

skin"? Yet Jude says this kind of leader would infiltrate the ranks of the church!

How can this be? It gets down to a question of lordship. Is Jesus truly Lord, or are we free to concoct our own theology and put His name on it? It's time to ask ourselves Jesus' famous question again today: *"Why do you call Me 'Lord, Lord,' and not do the things which I say?"*(Luke 6:46).

It gets down to this: How can we call ourselves followers of Jesus if our beliefs and our lives are contrary to much of what He taught? And if today's "Christian leaders" in America are truly men and women of God, why do they end up embracing political philosophies that are diametrically opposed to one another?

Liberals and progressives like Barack Obama, Jeremiah Wright, Jim Wallis, Jesse Jackson, and Al Sharpton all claim to be followers of Christ. But so do many people such as staunch conservatives like Rush Limbaugh, Glenn Beck, Bill O'Reilly, Sean Hannity, Rick Santorum, and Sarah Palin.

Something just doesn't add up here.

And just as some people blindly follow "Christian" pied pipers on the left or on the right, others seem to be swayed by the anti-God rants of media pundits like Bill Maher. Although he says he's an agnostic rather than an atheist, he received the 2009 Richard Dawkins Award from the Atheist Alliance International. Critical of organized religion, he says, "Religion to me is a bureaucracy between man and God that I don't need." His 2008 documentary *Religulous* was described by *Variety* magazine as a film "that spoofs religious extremism across the world."

The point in bringing up Bill Maher is that you can find a pied piper to lead you in just about any direction you are willing to go. Too many people today are spiritually gullible. Unclear about what they really believe, they are blown about by every new cultural fad.

Even Christians—who surely should know better—too often are standing on shifting sands rather than settled truth.

Which Voice Are You Following?

I love the story of Paul and Silas preaching in the town of Berea. (See Acts 17:10–11.) Rather than accept the teachings of Paul and Silas as accurate theology, these believers *"searched the Scriptures daily to find out whether these things were so"* (Acts 17:11).

Have you done that lately, my friend? As you're listening to Rush Limbaugh or watching *Morning Joe*, Al Sharpton, Rachel Maddow, or *The Daily Show*, do you search the Bible to see whether their philosophies line up to what it says? Despite all of the "God talk" that still occurs in America today, most people are woefully ignorant about what the Word of God really teaches.

The Bible says people tend to be like sheep. That is a *good* thing if we are faithfully following Jesus, the Good Shepherd. But, too often, we are hoodwinked by wolves in shepherd's clothing. They may have "Reverend" or "Pastor" or "Bishop" in front of their name, but that doesn't guarantee that they're the real deal. Some are merely thieves, robbers, or hirelings, as Jesus called them. (See John 10:1, 12.)

With so many voices in the world today, it's urgent for the people of God to get to know *His* voice. Look at how Jesus described the relationship we should have with Him as our Shepherd:

> *The sheep hear his voice; and he calls his own sheep by name and leads them out....He goes before them; and the sheep follow him, for they know his voice. Yet they will be no means follow a stranger, but will flee from him, for they do not know the voice of strangers.* (John 10:3–5)

What voice are *you* following today? Is it truly the voice of the Savior, or is it *"the voice of strangers"*—false saviors who are drawing you toward dependence rather than abundance? Jesus warned us about these other voices, likening them to a thief who comes to steal, kill, and destroy. In stark contrast, Jesus said those who follow Him can experience *"more and better life than they ever dreamed of"* (John 10:10 MSG). If that's not the kind of life you are experiencing today, I encourage you to pause and ask yourself which voice you've been listening to.

Lessons from the Hamelin Story

You've probably heard the old German legend of the Pied Piper of Hamelin. When the town of Hamelin was suffering from a terrible rat infestation, a charismatic man dressed in multicolored clothing appeared, claiming to have a solution. The desperate townspeople gladly promised to pay him for his services, and the man proceeded to play a musical pipe to lure the rats into a river, where they drowned.

Despite this success, the mayor of the town refused to pay the piper the full amount of money due. The piper angrily left the town, vowing to return and seek revenge.

Sure enough, the piper came back, this time when the townspeople were in church. He played his pipe again, but not to lure away the rats. The seductive sound of his music drew the children of Hamelin out of their town and into a cave, and they were never seen again.

Why has this story endured for so many centuries? Because we've all experienced some version of this plot: Somebody hired to fix one problem ends up creating other problems that are even worse.

We see this in the biblical story of the woman who suffered with a hemorrhage for twelve years. We're told that she *"had suffered many things from many physicians. She had spent all that she had and was no better, but rather grew worse"* (Mark 5:25–34). Notice that this poor woman (1) suffered at the hands of the very ones who were supposedly trying to help her, (2) spent all her money on worthless cures, and (3) ended up getting worse instead of better.

And it's also crucial to notice that this woman apparently *persisted*—for twelve long years—in a treatment plan that actually made her situation worse. No doubt, her worthless (or evil) doctors assured her that improvement was right around the corner. "Just stay the course," they advised her. "We're surely making progress."

You see, there are pied pipers everywhere. Politicians, financial planners, sports coaches—we've all heard the "stay the course" message when it made no logical sense at all.

A Spirit of Stupor

Romans 11:8 describes a dangerous condition known as a *"spirit of stupor,"* spiritual blindness and insensitivity caused by people's idolatry, hardness of heart, and failure to seek God's ways. Those overcome by this spirit have *"eyes that could not see and ears that could not hear."*

Our English word *stupor* comes from the Latin *stupure*, meaning "insensible." Dictionaries define it as "a lack of critical cognitive function, where a sufferer only responds to stimuli such as pain"… "suspension or great diminishing of sensibility, such as the effect of narcotics or intoxicants (e.g., a drunken stupor)"…"mental apathy."

Just as a person usually needs several drinks to become inebriated, America's stupor didn't happen all at once. The pied piper spirit began to weave its seductive web decades ago, but its tune comes to a crescendo whenever skilled politicians intoxicate us with soaring rhetoric and with promises they are unable to keep.

If you see this as strictly a matter of party affiliation you've completely missed the point. There are pied pipers on all sides of the political spectrum. We have to address the spiritual roots of many people's trancelike political preferences. The stupor is, after all, a "spirit"—something that must ultimately be broken through prayer, fasting, and spiritual warfare.

Have you ever tried to persuade a drunken person to follow any kind of sensible path? Good luck on that. First, the intoxicated person must sober up and come to his senses.

In the same way, God graciously wants to return America to "sobriety" and sensibility. Prayer is a powerful thing, and the curse of spiritual stupor can be broken. But time is running out, and our children's future depends on it.

It's time for true Christians to return to the Lord as their Savior, trusting in Him instead of the politicians and political movements. We must boldly cry out to awaken those still mesmerized by the seductive spell of political pipers: *"Awake, you who sleep, arise from the dead, and Christ will give you light"* (Ephesians 5:14).

The Allure of Barabbas

We live in dangerous, deceptive times, when it has never been more important to be like the sons of Issachar, *"who understood the times"* (1 Chronicles 12:32 NIV) and knew what God's people should do. In recent decades, many Christians have been hoodwinked by smooth-talking, emotion-stirring politicians and philosophies. Too often, we've allowed feel-good rhetoric, Santa Claus handouts, or demonization of opponents to twist reality and sway us from biblical values.

I'm old enough to remember the old *To Tell the Truth* TV program, where three mystery guests claimed to be a certain person, and the four celebrity panelists had to guess which one of them was telling the truth about their identity. Each segment of the program culminated with the host saying, "Only *one* of these is the real _____, and the others are imposters. Will the real _____ please stand up!"

Matthew 27 tells a story remarkably similar to an episode of *To Tell the Truth*. Two men stood before the Roman governor (Pontius Pilate) and a large crowd of people. Both of these men were revolutionaries, but they advocated two very different kinds of revolution. Both were radical in their approach, but in completely different ways.

Pilate made it clear that only one of these men could be chosen: *"Which **one** do you want me to release to you: Jesus Barabbas, or Jesus who is called Messiah?"*(Matthew 27:17 NIV). The people had to carefully evaluate the claims of these two revolutionaries before making their all-important decision.

According to many early manuscripts, the full name of the first man was Jesus Barabbas. Jesus meant "savior," and Barabbas meant "son of the father" (*Bar* = Son, *Abbas* = Father). This man was widely known as an insurrectionist who had participated in a recent uprising against the Roman authorities. (See Mark 15:7.)

The message of Barabbas was clear: "You all could have a great life if it weren't for the Romans. They've victimized and oppressed you, making it impossible to be happy and productive. Let *me* come to your aid and get rid of the 'bad guys' who've ripped you off and done you wrong."

In some ways, Barabbas was probably ahead of his time. It was a message later echoed by countless revolutionaries and political movements throughout the centuries. You can hear threads of the Barabbas message in Occupy Wall Street protesters, anarchists, populists, progressives, and communists from Karl Marx to Fidel Castro and Hugo Chavez.

And, no doubt, there was a grain of truth in Barabbas' case, just as there have always been elements of truth in the manipulative arguments of political demagogues throughout the centuries. However, the cure he promised didn't address the more fundamental cause of people's misery.

A New Kind of Revolutionary

Standing next to Barabbas that day was a very different kind of revolutionary, though there were some intriguing parallels between the men. This radical young leader from Nazareth was also named Jesus, and His followers considered Him the Savior. And just as the name Barabbas meant "son of the father," this other Jesus was known by many as the Son of Father God. Ultimately he was referred to as Jesus the Christ, or Messiah.

Jesus had some fair-weather followers who probably weren't much different from the followers of Barabbas. They saw His miracles and hoped He would liberate them from Roman oppression and restore the independent Jewish nation. Mostly likely, this was their misguided motivation in shouting "Hosanna" (save now!) when He rode into Jerusalem on a donkey a few days earlier.

However, the message of *this* Jesus was much different than Jesus Barabbas. Instead of promising political solutions—salvation from the *outside*—He told His followers they must repent and receive God's kingdom on the *inside*. Rather than allowing His disciples to pity themselves and feel like victims, He challenged them to take the "logs" out of their own eyes and deal with any sin or selfishness that was preventing them from receiving true freedom and abundance.

The unfolding scene in Matthew 27 was almost unbelievable. Which "Jesus"—which savior—would the people choose: Jesus Barabbas or Jesus Christ? Would they opt for a political solution that let them off the hook in dealing with their own sinfulness and disobedience? Or would they embrace Jesus' promise of a new heart and a transformed life?

You see, two different gospels were presented by these two men. Both claimed to offer "good news" to those who would follow their pathway. Barabbas promised a better life once the Romans were defeated, while Jesus promised new life in a spiritual kingdom that transcended politics and earthly kingdoms.

To Pilate's shock, the people overwhelmingly voted for Barabbas and were content to send Jesus to crucifixion. How could this be? Were they simply deceived, lured by Barabbas' promise of sweet revenge against their oppressors? Were they paid off by the jealous religious leaders, who saw Jesus as a threat to their grip on people's lives? Or was the problem that most of Jesus' fans and followers simply failed to show up—or *speak* up—on that fateful day?

America's Valley of Decision

Today, America faces an eerily similar moment of decision. As in the days of Barabbas and Jesus, we face enormous economic and social challenges, causing many people to feel desperate for relief. If we are seduced by the promises of Barabbas, we will seek political saviors and opt for government solutions to our woes. We will listen to the alluring siren call of those who stoke the flames of victimhood and demonize opponents with a "divide and conquer" strategy.

In contrast, the pathway prescribed by Jesus seems much more costly and difficult. It beckons us to lay down our lives and trust God to meet our needs. Instead of permitting us to play the blame game, it points us to the ancient remedy prescribed in 2 Chronicles 7:14: We must humble ourselves, pray, seek God's face, and turn from our own wicked ways. Then, and only then, does the Lord promise to forgive our national sins and heal our land.

It's time to repent of any tendency to cast our nation's leaders in the role of our savior or source. There's only *one* true Savior and Source, and those who put their hope in *Him* will not be disappointed. (See Romans 10:11 NASB.) Every human substitute is just an imposter and counterfeit, shifting sand that will ultimately replace our soaring hopes with deep disappointment.

8

RECLAIM WHAT THE ENEMY HAS STOLEN

"The thief comes only to steal and kill and destroy; I came that theymay have life, and have it abundantly."

—Jesus (John 10:10 NASB)

Perhaps, as you read my description of demagogues, wolves, and pied pipers, you find yourself agreeing with my message. You see that you've been misled, lied to, and robbed—and by people you've trusted as your leaders.

It's discouraging to discover that you've been deceived and ripped off. In fact, perhaps you're feeling a little hopeless about the future prospects of your family or your nation. *It's too late, Bishop Bloomer*, you may be thinking. *The devil has already stolen from us and there's nothing we can do about it at this point.*

If you're having feelings like these, I have great news for you! Even though the thieves and demagogues may have robbed you, God wants to restore whatever has been stolen.

"How can that be?" you may ask. Well, let's look at some remarkable examples of this in God's Word.

In Genesis 14, Abraham's nephew, Lot, is taken captive by enemy armies, along with his family and his possessions. When

Abraham hears the news, he immediately gathers more than three hundred men to mount a counterattack.

Look at the fantastic result of Abraham's raid against the enemy forces: *"So he brought back all the goods, and also brought back his brother Lot and his goods, as well as the women and the people"* (Genesis 14:16).

What a great story! Although the enemy came as a thief, the counterattack recaptured everything that was stolen.

Ziklag

A similar story is told in 1 Samuel 30:1–9, where David and his men come to Ziklag and find that the Amalekites have invaded it and taken their wives and children captive. This was such a horrible situation that the men *"lifted up their voices and wept, until they had no more power to weep"* (verse 4).

David became *"greatly distressed"*—particularly when his men spoke of stoning him! Yet David was a man after God's heart, and he knew where his strength must come from: *"David strengthened himself in the LORD his God"* (verse 6).

If Satan has stolen something that belongs to you, I encourage you to follow David's example and find new strength in the presence of the Lord. And then you'll be ready for David's next step: *"David inquired of the LORD"* (verse 8). When you're facing spiritual attack, nothing is more important than seeking God's strategy for a counterattack.

Please notice that David wasn't passive when he was attacked by the enemy. Nor was he content to wallow in defeat or allow the enemy to keep what was stolen. After David prayed and got his bearings, he immediately went on the *offensive* and prepared his counterattack.

War in the natural realm is a violent and bloody endeavor, and the same is true of spiritual war. When David discovered the enemy encampment, he wasn't in the mood for compromise or negotiation: *"David attacked them from twilight until the evening of the next day. Not a man of them escaped, except four hundred young men who rode on camels and fled"* (1 Samuel 30:17). This was aggressive warfare, in the same kind of spirit we must have to overcome the powers and principalities of the devil.

But David's warfare wasn't only about revenge against the enemy; it also involved recapturing everything that had been stolen:

> So David recovered **all** that the Amalekites had carried away, and David rescued his two wives. And **nothing of theirs was lacking**, either small or great, sons or daughters, spoil or anything which they had taken from them; David recovered **all**.
> (verses 18–19)

This should be our vision as well: Recovering *all* that the enemy has stolen! Instead of accepting defeat, it's time to go on the offensive!

The Spoils of Battle

As wonderful as it is to recover what the enemy has taken from us, often the Lord wants to give us even *more* than that! The Old Testament law required a thief to pay back even more than was stolen:

> If a man steals an ox or a sheep, and slaughters it or sells it, he shall restore **five** oxen for an ox and **four** sheep for a sheep.... If a man delivers to his neighbor money or articles to keep, and it is stolen out of the man's house, if the thief is found, he shall pay **double**. (Exodus 22:1, 7)

This principle is demonstrated in the story of Job. Satan had stolen everything Job had: his family, his health, and his possessions. But even in a fierce spiritual battle like Job's, the enemy's attacks weren't the end of the story! God broke through in Job's life and gave him even more than he had lost: *"The LORD restored Job's losses....Indeed the LORD gave Job* **twice as much as he had before"** (Job 42:10).

Has Satan ripped you off in some way? Has he stolen your health, your finances, your relationships, your confidence, and even your sanity? If so, there's no need to get stuck in a "victim" mentality. God wants to bless you, restore what you've lost, and give you even *more* than you had before!

Restoring the Years

Some people have been victimized by the enemy for so long that their feelings of victimhood have become a "familiar spirit"— deeply ingrained in their hearts and minds. Instead of just losing a spiritual battle or two, they feel as if they have already lost the war.

If you've entertained this defeatist mentality, God has a new beginning for you today! He's able to restore even *years* of losses from the enemy.

In the days of the prophet Joel, the people of Judah faced several years of devastating attacks on their crops by locusts. Because these attacks were both severe and long-lasting, it was easy for people to lose hope:

> *What the chewing locust left, the swarming locust has eaten; what the swarming locust left, the crawling locust has eaten; and what the crawling locust left, the consuming locust has eaten....He has* **laid waste** *My vine, and* **ruined** *My fig tree; He has* **stripped it bare** *and* **thrown it away;** *its branches are made white.* (Joel 1:4, 7)

Perhaps the attacks of the enemy have left you feeling like this today: *"laid waste...ruined...stripped bare...and thrown...away."* But God knows about your situation and wants to restore everything you've lost:

> *I **will restore** to you the **years** that the swarming locust has eaten, the crawling locust, the consuming locust, and the chewing locust.* (Joel 2:25)

And when the Lord says He wants to restore what you've lost, this means a life of incredible blessing and abundance:

> *The threshing floors shall be full of wheat, and the vats shall overflow with new wine and oil....You shall eat in **plenty** and be **satisfied**, and praise the name of the LORD your God, Who has dealt wondrously with you; and My people shall never be put to shame.* (Joel 2:24, 26)

This kind of amazing breakthrough is God's will for *you,* my friend. And it's also His desire for our nation as we humble ourselves, pray, seek His face, and turn from our wicked ways. (See 2 Chronicles 7:14.)

Reversing Your Losses

If the devil has stolen something from you, it's easy to get stuck in negative thinking and assume you'll never regain what you've lost. But it's time to throw off that "stinkin' thinkin'" and remember what God's Word says:

+ Abraham recovered *everything* that the enemy stole from Lot.

+ David recovered *everything* that the enemy stole from Ziklag.

+ God's law says that a thief must pay back even *more* than what he stole.

+ Job was blessed with *double* of everything that Satan had stolen from him.

+ In the book of Joel, God promised to restore to us even *years* of the enemy's plunder.

Has the devil stolen something from your life? Your health? Your marriage? Your children? Your job? Your finances? Your vision? Your peace of mind?

If so, take a moment and commit that area of your life to the Lord. Ask Him to give you His perspective and His strategies for overcoming the enemy's attacks. Take Him at His Word that He will reverse your losses and bless you beyond your wildest dreams.

And while you are praying to regain your personal losses, don't forget to pray for God's grace and favor on your nation.

PART III:

Applying Kingdom Principles to the Hot-Button Issues
of Our Day

1

ARE YOU CONSISTENTLY PRO-LIFE?

*"Defend the poor and fatherless; do justice to the afflicted
and needy. Deliver the poor and needy; free them from
the hand of the wicked."*

—Psalm 82:3–4

How would you respond if I asked if you are pro-life? "Yes, I'm against abortion," you might respond. Or you might say, "No George, I'm pro-choice on the abortion issue."

While it's easy to wear a simplistic label, issues like this are anything but simple. Let me explain what I mean.

If you claim to be pro-life, you doubtlessly believe that abortion is wrong—the taking of a human life. Okay, but what if it's your daughter or your granddaughter who's pregnant. Perhaps she was raped, or maybe it's just a deadbeat boyfriend who got her pregnant, and now he's nowhere to be found. And what if your daughter or granddaughter is just a young teen, with her whole life ahead of her and no money to provide for a baby?

Would you still be pro-life under those circumstances? Or would you be tempted to waffle on the subject? And what if your daughter or granddaughter was adamant that she had decided to abort the baby—would you still love her and support her?

You see, it's one thing to be pro-life in a theoretical way, but it gets a lot more difficult when your loved ones are involved.

If you are pro-choice, you can get into uncomfortable ethical dilemmas too. You may be able to absolve your conscience if the fetus is just a few weeks old, but what if the pregnancy is nearly full term? Can you really argue that it's not truly a "baby" at eleven or twelve weeks? Even if you say you're pro-choice, doesn't your conscience cringe at the thought of partial-birth abortions?

No matter which side of the fence you're on, this gets messy in the "real world," doesn't it?

I have friends on both sides of the issue, and I've noticed something quite ironic: Pro-life and pro-choice people *both* claim to base their positions on compassion and the moral high ground. Pro-life folks tell me we should have compassion on the unborn; pro-choice folks say we should be compassionate to young women facing pregnancy in dire circumstances and abort their unwanted fetuses.

But true compassion must be demonstrated by our actions. If we say we are pro-life, what actions are consistent with that position? Voting for politicians who claim to be "pro-life"? Putting anti-abortion bumper stickers on your car? Picketing outside abortion clinics?

I always challenge my pro-life friends that if they *truly* have the compassion they claim, they need to show it by doing something *positive* to help pregnant moms who don't want their babies. Sometimes this means being willing to adopt an unwanted baby. At other times, the issue is mostly financial—the mother would be willing to carry her baby to term if she knew that financial provision would be available.

At any rate, if you claim to be pro-life, you can't just throw stones at women who want to abort their babies! If your compassion is genuine, you will be willing to get involved and put your time and money on the line to help bring relief.

And I challenge my pro-choice friends on the compassion issue as well. When you encounter a woman who doesn't want her baby, do you just send her down to the abortion clinic and wash your hands of the whole thing? Or do you probe a little deeper, exploring if perhaps there's a way to relieve the woman's concerns and save the baby?

Pro-Life on Other Issues

The more I study the Bible and church history, the more I'm convinced that being pro-life must go far beyond the issue of abortion. Personally, I believe we should do everything possible to protect the life of the unborn. But I *also* want to do everything in my power to extend hope and healing to the women involved in unwanted pregnancies or other difficult life circumstances.

In addition to endeavoring to reduce the number of abortions, those who are pro-life should be wresting with issues such as war, sex-trafficking, urban violence, domestic violence, and capital punishment.

In his 2012 book, *The Early Church on Killing*, historian Ron Sider makes the case that the early Christians weren't just against abortion. They took *"thou shalt not kill"* (Exodus 20:13 KJV) quite literally—not just as a prohibition against murder but as a broad imperative applied to killing in any form at all.

Sider provides evidence that although the believers had no power to stop Roman gladiator fights, capital punishment, or their military machine, they did everything possible to avoid their own participation. For example, in the early days of the church, they thought Christians should avoid careers such as being in the military or being an executioner. One of the church fathers, Origen, wrote that although it was legitimate for Jews to have an army and engage in capital punishment, under the new dispensation, Christians should not do such things.

But even if we are to refrain from killing on a personal basis, how should this apply to our political views? We live in a dangerous world in which many believe it's crazy to advocate a pacifist foreign policy. Nevertheless, author and Sojourners founder Jim Wallis has taken Christian pacifism to radical extremes. For example, after U.S. Navy SEALs tracked down and killed al-Qaeda leader Osama bin Laden in May 2011, Wallis said:

> Pumping our fists in victory or celebrating in the streets is probably not the best Christian response to anyone's death, even the death of a dangerous and violent enemy. The chants of "USA, USA, USA" are also not the best mantra for believers, who should know that they are meant to be Christians first and Americans second.

Wallis also said U.S. Christians should repent for having valued innocent American lives "more than the innocents who were in the way of our wars in response to the attacks against us." Many Conservatives express outrage at these kinds of "liberal" attacks on American militarism. But from Wallis' point of view, he was just trying to consistently apply Christian pro-life principles to the issues of our day.

So what do you think? Are Jim Wallis and similar liberal Christians naïve and foolhardy? Or should followers of Christ be more aggressive in advocating for peace by opposing violence in all its forms?

Of course, the Scriptures give us a very clear vision of a futuristic time of peace:

> *Many people shall come and say, "Come, and let us go up to the mountain of the LORD, to the house of the God of Jacob;*

*He will teach us His ways, and we shall walk in His paths."
For out of Zion shall go forth the law, and the word of the
LORD from Jerusalem. He shall judge between the nations,
and rebuke many people; they shall beat their swords into
plowshares, and their spears into pruning hooks; nation shall
not lift up sword against nation, neither shall they learn war
anymore.*   (Isaiah 2:3–4)

But how are we to live our lives as "peacemakers" today? Is it
really feasible to go ahead and beat our swords into plowshares
today?

To become total pacifists, we might have to become Amish,
drop out of modern society, and declare that we are conscientious
objectors from military involvement. We might even oppose the
War on Terrorism. I don't know about you, but I'm not willing to
go that far. Yet I think people like Jim Wallis rightly challenge us
to think twice before blindly supporting the military. Our primary
allegiance as Christians should be to the kingdom of God, not to
American patriotism, right or wrong.

The Death Penalty?

While we're on the subject of what it means to be thoroughly
pro-life, let's take a few minutes to consider capital punishment.
There's not time to analyze all the issues involved, but this is an
important issue for Christians to understand nevertheless.

I want to say right up front: I'm in favor of the death penalty, at
least for the most egregious crimes. Can we require anything less
than death for people like the Boston Bombers or Ariel Castro,
the Cleveland man who kidnapped and repeatedly raped several
young women for more than a decade?

But let me make a few observations and raise a few questions
about how biblical principles apply to this debate:

1. *Numerous Old Testament passages endorse the use of capital punishment.* What many people don't realize is that the Old Testament legal code prescribed the death penalty for many crimes other than murder. For example, you could be executed for such things as:

   + Worshipping or offering sacrifices to gods other than the Lord

   + Making false prophecies

   + Engaging in witchcraft, divination, spiritualism, or the occult

   + Blasphemy

   + Breaking the Sabbath

   + Rape

   + Adultery, premarital sex, and some forms of incest

   + Homosexual sex

   + Bestiality

   + Disrespecting, cursing, or assaulting a parent

   + Kidnapping

2. *ALL of us are deserving of the death penalty according to these commands.* What's stunning about this list is that *all* of us would be in jeopardy of execution for violating one or more of these commandments. We may not have committed murder or adultery, but Jesus showed in the Sermon on the Mount that we truly *have* violated these commands if we've hated our brother or looked at another person with lust. (See Matthew 5:21–30.) And who among us can say they have never engaged in any form of idolatry? Or disrespect toward their parents? Or breaking the Sabbath?

   You see, under God's perfect law, we're *all* deserving of death. The Bible makes this quite clear:

- *"There is **none** righteous, no, not one"* (Romans 3:10).

- *"**All** have sinned and fall short of the glory of God"* (Romans 3:23).

- *"**All** we like sheep have gone astray; we have turned, every one, to his own way; and the LORD has laid on Him the iniquity of us all"* (Isaiah 53:6).

- *"The wages of sin is **death**, but the gift of God is eternal life in Christ Jesus our Lord"* (Romans 6:23).

So the verdict is in. The bad news is that we're all under the death penalty, because *"the wages of sin is death."* But the good news is that because *"the LORD has laid on Him the iniquity of us all,"* and *"the gift of God is eternal life in Christ Jesus our Lord."*

3. *Jesus' example shows that mercy should triumph over judgment.* Jesus never explicitly told us whether the death penalty should be revoked after His death and resurrection. Yet we see His heart on the matter in John 8:3–11, when the religious leaders brought Him a woman caught in the act of adultery. It was a trap, of course. If Jesus merely overlooked her sin, He would be violating the Old Testament precept that adulterers should be put to death. But if He followed the law and stoned her, it would be clear that His "new order" was no different than the old one.

Jesus didn't just flaunt the law. He had already said in the Sermon on the Mount that His purpose in coming was not to abolish the Old Testament law, but rather to establish a *higher* law. (See Matthew 5:17–20.)

When this adulterous woman was brought before Him, Jesus didn't immediately respond. Instead, He *"stooped down and wrote on the ground with His finger"* (John 8:6). What was this all about it? Many commentators believe that Jesus was writing down the capital punishment requirements of the law—along with how each of the woman's accusers had violated those principles. Eventually the accusers were *"convicted by their conscience* [and] *went out one by one, beginning with the oldest"* (verse 9).

What a powerful example Jesus had given! In essence, He was saying, "Okay, you guys are right about what the law says. But let Me go ahead and apply it to *all* of you!"

After Jesus did this, only He and the woman were left. He asked her, *"Woman, where are those accusers of yours? Has no one condemned you?"* And she replied, *"No one, Lord"* (John 8:10–11).

Jesus then told her, *"Neither do I condemn you; go and sin no more"* (verse 11). Just as we're told in Romans 8:1, there is *"no condemnation"* anymore for those who are in Christ. But that doesn't mean that Jesus simply condones our sins. His final words to the woman were, *"Go and sin no more"* (John 8:11).

4. *Practical considerations about the death penalty can be argued on either side of the issue.* Many pages could be filled with information about the pros and cons of the modern death penalty. Here are some of the "talking points" on both sides:

    ✦   Aren't some crimes so egregious that anything less than the death penalty would be inadequate? What about serial killers and terrorists? Shouldn't they expect to die for their crimes against humanity?

    ✦   Is capital punishment truly a deterrent to future crimes? This could be argued either way. One of the problems with the modern death penalty is that the criminal justice system is simply too slow to scare anyone that they will be executed. Under the Old

Testament law, justice was swift, and those guilty of capital offenses were put to death quickly and publically. These procedures would have been much more likely to deter future offenders.

+ As numerous news stories have shown, many innocent people have been put on death row. Thanks to DNA tests, some people who were convicted many years ago have now been completely exonerated. One thing is for sure: If there is going to be a death penalty today, we must have mechanisms to be very sure that there's evidence of guilt "beyond a reasonable doubt." The Old Testament law tried to ensure this kind of certainty by requiring death penalty evidence to be based on *"the testimony of two or three witnesses"* (Deuteronomy 17:6). One witness wasn't enough. And to further ensure the accuracy of the testimony, a false witness in a death penalty case would himself be executed. (See Deuteronomy 19:15–21.)

+ Historically, most societies have used capital punishment at least for certain heinous crimes, but the trend is in the other direction. From what I can tell, fifty-eight nations still actively impose the death penalty, while ninety-eight nations have abolished it. Meanwhile, the United Nations General Assembly has passed several non-binding resolutions calling for a global moratorium, and eventual abolition, of executions.

5. *Regardless of what cultural trends may be, Christians should seek to address capital punishment from a biblical perspective.* I fully recognize that believers may differ on whether the death penalty is a good thing or not. But there are some things we should *all* be able to agree upon:

+ God is a redemptive God, able to forgive and transform a person into a *"new creation"* (2 Corinthians 5:17) in

Christ. This means that, until a person takes their last breath, there is always hope for a new beginning.

+ Instead of merely being bystanders to the debate over our country's criminal justice system, the Bible commands us to get *involved*. Jesus' disciples must have been puzzled when He told them, *"I was in prison and you came to visit me"* (Matthew 25:36 NIV). But then He made His point clear: *"Truly I tell you, whatever you did for one of the least of these brothers and sisters of mine, you did for me"* (verse 40 NIV). Whether a person is on death row, in federal prison, or just in the county jail as a common criminal, believers should do what they can to reach out with the love of Christ.

+ While some legislators would replace the death penalty with endless incarceration, Christians should advocate programs that give hope for true rehabilitation and eventual release. Sadly, the penal system in the United States offers almost no hope for any kind of positive life transformation or rehabilitation. Prisons are overflowing, but most prisoners are being changed for the worse instead of the better as they learn "the tricks of the trade" from other criminals. Meanwhile, people released from prison usually struggle to find honest jobs, and often they end up being incarcerated again. Believers have a tremendous opportunity to get involved in a positive way—both to bring transformation to prisoners and to help those who are released find a new life as they reenter society. I've known a number of convicts over the years, including people who are still on death row. My heart goes out to them. They need the kind of hope and rebirth that only God can give.

Speaking Words of Life

No matter which "pro-life" issue we are debating, it's important to recognize the power of our *words* to either bring healing or bring unnecessary pain. Jesus addressed this in His own ministry when He said, *"The Spirit gives life; the flesh counts for nothing. The words I have spoken to you—they are full of the Spirit and life"* (John 6:63 NIV).

Unfortunately, some of us who claim to be "pro-life" on the issues are "pro-death" when it comes to our attitudes and our words. While we may technically be correct on the issues, our positions are undercut because we engage in personal attacks and use unkind and incendiary words.

Christians need to regain an understanding of the power of our tongue. We probably all grew up with the old saying, "Sticks and stones may break my bones, but words can never hurt me." Yet we all know that this isn't true, don't we? Words definitely *can* hurt—and often they hurt *a lot*.

Solomon explained it this way: *"Words kill, words give life; they're either poison or fruit—you choose"* (Proverbs 18:21 MSG). So let's choose our words carefully when we address the hot-button issues of our day. This doesn't mean we must compromise the truth or back down from our convictions. It's simply an application of God's wisdom: *"The wise in heart will be called understanding, and sweetness of speech increases persuasiveness"* (Proverbs 16:21 NASB).

So no matter what pro-life positions you're seeking to promote, *"sweetness of speech"* will increase your persuasiveness. As the old maxim says, "You can catch more flies with honey than with vinegar." That's great advice to remember when you're confronting the important social issues of our times.

2

TRAYVON OR ZIMMERMAN: WHO WAS RIGHT?

"Justice cannot be for one side alone, but must be for both."

—*Eleanor Roosevelt*

A lot of important questions are raised by the shooting of Trayvon Martin and George Zimmerman's subsequent acquittal of murder charges. Is there any fairness in the American justice system? Can people of every ethnic group be confident that they will receive equal treatment under the law?

Unfortunately, how you answer these questions will largely be determined by your skin color, your upbringing, and whether you grew up in the inner city or the suburbs. Remember the Rodney King police brutality case and the O. J. Simpson murder trial? It was amazing that people who watched exactly the same evidence often came to entirely different conclusions.

Before I say more about Trayvon Martin and George Zimmerman, let me share a story from my own life that will help you better understand my vantage point.

Several years ago, I had finished preaching at a church near Fayetteville, North Carolina. I had two other men in my Mercedes as we began our trip back home along some dark country roads in the middle of nowhere.

For a reason that is still unclear to me, a police cruiser behind me turned on his swirling lights in an effort to get me to pull over. Okay, *you* probably would have complied immediately, but I decided to continue driving slowly until we reached a lighted gas station several miles ahead. I guess I had already seen enough questionable behavior by law enforcement officials to be a little nervous about encountering one on a narrow, pitch-black road.

To my shock, when I pulled into the Kangaroo gas station, I wasn't just greeted by this one police cruiser. The officer had called for backup, and four other cruisers surrounded my car, as if I was a notorious drug dealer or terrorist.

I was a little bit alarmed at this point, but I knew how to handle the situation. I told the other two men to remain calm and put their hands in plain view so the officers could clearly see them. The guy in the front passenger seat listened to me, but the one in the backseat didn't. He had a criminal record from his previous life, and he allowed himself to get really agitated by encounters with the police.

After the officer asked for my license and registration, he shined his flashlight directly into the eyes of Edward, the man in the back. That made Edward even angrier, and things got completely out of hand when the officer commanded us all to get out of the car.

At this, Edward became increasingly ballistic. Loudly protesting, he cussed at the officer with all kinds of speech not befitting a Christian. The officer saw how unhinged Edward was becoming, and he chose to use his stun gun on *all three of us!*

Fortunately, it was *just* a Taser that the officer used, not a billy club or pistol. But it was painful and degrading nevertheless—an experience I will never forget.

We were then taken to the police station and released after a few hours. The magistrate on duty recognized me, and was sympathetic to my explanation of how we were treated.

The officer who took us into custody made a rather lame attempt at an apology, saying, "If I would have known who you were, I would have handled things differently." That statement has stuck in my mind ever since, and I find it very troubling.

In essence, the officer was saying he would have treated me with more courtesy if he knew who I was, but it was perfectly fine to treat *other* suspected criminals the way he did (especially if they are black?). Is *that* the kind of criminal justice system we want in this country?

What about Trayvon and George?

When I think about the Zimmerman murder trial, it's hard for me not to view it through the eyes of my own experience with "law enforcement" that night on the country road. Had the officers "profiled" the three of us in the car that night? Perhaps they impulsively concluded, "Three black men in a Mercedes late at night— there must be something fishy going on here."

Hopefully, you've never had this kind of experience with the police, but many of us Blacks have, especially if we've spent any time in the inner city.

George Zimmerman may have been well-meaning. I can't judge his motives or intentions. But like the police officers who wrongly judged us that dark night near Fayetteville, he clearly seems to have made incorrect, racially biased assumptions about this young black boy with a hoody, walking through the neighbor-hood on a dark February night.

Since Zimmerman's acquittal, he has continued to display erratic behavior and have brushes with the law. Although it's hard to say he should have been found guilty of *murder*, it's also hard for me to accept the fact that the legal system basically exonerated him from any wrongdoing at all.

I also can see why some Blacks openly ask whether the result would have been the same if the shooter was Trayvon and the victim was Zimmerman. Would the jury acquit a black man of shooting a white person under the same circumstances? It's hard to say, but you can see why such things touch a nerve in many us.

Bishop T. D. Jakes made some waves on this subject when the Religion News Service ask him in 2013 whether he thought justice was upheld in the Zimmerman case:

> I think the problem here is that America must realize that
> the law can be adhered to and justice still not be accom-
> plished. There is often a gulf between the two. And that
> is particularly resounding among African-Americans,
> where just a few years back, we were being beaten, and it
> was legal. Where we couldn't vote, and it was legal. So the
> real question is whether there is equality between the law
> and justice.

> This is bigger than black and white. It is a clarion call to
> dispel the increasing disparity between what is legal and what
> is just.

Bishop Jakes is making an insightful point here. Sometimes true "justice" is not done, even when the law has been faithfully adhered to.

My Friend's Contrary View

I have a white friend named Jim who wrote a blog about this case. Like me, he's a preacher and writer, and we find ourselves in agreement on most issues. But it was amazing to read how differently he viewed George Zimmerman.

I'll let you read Jim's article for yourself, and you can see which of us you agree with. Each of us is viewing the case from the vantage point of our own experiences, but perhaps we each have blind spots as well.

Here's what Jim wrote:

I find myself sympathetic to George Zimmerman, because I made some of the same fundamental errors many years go. No, I didn't kill anyone, nor was I in reasonable fear that my own life would end. And thankfully, my fiasco didn't spark a media circus.

No racial overtones were involved in my errors. I was just dumb.

I don't believe George was guilty of murder, manslaughter, or even a civil rights violation. But when you hear my own story, I think you'll see that he probably did break some cardinal principles for successful leadership.

I wasn't the coordinator of Neighborhood Watch, as George was. Instead, my first leadership assignment occurred at age ten when I was appointed as one of the "Safety Guards" on the playground of my elementary school.

I'll admit, I was rather proud of myself when they handed me my red armband, the symbol of authorityto keep order on the playground. And after only two days of patrolling, I had the first major opportunity to exercise my authority.

I happened to spot a disgruntled-looking student walking by himself and throwing stones at the ground. *Here is my chance to straighten this guy out*, I reasoned. The boy was much bigger than I was, but I figured there was no reason to worry. After all, I was the one with the red armband.

In retrospect, I can see that the stones weren't really a threat to anyone's safety. He might as well have been throwing Skittles to the ground. But at the time, it seemed perfectly reasonable to stop a kid from throwing stones in the playground.

However, this angry young man refused to listen to my demand that he immediately stop his behavior. Not only that, but my effort to exercise my authority as a Safety Guard resulted in a serious punching match—one he got the better of.

Frankly, I don't even remember the punching match. I just remember sitting in the school office with bumps all over my head, while the secretary called my mother to come and pick me up early. As Mom later put an ice pack on my aching head, I tried to explain to her that I was just trying to exercise my authority as a good Safety Guard.

I don't think she understood.

In retrospect, I bet George Zimmerman wishes he would have handled his encounter with Trayvon differently. But the slow motion perspective of hindsight is always a lot clearer than what we see on the spur of the moment."

Lessons from Jim's Playground Rumble

Although I think Jim was being far too easy on George Zimmerman, I agree with the leadership lessons he gleaned from his painful experience as a Safety Guard. These are lessons we should all take to heart as we seek to be truth-tellers and difference-makers in our world:

1. *Authority must be based on more than titles or outward symbols.* Jim says he was thrilled when they called him a Safety Guard and gave him an armband so everyone would know of his authority. But he found that true authority is much more than that. Even though we may have a badge, a diploma, a clerical collar, a special robe, or some other emblem of our office, we cannot naively assume that everyone will follow our leadership.

2. *To some extent, authority is not merely delegated, it must be earned.* Although the Bible teaches the principle of delegated authority, Jim learned a practical lesson from the "real world" of leadership: People will not wholeheartedly follow a leader unless they see that the leader has "paid the price" and laid down his or her life for them in some way. Paul says in 1 Corinthians 10:2 that the Israelites were "*baptized into Moses in the cloud and in the sea*" (NASB), which seems to mean that Moses' credibility as a leader was not really established among the people until they saw how he handled the crossing of the Red Sea.

3. *Authority is best exercised where there is a relationship.* If Jim had *known* the guy throwing the stones, I'm sure he could have worked out something without the necessity of a brawl. In the same way, Trayvon would still be alive today if George Zimmerman had made an effort to get to *know* him, not just *confront* him. Authority that is impersonal, driven by titles rather than a relationship, will

almost always result in rebellion or resentment toward the authority.

4. *The manner in which the authority is exercised is nearly as important as having the authority itself.* Jim's problem as a Safety Guard wasn't a lack of valid delegated authority. Instead, his problem was in knowing how to properly *exercise* the authority he had been given. Leadership mishaps are likely to happen when people are given authority but never trained in how to handle it. I highly doubt whether either George Zimmerman or the officer who stopped my car and shocked me with a stun gun had received adequate training in how to enforce neighborhood regulations or criminal laws.

5. *The timing in which authority is exercised is often crucial.* As Jim looks back, he says he can see that he was much too eager to exercise his new authority as a Safety Guard. If he had just taken time to pause briefly and better assess the situation, he would have recognized that the guy throwing the stones wasn't really endangering anyone. Some leaders, like Jim was that day, tend to be much too eager and hasty in using their authority.

What about *you?*

Perhaps you don't think these three stories—about Trayvon, me, and my friend Jim—are relevant to you at all. But we need to grasp the wisdom of Martin Luther King Jr. when he warned, "Injustice anywhere is a threat to justice everywhere."

If you only care about getting justice for *yourself,* your perspective is both selfish and shortsighted. We should all be challenged by these powerful words credited to Martin Niemöller, a German church leader who stood with Dietrich Bonhoeffer against Hitler's control of the church before and during World War II:

First they came for the Communists, but I was not a Communist so I did not speak out. Then they came for the Socialists and the Trade Unionists, but I was neither, so I did not speak out. Then they came for the Jews, but I was not a Jew so I did not speak out. And when they came for me, there was no one left to speak out for me.

By speaking out against Nazi injustice, Niemöller landed in the Dachau concentration camp—in contrast with other church leaders who cowered before the injustices of the Third Reich.

My friend, I challenge you to care about injustice wherever you find it. And when you see people mishandling their authority, take a moment to search your own heart to see whether you are properly exercisingthe authority *you've* been entrusted with. Make sure you're not hastily profiling people, consciously or unconsciously, because of the color of their skin, the car the drive, or the clothes they wear.

We need to pray for George Zimmerman and the family of Trayvon Martin. I've pretty much recovered from my ordeal with the police near Fayetteville. And Jim tells me he has no lasting effects from his painful introduction into leadership as a Safety Guard. But the lives of George Zimmerman and the Martin family will never be the same.

3

IS THE INCOME INEQUALITY
DEBATE A RUSE?

"He called his servants together and delegated
responsibilities. To one he gave five thousand dollars,
to another two thousand, to a third one thousand,
depending on their abilities."

—Matthew 25:14–15 (MSG)

One of the most divisive issues in our nation in recent years is the debate over "income inequality." Perhaps you've never given this much thought in the past, but the issue started bubbling to the surface in the national consciousness in September 2011, when the Occupy Wall Street movement launched a few months of protests in Zuccotti Park, near New York City's Wall Street financial district. Their slogan was "We are the 99 percent" and they vilified the wealthiest 1 percent of the American population as greedy, unfeeling, and corrupt.

Politicians have continued to fan the flames of class warfare with this polarizing subject, from President Obama to New York City's mayor, Bill de Blasio. Look at these words from the president's State of the Union address in January 2012:

We can either settle for a country where a shrinking number of people do really well, while a growing number

241

of Americans barely get by, or we can restore an economy where everyone gets a fair shot and everyone does their fair share.

On a surface level, much of this statement by the president seems perfectly reasonable. After all, who could oppose the grand objective that "everyone gets a fair shot and everyone does their fair share"? Can't really argue with that, can we?

However, the president's argument here, as on many other issues, is based on a false premise. The facts do not support his assertion that a "shrinking number of people do really well." Nor is it true that "a growing number of Americans barely get by." Despite these common misconceptions, the data shows that *many* people are doing really well, and the overall poverty rate has decreased rather than increased in the past several decades.

Faulty Analysis, Faulty Solutions

Is there income inequality in America today? Of course there is! There has never been a major world power in history that enjoyed economic prosperity and freedom without some people making more than others.

Did you know that Finland has less income inequality than the United States? That may sound wonderful, but not when you find out that the per capita income is much lower for *everyone* in Finland.

And a few years ago, Greece managed to substantially reduce its income inequality—because the nation was in a dire economic crisis. Instead of being a model we should envy, the citizens of Greece were faced with little money, scarcity of goods, riots in the streets, and economic opportunity limited to those partaking in corruption.

Whenever governments have tried to redistribute wealth and create equality of outcomes, the results have been catastrophic.

Everyone suffered. The only people who prospered were the corrupt politicians who ran the system. Instead of sparking widespread prosperity, the result of forced "equality" was to pull everyone down to a subsistence level.

When government inserts itself into the income inequality debate, the result is always less economic freedom and less overall prosperity. The Robin Hood philosophy may sound good on paper, but it becomes totalitarianism when taken to its logical conclusion. Stealing from the rich to give to the poor is still *stealing*.

In the end, it does little good for those in poverty to be given handouts, if they never learn how to make it on their own. Of course, there are exceptions. We need a safety net for people who are truly incapable of working. But beware of political demagogues who advocate "sticking it to the rich" as if that somehow would help "the little guy" get out of poverty.

Level Opportunities, not Outcomes

President Ronald Reagan once said, "The American dream is not that every man must be level with every other man. The American dream is that every man must be free to become whatever God intends he should become." Government can strive to create a somewhat level playing field where everyone plays by the same set of rules. There should be economic mobility and equal opportunities to succeed. But that certainly doesn't mean there will be "level" results and equality of outcomes.

You may have heard this quote, which often has been incorrectly attributed to President Abraham Lincoln:

You cannot bring about prosperity by discouraging thrift.
You cannot strengthen the weak by weakening the strong.
You cannot help the wage earner by pulling down the
wage payer. You cannot further the brotherhood of man

by encouraging class hatred. You cannot help the poor by destroying the rich. You cannot keep out of trouble by spending more than you earn. You cannot build character and courage by taking away man's initiative and independence. You cannot help men permanently by doing for them what they could and should do for themselves.

Instead of being the words of President Lincoln, they actually were penned more than fifty years after his death by an obscure Presbyterian minister named William John Henry Boetcker. Although Boetcker obviously doesn't carry as much weight as Lincoln, his maxims here are important nevertheless.

When the debate about income inequality comes up, there are always some people who propose that we try to "strengthen the weak by weakening the strong" or "help the poor by destroying the rich." As Boetcker pointed out, such an approach will never work.

He also correctly warned against poverty solutions that end up making people more dependent instead of self-reliant: "You cannot build character and courage by taking away man's initiativeand independence. You cannot help men permanently by doing for them what they could and should do for themselves."

In many ways, Boetcker was just stating common sense. Yet our country would have been smart to pay more attention to the wisdom he voiced.

Simple Keys for Avoiding Poverty

Art Laffer, one of President Reagan's chief economic advisors, recently weighed in on the income inequality debate:

I don't mind inequality if people are rising in incomes in all groups. I do mind equality when everyone's brought down to the lowest common denominator. You don't want to make the rich poor; you want to make the poor richer. These inequality specialists all around the place aren't proposing that. In all the quest to achieve less inequality, they are creating equality by lowering everyone. And that's silly.

Economist Robert Samuelson points out that the wealthiest 1 percent are "convenient scapegoats" for America's economic problems. However, he says, "the poor are not poor because the rich are rich." The economic data shows that while the income of the rich has grown faster than the income of the poor, *both* have seen gains in the past several decades.

So if the rich aren't really to blame for the poor being poor, what are the factors that keep many people locked in the grip of poverty? I could write an entire book on that subject, for there are numerous aspects to the problem. But let me just make a rather fundamental observation, based on a study by the Brookings Institution.

According to Brookings, you can avoid poverty by:

1. Graduating from high school

2. Waiting to get married until after age twenty-one and not having children till after being married

3. Having a full-time job

If you just do all three things, your chance of falling into poverty is just 2 percent. And you'll have a 74 percent chance of being in the middle class.

Isn't that good news? The solution to poverty and income inequality is not a matter of retribution against the "evil rich." In most cases, the solution is personal responsibility. In addition to the three-prong formula suggested by the Brookings study, I would include a few other Bible-based traits that are important for success:

+ Abstain from illegal drugs or drunkenness

245

+ Avoid criminal activity

+ Be honest and dependable

+ Have a good work ethic

It's really that simple. By just a few key lifestyle decisions, a person can nearly always avoid the trap of long-term poverty.

An Important Parable

I'm astounded by how many preachers and Christians have succumbed to the class-envy arguments of the demagogues who bemoan America's income equality. Haven't they ever read Jesus' Parable of the Talents in Matthew 25:14–30?

You probably know the story, but perhaps you've never thought of it in terms of income inequality. A wealthy man was going on a long journey, so he entrusted his belongings to three of his servants. He gave one of them five bags of silver, another two bags of silver, and the third servant just one bag of silver.

You see, these servants weren't entrusted by their master with the same amount. The point of the story is that the first two servants were faithful to invest and increase what they had been given, but the third servant just buried his silver in the ground.

Perhaps the third servant felt the master hadn't given him his "fair share." Yet he failed to see his grand opportunity to invest and increase what he had. His dismal condition at the end of the story wasn't the fault of the wealthy man—it was his *own* fault, based on fear and negligence.

If you don't like your current financial condition, you have a choice to make. You can either find some straw man to blame for your plight, or you can accept responsibility for your actions and take positive steps to better your circumstances. It's time to drop the excuses and trust God for a new beginning.

4

WHO WON THE WAR ON POVERTY?

"I am for doing good to the poor, but I differ in opinion
about the means. I think the best way of doing good to
the poor is not making them easy in poverty, but leading
or driving them out of it."

—*Benjamin Franklin*

In his first State of the Union address, President Lyndon Johnson
declared an "unconditional war on poverty in America." Now,
more than fifty years later, people still debate whether this ongoing initiative has been a success, a dismal failure, or simply a mixed
bag.

To you, the War on Poverty may just be something you read
about in a history book, but I'm one of the survivors of that war.
Raised on welfare, I know what an entitlement mentality can do to
a person's work ethic and self-esteem.

The Bible makes it absolutely clear: *The one who is unwilling
to work shall not eat"* (2 Thessalonians 3:10 NIV). But this principle is violated every day by the welfare system. It's one thing to
help people who are going through a temporary crisis, but now the
system is like a drug dealer—keeping many people permanently
hooked, generation after generation.

Just like a prison cell, everything is provided by the government: healthcare, food stamps, rent, utilities, and subsistence wages. But just like a prison cell, people are in bondage rather than living in freedom, self-reliance, and self-respect.

And one of the most diabolical aspects of this is how it has wrecked inner-city families. Do you know how you can get a "raise" in the amount of your entitlement check and food stamps? Have more babies! And it pays to lock the father out of the house, because he puts your welfare benefits in jeopardy.

These policies send a terrible message. No wonder there are so many out-of-wedlock births. It's not because of a lack of access to birth control—it's because that's the ticket to increased government benefits. Instead of promoting marriage and strong families, the current policies are extremely detrimental.

Well, these are some of my personal observations. But let's look at the War on Poverty from a more objective viewpoint.

A Cost-Benefit Analysis

Like any "war," the War on Poverty has had an expensive price tag. Over the past fifty years, the government has spent roughly $20 trillion to eradicate poverty. In 2012, the federal government spent $668 billion to fund 126 separate anti-poverty programs. State and local governments kicked in another $284 billion, bringing total anti-poverty spending to nearly $1 trillion. That amounts to $20,610 for every poor person in America and $61,830 per poor family of three.

Yet 15 percent of Americans still live in poverty, only marginally better than the 19 percent living in poverty at the time of Johnson's speech. Nearly 22 percent of children live in poverty today, versus 23 percent when the War on Poverty was enacted in 1964. And the statistics are much worse for minority children:

38 percent of our African-American children and 34 percent of our Hispanic children live in poverty.

How could we have spent so much and achieved so little? President Bill Clinton voiced this conclusion in 1996: "All Americans, without regard to party, know that our welfare system is broken, that it teaches the wrong values, rewards the wrong choices, hurts those it was meant to help. We also know that no one wants to change the current system in a good way more than people who are trapped in it."

If you are on the conservative side of political spectrum, you no doubt are saying at this point, "It's obvious why the War on Poverty has failed. It *never* works in the long-term to just give people handouts."

Yet the original rhetoric of the War on Poverty claimed that it was designed to *reduce* rather than expand government dependence. When the War on Poverty was launched, President Johnson pledged "not only to relieve the symptom of poverty, but to cure it and, above all, to prevent it."

African-American economist and author Thomas Sowell describes these original good intentions:

> Its mission was not simply to prove that spending money on the poor led to some economic benefits to the poor. Nobody ever doubted that. How could they?

> What the War on Poverty was intended to end was mass dependency on government. President Kennedy said, "We must find ways of returning far more of our dependent people to independence."

> The same theme was repeated endlessly by President Johnson. The purpose of the War on Poverty, he said, was to make "taxpayers out of taxeaters." Its slogan was, "Give a hand up, not a handout." When Lyndon Johnson signed

the landmark legislation into law, he declared: "The days of the dole in our country are numbered."

Now, 50 years and trillions of dollars later, it is painfully clear that there is more dependency than ever.

I'm stunned every time I read President Johnson's prediction that "The days of the dole in our country are numbered." A similar statement was made by President Bill Clinton thirty-two years later when he said, "The era of big government is over."

Whatever you may think of the accomplishments of Presidents Johnson and Clinton, one thing is for sure: They weren't very good at prophesying the future of poverty and welfare in America.

Unintended Consequences

My intention is not to berate the intentions of the War on Poverty. Poverty is a very real problem, in our country and every country. And there is no doubt that some people have truly been helped by government programs such as Medicare, Medicaid, Head Start, Job Corps, food stamps, VISTA, and the Elementary and Secondary Education Act.

But why does poverty persist when we are annually spending $20,610 for every poor person in America and $61,830 per poor family of three? Doesn't that suggest that there is considerable inefficiency, if not corruption, in the welfare system?

In addition, an increasing number of commentators are pointing to possible unintended consequences of the government's well-meaning efforts to alleviate poverty. For example, the following statistics hardly seemly like just a coincidence:

+ When the War on Poverty began, only 6.4 percent of all children in America were born outside marriage. Since the mid-1960s, unwed childbearing has skyrocketed to more than 40 percent of all births, and from 25 percent to about 73 percent among black children. Is it possible that many of our current welfare programs actually subsidize out-of-wedlock births?

+ Children growing up in a single parent family are almost five times more likely to be poor than children growing up in married-couple families. In fact, 30 percent of America's single-parent households live below the poverty line. And roughly 63 percent of all poor children reside in single-parent families.

+ Since the War on Poverty was launched, America has witnessed an unprecedented rise in cohabitation and divorce. Today 52 percent of American adults are married, while just a half-century ago, 72 percent were.

Did a culture of government dependency have anything to do with these rapid and unfortunate shifts in our society? The debate will no doubt continue. But we need to make sure that our programs incentivize work rather than dependence, marriage rather than single parenthood, and education rather than dropping out.

Michael D. Tanner of the Cato Institute provides this accurate summary of the good, the bad, and the incomplete record of the War on Poverty's legacy these past five decades:

> *The vast majority of current programs are focused on making poverty more comfortable—giving poor people more food, better shelter, health care, etc.—rather than giving people the tools that will help them escape poverty. As a result, we have been successful in reducing the worst privations of poverty. Few Americans live without the basic necessities of life, yet neither do they rise out of poverty. Moreover, their children are also likely to be poor.*

But what does this mean for the future of the welfare state? Are we to continue down the same road, spending billions of dollars in order to reduce "the worst privations of poverty"—even though the poor generally are remaining poor for endless generations?

President Johnson said, "The richest nation on earth can afford to win the war on poverty. We cannot afford to lose it." While that may be true, it's time to access whether our current strategies are having the intended results in this epic battle. Otherwise, we will find ourselves modeling Einstein's definition of insanity—doing the same things over and over, but expecting different results.

Good Intentions Gone Awry

Should the War on Poverty be judged by its intentions or its fruit? Thomas Sowell paints a bleak picture of how good intentions have resulted in economic dependence rather than freedom:

> Never had there been such a comprehensive program to tackle poverty at its roots, to offer more opportunities to those starting out in life, to rehabilitate those who had fallen by the wayside, and to make dependent people self-supporting. Its intentions were the best. But we know what road is paved with good intentions...

> The black family, which had survived centuries of slavery and discrimination, began rapidly disintegrating in the liberal welfare state that subsidized unwed pregnancy and changed welfare from an emergency rescue to a way of life.

You might prefer to characterize the War on Poverty in more positive terms. But can you really deny his conclusion that the welfare state has, in effect "subsidized unwed pregnancy" and changed government handouts into "a way of life" for many people?

Sowell takes the creators of the War on Poverty at their word that they never intended to foster greater government dependence. In fact, they argued just the opposite—that the War on Poverty would ultimately set people free from reliance on government programs:

> Its mission was not simply to prove that spending money on the poor led to some economic benefits to the poor. Nobody ever doubted that. How could they?

> What the War on Poverty was intended to end was mass dependency on government. President Kennedy said, "We must find ways of returning far more of our dependent people to independence."

> The same theme was repeated endlessly by President Johnson. The purpose of the War on Poverty, he said, was to make "taxpayers out of taxeaters." Its slogan was, "Give a hand up, not a handout." When Lyndon Johnson signed the landmark legislation into law, he declared: "The days of the dole in our country are numbered."

> Now, 50 years and trillions of dollars later, it is painfully clear that there is more dependency than ever.

It's hard to contest Sowell's analysis. And the editors of *National Review* wrote a similar obituary for the War on Poverty in their January 8, 2014, edition: "The main beneficiaries of the war on poverty have not been and will not be the poor; the beneficiaries are the alleged poverty warriors themselves. The war on poverty is war on the Roman model in which soldiers are paid through plunder."

In other words, the War on Poverty has become a lucrative business for entrenched government bureaucrats. It would have been more efficient just to eliminate the bureaucratic red tape entirely, automatically sending money toevery man, woman, and child in the country.

But if government programs are not the answer—well intentioned as they may be—how will the very poor be helped? We can't just turn a blind eye to the needs of the poor, especially when many of them are innocent children.

Where's the Church?

There's plenty to criticize about America's welfare system. I'm sympathetic to the concerns of people who say that the government has, too often, replaced the role of fathers in the Black community.

And instead of being self-reliant, God-reliant, or looking to family members or faith communities for assistance, it's sad that government has become some people's default Provider. No wonder some preachers and talk-show pundits say America is in danger of becoming a "nanny state."

However, I also get really irritated when people criticize the welfare system without getting involved and providing alternatives. Hey, some folks *need* a "nanny" for a while. If you don't like to see the government in that role, I can understand. But what are *you* doing to help the plight of the poor? How is *your* church or community organization reaching out to alleviate poverty in our nation?

And I'm not sure how helpful it is for a conservative commentator like Fox News' Bill O'Reilly to make simplistic statements like this about how to alleviating poverty:

> It's hard to do it because you gotta look people in the eye and tell 'em they're irresponsible and lazy. And who's gonnawanna do that? Because that's what poverty is, ladies

and gentlemen. In this country, you can succeed if you get educated and work hard. Period. Period.

Not long ago, I heard another conservative political commentator quote, or rather misquote, the words of Jesus on this issue. *"You will **always** have the poor among you"* (NLT), he declared, citing Jesus' words in Mark 14:7. "No wonder the War on Poverty hasn't worked!"

However, if you turn in your Bible to Mark 14:7, you can see that Jesus' statement didn't end there. Yes, there will always be poor people, for a variety of reasons. Yet Jesus didn't point this out as an excuse for our inaction. In fact, His sentence ended with an expectation that we would be involved in helping them: *"You can help them whenever you want to."*

You see, from cover to cover, the Bible tells us to help the poor in every way we can. I honestly have never counted the Bible verses on God's concern for the poor and for social justice, but some people say there are more than *2,000 verses* on the subject. Yet many evangelical churches rarely preach on this at all.

James writes, *"Pure and genuine religion in the sight of God the Father means caring for orphans and widows in their distress and refusing to let the world corrupt you"* (James 1:27 NLT). This is quite a statement, isn't it? If you and your church aren't involved in caring for needy people like *"orphans and widows,"* you might want to question whether your religion is *"pure and genuine."*

Jesus never anticipated that His people would "leave it to the government" to care for poor folks. Quite the contrary, He said our service to the poor should be seen as the same as ministering to the Lord Himself:

Then the King will say....."I was hungry and you gave Me food; I was thirsty and you gave Me drink; I was a stranger and you took Me in; I was naked and you clothed Me; I was sick and you visited Me; I was in prison and you came to Me." Then the righteous will answer Him, saying, "Lord, when did we see You hungry and feed You, or thirsty and give You drink? When did we see You a stranger and take You in, or naked and clothe You? Or when did we see You sick, or in prison, and come to You?" And the King will answer and say to them, "Assuredly, I say to you, inasmuch as you did it to one of the least of these My brethren, you did it to Me."

(Matthew 25:34–40)

It's clear from Jesus' story here, as well as countless other scriptures, that this is a very serious matter. In fact, part of our final judgment will involve the question of whether or not we cared for the poor and needy.

A New Paradigm

If throwing money at poor people would make poverty go away, that would have happened a lot time ago. But poverty is not just a material problem. It involves issues that are spiritual, emotional, relational, and moral.

Government programs are relatively good at distributing large amounts of money to a wide cross-section of those in need, but the church has a different skillset. We can care for the spiritual, emotional, relational, and moral needs much *better* than any government programs, no matter how well intentioned those programs may be. While it would be great if the government incentivized sexual abstinence before marriage, strong families, the role of fathers, two-parent homes, freedom from addiction, and other wholesome values, the church is clearly in a much better position to help promote such objectives.

Many churches are already doing a great job with such things, but others have chosen to abandon the cities and find safer, more comfortable, and more lucrative venues in wealthier areas. So, for some middle-class or upper-class Christians these days, it's "out of sight, out of mind" when it comes to the poor.

And although I am grateful for the "soup kitchen" approach that many ministries have used to at least give needy people a warm meal, the situation really requires a deeper level of involvement than that. Just as people need more than money, they also need more than food. That's why churches can provide vital help through such things as mentoring, after school programs, Big Brother/Big Sister involvement, job training, helping the unemployed prepare and place their resumes, visiting the incarcerated, and assisting single moms with childcare, home or car repairs, and housework.

No, the War on Poverty is not over yet. Nor will it ever be until Jesus returns. But it's a war we must *all* be involved with. It's not something we can just delegate to the government and then absolve ourselves of responsibility. The Lord didn't leave us that option.

5

DOES GOD APPROVE OF GAY MARRIAGE?

"It's the Holy Spirit's job to convict, *God's job* to judge, and my job to love."

—*Billy Graham*

World Vision's American branch recently shocked the Christian world by announcing that it will no longer require its more than one thousand employees to restrict their sexual activity to marriage between one man and one woman. Although abstinence outside of marriage remains the rule, the new policy will permit gay Christians in legal same-sex marriages to be employed at one of the world's largest Christian charities.

It was shocking enough when Queen Latifah performed a mass gay wedding service at the 2014 Grammy Awards, but you have grown to expect bizarre events from Hollywood and the music industry. However, it's even more bewildering when political correctness strikes major Christian organizations like World Vision.

Although a growing number of Christian leaders choose to be silent on the issue, Samaritan's Purse president Franklin Graham issued a stern rebuke to World Vision and its president, Richard Stearns:

World Vision maintains that their decision is based on unifying the church—which I find offensive—as if supporting sin and sinful behavior can unite the church. From the Old Testament to the New Testament, the Scriptures consistently teach that marriage is between a man and woman, and any other marriage relationship is sin.

Wow. What an explosive subject. Franklin Graham's criticism of World Vision prompted the Charlotte Observer to run a feature story about "his litany of controversial condemnations of gays and lesbians, Islam, and President Obama." Interesting characterization, to say the least. The newspaper is, in effective, condemning Graham for his remarks.

In response, Franklin Graham said he was only speaking out like his father would have in his younger days. He pointed out that Billy Graham took unpopular moral stands against such things as racial segregation and poverty. "You talk about controversy—my father stood with Martin Luther King Jr. in the early 1960s," Franklin explained to the Observer.

Instead of being a hater, as his critics might charge, Franklin Graham said, "I love people enough and care enough to warn people that if they choose to continue to live in sin, God is going to judge them one day, and they'll be separated from Him for eternity in hell."

Perhaps the secular media is more offended by what the *Bible* teaches than by what a preacher like Franklin Graham says. Meanwhile, just a few days after announcing their decision, World Vision reversed itself in the face of a groundswell of protest from its donors. Instead of ending people's concern, however, their flip-flop made it look like they have no *convictions* on the subject at all—just a concern to keep their donor basis intact.

Is that how far we've sunk in our handling of moral issues in our country, willing to change positions according to the highest bidder?

Of course, the media will continue their attempts to trap prominent TV preachers with questions about gay marriage or whether gays will be in heaven. It's a no-win situation, really. If the preachers quote the Bible in condemnation of gay marriage, they are branded as narrow-minded bigots. But if they compromise and adopt the socially acceptable position that a person's sexual expression isn't really a moral issue at all, the preachers offend God and outrage their conservative followers.

A Personal Issue

This is a very personal issue for me. I lost a brother to AIDS. Another brother is involved in the gay lifestyle, and he broke my heart when he left the church because he thought it was too judgmental. *I* had been judgmental too, preaching that gays would all burn in hell.

So this may be just a theoretical issue for you, but for me it gets close to home. If I truly believe in heaven—and I do—then I want to do everything possible to secure the eternal destiny of my loved ones. Of course, I want to be "nice" to them as well, but not at the expense of the truth.

And as a pastor, I'm also concerned about my parishioners. Pastors may pretend their churches are composed only of those who are straight and monogamous—or ex-gays who've been "saved and sanctified"—but the reality isn't as simple as our rhetoric. Homosexuals are *everywhere* in today's churches. Will they be in heaven too?

If we believe anything about what the Good Book says about heaven, it's a holy and happy place that *none* of us really deserves. That's right, gays *don't* deserve to go to heaven. But neither do those who are straight. No matter *how* you classify yourself, you had better depend on God's mercy instead of your inherent goodness.

Is homosexuality an unforgiveable sin? No, the only unforgiveable transgression is to smugly refuse to bow before your Creator. And that arrogance certainly isn't limited to any particular sexual orientation, nor to any particular kind of sin.

Gays aren't the only ones who engage in destructive thoughts, attitudes, or behaviors. I'll never forget the woman who wanted me to cast a "homosexual demon" out of her son—while her hands shook uncontrollably for want of a cigarette.

So why not deal with your *own* issues? Instead of focusing on the lofty question of whether God will let gays into heaven, how about personalizing the debate: Are *you* ready to step into eternity and face your Creator and Judge?

Sometimes people ask me whether people are more forgiving than God. Let me be clear: *No one* is more forgiving than God. But you can't receive His forgiveness unless you're willing to humble yourself and admit you need it—whether you're gay or straight.

Moral Crusaders

If I told you I'm opposed to same-sex marriages, you probably would assume I hate gay people and am on a crusade to make their lives miserable. But that's not it at all. I *love* homosexuals and want the *best* for them.

And even though I don't favor gay marriages, I also have reservations about the "Marriage Protection Acts" some states still have in place to strictly define marriage as between one man and one woman.

Have I confused you yet?

The problem with the federal Defense of Marriage Act (DOMA) and the state laws is that they make the *government* the chief definer of sexuality and morality. As a minister of the gospel, I have very strong views on what the Bible says about sexual conduct, but I don't really want the government—or even a majority of the people—telling me what's right and wrong in private, consensual activities between consenting adults.

Let me be clear: We *will* answer to Almighty God one day for our private conduct, but it's a slippery slope for any human government to define such things.

Of course, a country without a constitution and basic moral standards would be like the wild, wild West. There *must* be laws to protect us from one another in matters of such things as violence or theft.

But there seldom has been a good outcome when moral crusaders impose their personal views on the populace. Remember the time in America when it was against the law for whites to marry blacks and for blacks and women even to vote? When children went to segregated schools and blacks were barred from some restaurants and public accommodations? Strangely, proponents of such twisted policies often quoted Bible verses in their support.

Do you see why we should be cautious about enacting our personal preferences and prejudices into the law of the land?

Yet even though I'm uncomfortable with the government defining personal matters such as marriage, there's one major reason why I *also* fear the consequences of widespread acceptance of gay marriage. The problem is not that same-sex marriages would pose a serious danger to the institution of heterosexual marriage. Heterosexuals have already done *plenty* to damage the institution of marriage without the assistance of any gays!

My concern involves a bigger question: Does it matter if a child is raised by two moms or two dads? I believe it does. The ideal home has both a father and a mother, and fatherless homes have been shown to produce more high school dropouts, drugs, incarceration, and abuse.

But ideal homes are hard to find these days. In the beginning, God Himself defined marriage. Sadly, both heterosexuals and homosexuals have strayed from His plan—with tragic results for all. The LGBT community scoffs at Christians when we say gay marriage isn't God's plan.

Sadly, they correctly point out that many of our heterosexual marriages aren't working out too well these days either.

One thing we should all ask is this: What will it take to get the full blessing of God on our marriages? Well, first we should lay down our own views and feelings and seek out His plan. Marriage is a difficult thing, and we all need His help if our marriage is to be successful. Ecclesiastes 4:12 says, *"A threefold cord is not quickly broken."* Without the involvement of God as the third strand in our marriage cord, we're *all* on shaky ground.

Slippery Slope

People in the LGBT community typically go ballistic when someone raises a very important question: If we allow gay marriages based on a "freedom of choice" argument, why wouldn't we also allow other forms of marriage unions as well—including polygamy, incest, even bestiality. Proponents of gay marriage usually say that such an argument is outlandish. How could a critic dare equate a gay marriage with a marriage to multiple people... or to one's *pet*?

But things are changing rapidly on the cultural landscape.

Perhaps you heard the 2014 story of Amanda Rodgers, a 47-year-old British woman who divorced her husband and married her dog Sheba, a four-year-old Jack Russell terrier. Explaining that she had finally found the true meaning of love and marriage, Rodgers said, "I fell in love with Sheba and knew we were meant to be." Two hundred guests attended the peculiar ceremony.

Is this the new frontier of personal freedom? The wave of the future for marriage equality? Maybe so.

Aparecido Castaldo is a Brazilian man who decided to marry his pet goat, named Carmelita. Describing why the goat was so appealing, Castaldo said, "She doesn't speak and doesn't ask for money." Unfortunately, Carmelita ate her first wedding dress, but another dress was found for this very special occasion.

Where will this ever end? I can understand why gay people get offended at the suggestion that their relationship has similarities to marrying multiple partners or marrying one's pet. But don't we have to ask: Where is this newfound "freedom" headed, and how will it impact our society as a whole?

God's Agenda

If the LGBT community has an agenda, so does God.

Commenting on Paul's words in Romans 5:8–10, writer Paul Jenkins describes God's plan to interact with gay people:

> Make no mistake: God loves his enemies. I'm proof of that, because I was born his enemy, and every desire I had at birth not only took me farther from God, but also made me his killer when I got close to him. Asking whether or not we were born gay or straightis the wrong question because the answer will always be that we were born sinners and enemies of a God who always meant for us to be his children. That's why he sent Jesus to die on a cross. It wasn't to make gay people straight. It was to make dead people live.

> It was a clear statement that, while the world loves homosexuality, God loves homosexuals. It's the difference between an agenda and a Savior.

But amid the cultural haze that shapes debate on this issue, both the LGBT community and Christians often misunderstand

God's agenda. As a result, they can be hypocrisy on both sides, as Alveda King points out: "It's sadly hypocritical to publicly proclaim that 'God hates the sin but loves the sinner,' while all the time we secretly sneer and use ugly names to brand others. On the other hand, it's critically intolerant to bad mouth Bible believers and deny our Constitutional rights for holding to our standards of faith while insisting that we be tolerant of contrasting views."

In her 2014 article, "As the Marriage Battle Rages, Let Mercy Prevail," provides this excellent quote from C. S. Lewis: *"The miracle of the redemptive reality of God is that the worst and vilest offender can never exhaust the depths of God's love."* So true. I need the mercy of God, and so do you.

I'll close this chapter with a quote from Dietrich Bonhoeffer's challenging book, *The Cost of Discipleship*: "Judging others makes us blind, whereas love is illuminating. By judging others we blind ourselves to our own evil and to the grace which others are just as entitled to as we are."

Let's be bold in speaking out against sin, but just as bold in extending grace to the offenders.

6

DO WOMEN NEED AN EMANCIPATION PROCLAMATION?

"You don't always see was what it took for many of us to get to where we are today. You don't always see the thousands of hours that were spent studying or practicing or rehearsing, the years spent working for that promotion, the hammers used to break glass ceilings."

—*Michelle Obama*

President Lincoln issued the Emancipation Proclamation on January 1, 1863. Although the slaves were technically freed by this bold executive order, the ramifications of racial prejudice were not so easily or quickly shaken.

Feminists have pointed out some parallels with the struggle for women to gain full equality. After years of opposition, President Woodrow Wilson changed his position on women's suffrage in 1918, and the Nineteenth Amendment finally granted it throughout the country in 1920.

You might be surprised to find out where the battle lines had been drawn in the U.S. Senate debates on this issue. The pivotal vote came on June 4, 1920, when the amendment was approved in the Senate by a vote of 56 to 26 after four hours of debate. Democratic senators had originally filibustered to prevent a vote. When a vote on the suffrage amendment was finally taken, the ayes included 36 Republicans (82 percent of party's votes) and 20 Democrats (54 percent of party's votes). The nays comprised 8 Republicans (18 percent of party's votes) and 17 Democrats (46 percent of party's votes).

So women had officially had a right to vote for more than ninety years. But some would argue that there are still "glass ceilings" in many organizations and corporate boardrooms.

According to the most recent information available, there are only nineteen female presidents and prime ministers that have been elected into power around the globe. In the business world, women currently hold only 4.6 percent of Fortune 500 CEO positions and the same percentage of Fortune 1000 CEO positions. As women continue their upward trajectory in the business world, they have yet to be fully appreciated for the unique qualities and abilities they bring to the workplace.

And what about the church? Although there are thousands of women pastors, especially in the Black community, some denominations and churches still have strong convictions that pulpits should be reserved for men.

What is the correct view on this? Of course, the politically correct beliefs of our society are moving steadily toward the "unisex" position—that gender is irrelevant and should not be considered a factor in any job or ministry qualification. This is forcing the church to take a new look at what the Bible says about women and men in the church.

Two extreme views both use Scripture proof texts to support their positions. Some commentators glibly quote 1 Corinthians 14:34, *"Let your women keep silent in the churches,"* and 1 Timothy 2:12, *"I do not permit a woman to teach or to have authority over a man."* This should end any discussion of women in the pulpit, they say.

However, there's another side on this. You've probably met people who ignore all passages that make gender distinctions, using Galatians 3:28 as their battle cry: *"There is neither male nor female; for you are all one in Christ Jesus."*

There are still deep divisions on this issue, and I probably won't be able to sway your opinion in just a short chapter. But before you close your mind on the subject, let's at least consider some simple observations.

1. *An increasing number of women are successfully engaging in leadership roles, in the business world, in politics, and in the church.*

    While some people still want to debate the theology of the matter, here's a fact we can't ignore: Many women are already having a great impact, whether in business or in ministry. In the business world, we've seen powerful women like Sheryl Sandberg, Meg Whitman, and Carly Fiorina. In the political world, powerful women include Hillary Clinton, Sarah Palin, Condoleezza Rice, Ruth Bader Ginsburg, Sonia Sotomajor, and Elena Kagan.

    Likewise, some of the most effective preachers of the gospel today are women. The list is long, but some examples include Joyce Meyer, Beth Moore, Marilyn Hickey, and Kay Arthur. According to the U.S. Department of Labor, 11.1 percent of the women in America describe their occupation as "clergy." The Assemblies of God and United Methodist denominations each have more than four thousand women who have ministerial credentials. The African Methodist Episcopal Church estimates that women make up one-third of it's a hundred and twenty nine thousand ministers.

2. *It is clear that many women in the Bible had prominent leadership roles.*

In addition to women such as Miriam, Deborah, Esther, and Huldah in the Old Testament, the pages of the New Testament are filled with women who made tremendous contributions. Following Mary, Jesus' mother, we could list women such as Anna the prophetess, Mary Magdalene, Joanna, Susanna, Priscilla, Phoebe, Chloe, Euodia, Syntyche, Nympha, Junia, Julia, and Philip's prophetess daughters—a long roster indeed.

Some of these, such as Joanna and Susanna, could be written off by "let the women be silent" advocates as merely being players of supporting roles. Others, though, are specifically described as operating in roles analogous to the Ephesians 4:11 and 1 Timothy 3:1–13 ministries often reserved for men:

APOSTOLIC MINISTRY: In Romans 16:7, Junia (a female name) is described as *"of note among the apostles."* Also, Priscilla and her husband seem to have functioned as an apostolic couple who were *"fellow workers"* with Paul. (See Romans 16:3–4.)

PROPHETIC MINISTRY: Anna in Luke 2:36 and Philip's daughters in Acts 21:8–9 are recognized as having prophetic ministries. And an *increase* of such roles for women is foretold by Peter's message at Pentecost: *"Your sons and your daughters shall prophesy"* (Acts 2:17).

EVANGELISTIC MINISTRY: Euodia and Syntyche are described by Paul in Philippians 4:2–3 as laboring with him in the gospel. It should not be surprising that women were involved in evangelistic ministries, because Mary Magdalene was the first person to see and proclaim the risen Savior. (See John 20:1–18.)

PASTORS AND TEACHERS: Though some

would claim that 1 Timothy 2:12 prohibits women from serving in pastoral roles over men, there is no doubt that, at the very least, they can serve in such roles over the younger women. (See Titus 2:3–5.)

But what about the issue of whether women should be allowed to teach men? Those who take a strict view against this should consider the scriptural examples on the other side: Priscilla apparently felt no qualms when she took the erring Apollos aside and *"explained to him the way of God more accurately"* (Acts 18:26). Also, Timothy's grandmother Lois and his mother, Eunice, taught him the Scriptures from childhood. (See 2 Timothy 1:5.)

DEACONS: From the example of Phoebe in Romans 16:1–2, it's hard to dispute that women should be allowed to serve as deacons. Although the common term in the church today is "deaconess," the Greek word used to describe Phoebe, *diakonos*, is exactly the same word used in 1 Timothy 3:8 for male deacons.

3. *Though the Bible makes it clear that women may be actively involved in leadership and ministry, it also describes gender differences that remain.*

Some women, in their zeal to break loose from oppressive views that would seek to muzzle them, have perhaps gone too far. Desiring to prove that there should be absolutely no gender distinctions, they have grabbed Galatians 3:28 as a proof text and mantra: *"There is neither Jew nor Greek, there is neither slave nor free, there is neither male nor female; for you are all one in Christ."*

This is indeed a wonderful and liberating verse, but let's be honest about its context. Rather than being a conclusive statement on church government or a woman's role in society, its scope is primarily focused on the standing of men and women as equals in Christ. For example, even though Paul says there is neither Jew nor Greek, in other passages he makes practical *distinctions*: The gospel is *"for the Jew first and also for the Greek"* (Romans 1:16). And Romans chapters 9–11 contrast God's separate dealings with the Jews and with the Gentiles.

Likewise, although Paul says that in Christ there is neither slave nor free, that did not stop him from separately addressing the different situations in which slaves and masters found themselves in the culture of his day. (See Ephesians 6:5–9.) We shouldn't think it unusual, therefore, that Paul could say there is neither male nor female, yet still give separate instructions to both genders in his letters—especially within the context of marriage.

Yes, men and women are of equal value in God's eyes. But that doesn't mean they are exactly the *same*, as any honest assessment will conclude. The emancipation of women into God's fullest intentions should not erase all distinctions—for those distinctions were designed by the Lord Himself. Women cannot make their greatest contribution to the world by imitating men, but rather by shining with the special qualities that men do not have.

The Impact of Genesis 3

Having said that men and women offer unique attributes is not to imply in any way that one is inferior. In fact, some commentators have pointed out that only after sin entered the world in Genesis 3 was there a need to clarify the role of women as being under the leadership of their husbands.

Although the distinction between male and female is part of God's original creation, there initially was such harmony, oneness, and teamwork between the genders that the Lord could consider them both as having the same name: *"Adam"* (Genesis 5:2 KJV). Not until they fell into sin did it become necessary to give the woman a separate name: *"Eve"* (Genesis 3:20).

We should be wary of our society's push toward the view that men and women are completely interchangeable, except for differently shaped bodies. Yet Jesus indeed points to a day when we all will be *"like the angels"* (Matthew 22:30 NIV), and gender apparently will not be important.

Meanwhile, history reveals a fascinating principle: In times of revival and spiritual awakening, gender distinctions are minimized; in times of spiritual decline, we are more aware of our differences and come up with oppressive traditions and regulations to keep everyone in their places.

Women clearly were given wide latitude in the pages of Scripture, and they should have wide latitude today. Some would suggest that women should have even *greater* liberty today, since the surrounding culture is much more favorable to women in leadership roles.

Of course, sincere believers will differ on these issues. Our commitment should be to affirm anyone who genuinely desires to serve Christ, regardless of whether we personally agree with every aspect of how they conduct their businesses or ministries. And if we err, we should err on the side of granting as much liberty as possible.

Principles for *Everyone*

One of the saddest and most hypocritical aspects of the debate over women in leadership is the way men have often preached on the requirement for women to be accountable and "under submission," while the men ignore similar principles the Bible addresses to *them*. Here are some notable examples:

- *All* ministers are warned not to be *"lords over"* (1 Peter 5:3) those entrusted to them, but to lead by example.

- We are *all* to submit to God and humble ourselves under His mighty hand. (See James 4:6–7; 1 Peter 5:6.)

- We *all* must give an account for our ministries. (See Hebrews 13:17.)

- Although we may be leaders, we must *all* be careful that we are not guilty of *"insubordination"* (Titus 1:6 NIV).

- *All* ministers must be careful not to neglect their own families. (See 1 Timothy 3:4–5; Titus 1:6.)

- *All* those in ministry should heed the character qualities listed as prerequisites to leadership, which include having a good reputation, being selfcontrolled, controlling their temper, not being quarrelsome or violent, not being addicted to wine or other substances, not being greedy or dishonest, and not being conceited. (See 1 Timothy 3:1–13; Titus 1:5–9.)

- *All* leaders must beware of seeking their own prominence or positions or titles. (See Matthew 23:5–12; 3 John 1:9.)

- The bottom line for *all* greatness and leadership, according to Jesus, is that we be willing to lay our lives down and be servants. (See Matthew 20:20–28.)

The Spirit of God is grieved when men try to suppress women who aspire to roles of leadership or ministry, while the men themselves are insubordinate and unwilling to be accountable to any other leaders. God exalts those who humble themselves, *regardless* of their gender. Many women have the humble hearts and a desire to see Jesus exalted above all else—and there is scarcely any limit to the heights God can lift them to.

This is an important issue. Emancipating women to their rightful places of leadership and ministry is a crucial key to unlocking the full potential both of our society and of the church. We cannot afford to be without the valuable contribution women can make by their full participation in business, politics, media, the arts, and ministry.

7

IS GOD A MEMBER OF THE
MILITARY-INDUSTRIAL COMPLEX?

"In the councils of government, we must guard against
the acquisition of unwarranted influence, whether sought
or unsought, by the military-industrial complex.
The potential for the disastrous rise of misplaced
power exists and will persist."

—*Dwight D. Eisenhower*

President Dwight Eisenhower had spent most of his life as a
military man. Before becoming the United States president
and commander in chief in 1953, he had served as supreme commander of the Allied Forces in Europe during World War II, as
the first supreme commander of NATO, and as Army Chief of
Staff under President Truman.

So Dwight Eisenhower's military credentials were impecca-
ble. No one in his generation knew the military better or loved
it more. Yet when his two terms as president were coming to an
end, Eisenhower chose to warn people about the danger posed by
the military, especially because of its economic ties with American
industry.

In his farewell address to the nation on January 17, 1961,
Eisenhower first acknowledged the important role of the military
in protecting our nation from aggressors:

A vital element in keeping the peace is our military establishment. Our arms must be mighty, ready for instant action, so that no potential aggressor may be tempted to risk his own destruction.

But then his tone changed, and he drew attention to a major shift that had occurred in the military over his lifetime. He pointed out that America had no permanent armaments industry until World War II. But by the time he left office, the defense establishment and arms industry were huge, both in manpower and in expenditures. Eisenhower said although there was an "imperative need" for this expansion, it also had "grave implications" for the country's future:

> Our military organization today bears little relation to that known by any of my predecessors in peacetime, or indeed by the fighting men of World War II or Korea.

> Until the latest of our world conflicts, the United States had no armaments industry. American makers of plowshares could, with time and as required, make swords as well. But now we can no longer risk emergency improvisation of national defense; we have been compelled to create a permanent armaments industry of vast proportions. Added to this, three and a half million men and women are directly engaged in the defense establishment. We annually spend on military security more than the net income of all United States corporations.

> This conjunction of an immense military establishment and a large arms industry is new in the American experience. The total influence—economic, political, even spiritual—is felt in every city, every State house, every office of the Federal government. We recognize the imperative need for this development. Yet we must not fail

to comprehend its grave implications. Our toil, resources and livelihood are all involved; so is the very structure of our society.

In the councils of government, we must guard against the acquisition of unwarranted influence, whether sought or unsought, by the military-industrial complex. The potential for the disastrous rise of misplaced power exists and will persist.

We must never let the weight of this combination endanger our liberties or democratic processes. We should take nothing for granted. Only an alert and knowledgeable citizenry can compel the proper meshing of the huge industrial and military machinery of defense with our peaceful methods and goals, so that security and liberty may prosper together.

Eisenhower's message was a profoundly prophetic warning, especially in light of his own military background. He was absolutely correct in recognizing that "The potential for the disastrous rise of misplace power exists and will persist." And, as if to envision our debates over the Patriot Act and NSA surveillance since 9-11, he wisely saw how difficult it would be for "security and liberty" to "prosper together."

Money Talks, Power Corrupts

Eisenhower understood that the military-industrial complex would become increasingly powerful and persuasive in American politics. Millions of jobs and enormous amounts of money are at stake in how the Pentagon and its contractors do their business.

Take a few minutes to review American military history since Eisenhower left office:

+ The Vietnam War was a catastrophic blunder. More than fifty-eight thousand Americans lost their lives, and over a million Vietnamese, Cambodians, and Laotians were killed as well, including both soldiers and civilians.

+ The war in Afghanistan has not brought lasting peace or stability to that nation. While propping up a corrupt regime, Coalition fatalities have exceeded thirty-four hundred, and many civilians have been caught in the crossfire.

+ We've been involved in two costly wars in Iraq, and still the nation does not have true peace or democracy. Since 2003, more than forty-four hundred U.S. soldiers were killed, and many others we permanently disfigured and disabled. Many estimates say that over one hundred thousand Iraqi lives have been lost as a result of the war.

+ Arguably, billions of dollars have been squandered through corruption or ill-advised military procurements.

So what are we to make of all of this? Candidates of both parties generally claim to favor "peace and security" during their campaign, saying they will keep us out of war or get us out of a war we're already in. Yet once they get elected, it becomes apparent that the campaign slogans are out the window, and nothing has significantly changed. How can that be? Is it because *both* parties, in the final analysis, are controlled by special interests and lobbyists from the military-industrial complex?

And what should our posture be as followers of Christ in dangerous and war-prone world? Some Christian traditions in the U.S. have been extremely pro-military. "Support Our Troops!" they proudly say. Others traditions, such as the Mennonites and the Friends (Quakers), say Christians should be pacifists and avoid military service altogether. Some of these have been "conscientious objectors" in wartime.

Still others have sought to follow the "just war theory" originally proposed by Augustine of Hippo. Augustine asserted that if certain criteria were met, a Christian could be a soldier and serve both God and country honorably. Based on Romans 13:4, he claimed that God has given *the sword* to government, and Christians should not be ashamed to participate in the protection of peace and the punishment of wickedness.

When Is a War "Just"?

I don't dispute that some wars are "just." I'm certainly glad we had the guts to stand up to Hitler, for example. However, this kind of thinking is extremely difficult to apply in the real world. Every leader who launches a war—including Hitler himself—claims that righteousness is on his side!

It's also bewildering to see how leaders often change their tune between their campaign slogans and their policies once in office. For example, George W. Bush was very clear during the presidential debates in 2000 that he opposed America's participation in "nation building" in far-off countries. The U.S. military, he said, should be used to defend the American country, not endeavor to create democracy in nation's that had no previous foundation of freedom.

Bush probably meant what he said in those debates. I'll give him the benefit of the doubt. However, once elected and faced with the events of 9-11, he chose to engage in nation building in both Afghanistan and Iraq. From any objective analysis, the results have not been good in either case.

So who should we blame for these misguided missions? Our presidents? Military hawks in Congress? The military-industrial complex?

And what are we to do in the face of wars we disagree with? Do we need to become peaceniks and launch a new round of anti-war protests? Toward the end of his life, MLK spoke out against the Vietnam War. In a speech called "Beyond Vietnam," delivered on April 4, 1967, Dr. King told three thousand people at Riverside Church in New York City that there was a common link forming between the civil rights and peace movements. He proposed that the U.S. stop all bombing of North and South Vietnam; declare a unilateral truce in the hope that it would lead to peace talks; set a date for withdrawal of all troops from Vietnam; and give the National Liberation Front a role in negotiations.

To Martin Luther King Jr., nonviolence wasn't a conservative or a liberal issue. Like civil rights, peace was a *moral* issue. He came to his conclusions through his convictions as a man who desired to follow the precepts of Scripture.

What convictions do *you* have about war and the military? Are you able to extend love and compassion to members of the military—especially the wounded warriors—without necessarily supporting all facets of the military-industrial complex?

More Advice from Eisenhower

This chapter began with President Eisenhower's warning about the dangerous power when military might and industrial interests are combined. I want to share another nugget of his wisdom from the same speech, even though it is on a completely different subject.

Eisenhower, again with prophetic foresight, shared his concern about the legacy of debt we were leaving the coming generations:

As we peer into society's future, we—you and I, and our government—must avoid the impulse to live only for today, plundering, for our own ease and convenience, the precious resources of tomorrow. We cannot mortgage the material assets of our grandchildren without risking the loss also of their political and spiritual heritage. We want democracy to survive for all generations to come, not to become the insolvent phantom of tomorrow.

Although our chronic national budget deficits are in many ways a completely different matter than the military-industrial complex, there is clearly some overlap. Our deficits would be much smaller—some would argue that they would be non-existent—if it weren't for our ill-advised and poorly executed military ventures in recent decades.

Of course, conservatives generally see things much differently on the debt issue. Under the Constitution, they point out, the national defense is the federal government's most significant role. So, for hawkish Congressional leaders, we must spend "whatever it takes" to keep our country safe. This view still has many support- ers, but I believe it's time for a new approach. Keeping America safe is a crucial objective, but one that is not necessarily advanced by preemptive military campaigns.

It's interesting that there tends to be some common ground between liberals and libertarians on the issue of curbing the mil- itary-industrial complex. Conservatives are prone to cut social programs, while liberals are generally willing to trim the military. Libertarians and strict constitutionalists, like Ron Paul, would say that both social entitlements and undeclared wars are outside of the government's authority under the Constitution.

A Higher Constitution

The American Constitution has served our country well for the most part. There is much wisdom in its principles of checks and balances and division of powers among the executive, legislative, and judicial branches.

But as Christians, we must give our allegiance to a *higher* constitution—the Word of God. Although I'm sure the Lord calls some people to serve in the American armed forces, *all* of His people are called to serve in the army of salvation. Instead of bearing arms to secure earthly kingdoms, we are called to lay down our lives for a kingdom that is eternal.

From my perspective, it was tragically misguided for church folks in the Middle Ages to launch the Crusades in order to win back territory from the Muslims. Can you picture Peter, Paul, John, or the other apostles in the first century leading such a military campaign? No way. To the contrary, Paul wrote that *"we are human, but we don't wage war as humans do. We use God's mighty weapons, not worldly weapons, to knock down the strongholds of human reasoning and to destroy false arguments"* (2 Corinthians 10:3–4 NLT).

You see, Jesus made it clear: *"Blessed are the peacemakers, for they will be called children of God"* (Matthew 5:9 NIV). The Prince of Peace enlists us to into His army to make peace rather than war. Yes, we may need to fight at times, but our highest objective should be to fight for His kingdom rather than the kingdoms of men.

8

THE ONLY GUN CONTROL LAW
THAT WILL WORK

*"The fruit of the Spirit is love, joy, peace, longsuffering, kind-
ness, goodness, faithfulness, gentleness, self-control. Against
such there is no law."*

—Galatians 5:22–23

Do you own a gun? Are you a hunter? Have you ever been the
victim of gun violence?

How you answer questions like these will shape your perspective on the gun control debate. Personally, I'm certainly grateful
for the protections of the Second Amendment, but I also would
love to keep assault weapons out of the hands of crazy people.

There have been crazy people with guns throughout history,
but some of the gun violence in recent decades has been particularly heart-wrenching: innocent school children, college students, movie patrons, post office workers, military base personnel.
Craziness seems to have no limits these days.

But the craziness problem isn't confined to guns. We've seen
the terrorists fly airplanes into buildings, bombers bring devastation to the Boston Marathon, and parents drown their own
children.

When gun violence occurs, it's understandable that we would be outraged and demand that "somebody" do something. Surely there must be a solution.

Yet some of the *worst* gun violence has occurred in "gun-free zones" like schools, where guns are prohibited. Criminals don't seem to pay much attention to such prohibitions, and perhaps they are even *drawn* to such areas, knowing that no one is likely to be armed.

The Price of Freedom?

I'm sympathetic to the argument that America's founders never envisioned assault weapons when they wrote the Second Amendment. But I'm even *more* concerned about a very disturbing trend in our country:

- Individuals have fewer and fewer rights.
- States have fewer and fewer rights.
- The federal government has rapidly increasing rights.

I don't like the trajectory of these trends, particularly when the top person in power has openly criticized "those who cling to their guns and religion."

But what about stricter gun control laws? For the sake of the *children*, after all.

Although I'm pretty wishy-washy on the subject, it seems that even the most ardent gun control fans will have to admit that the numerous laws already on the books haven't been particularly effective. Some of the cities with the worst gun violence, in fact, are the ones with the *strictest* laws.

Shouldn't law-abiding citizens who pass background checks be allowed to own guns in order to defend themselves? You know what the bumper stickers say: "When guns are outlawed, only the outlaws will have guns."

Bible Insights

The Bible provides some very insightful observations about all of this:

+ The first murder in history occurred in Genesis 4, when Cain killed his brother Abel. There were no laws against guns, nor were any guns even invented yet. However, Cain found a way to kill his brother anyway. There wasn't actually a "law" against murder at the time, but God assumed anyone walking in a close relationship with Him would certainly know better.

+ When the Ten Commandments were given in Exodus 20, murder was on the short list of things people shouldn't do. However, that didn't do much to solve the murder problem. Nor did people quit making idols, worshiping other gods, committing adultery, violating the Sabbath, lying, or being jealous of their neighbors. Although the Law came with great fanfare, I guess you could say it didn't really work.

To summarize these examples: It didn't work to not have any law, and even after the Law was finally given, it proved unsuccessful in putting an end to the things it prohibited.

Based on these facts, I don't have a lot of optimism that a new gun control law today will save any lives. While it's terrible to let insane people have guns, it's *also* terrible to allow grandstanding politicians to demagogue the issue and enact insane laws that have no chance of actually fixing the problem.

Of course, the *ultimate* form of gun control is *self-control* and *sound minds*. (See 2 Timothy 1:7.) Under the new covenant, there is an *internal* law instead of an *external* one. God says, *"This is the covenant that I will make…I will put My law in their minds, and write it on their hearts; and I will be their God, and they shall be My people"* (Jeremiah 31:33).

If laws engraved by God on tablets of stone didn't work, it's highly unlikely that new laws from Washington will work either. We need a revival in the land, changing people's hearts, restoring families, and putting a hedge of protection around our children.

9

SHOULD PASTORS LIVE IN (VERY BIG) GLASS HOUSES?

"Taking precaution so that no one will discredit us in our administration of this generous gift; for we have regard for what is honorable, not only in the sight of the Lord, but also in the sight of men."

—2 Corinthians 8:20–21 (NASB)

Let me just say from the beginning: I'm a preacher and I live in a big house. Is that okay with you? Or is that a problem?

There used to be stories in the press about how ministers of the gospel lived in "glass houses." In other words, because of their public profile and profession of spirituality, they and their families were under constant scrutiny by a watching world. There's no real privacy in a glass house, you see.

You've also probably heard the related maxim, "Those who live in glass houses shouldn't throw stones." This clever statement is used to intimidate truth-speakers from challenging the morality of others. It's as if to say, "Hey, you better not criticize *my* lifestyle, when you have so many visible flaws in your own life."

Remember the TV preacher years ago who went on rants against pornography—only to have it revealed that he himself was paying visits to a prostitute? Yes, if we are going to be preachers of righteousness, we had better be living a life of righteousness. But that's not really my main point in this chapter.

Instead of focusing on glass houses, I want to address one of the thorniest issues in the church today: Is it alright for pastors to live in very big and extravagant homes?

Critics of a Carolina Pastor

You probably heard the story that broke in the fall of 2013 about one of my fellow North Carolina pastors who was building a 16,000-square-foot house on nineteen acres of land. It turned out that the house wasn't quite as big as originally reported. It "only" had eighty-four hundred square feet of heated living area, and the rest of the space was composed of a basement, attic, garage, and porch.

When the story was about to break, the pastor warned his congregation that helicopters were flying over his new home and were about to broadcast a critical story about how big it was. He first tried to argue that the house wasn't "*That* big...there are other houses that are bigger." But this approach completely backfired when people saw pictures of the massive house.

So he tried a new approach the next time he addressed the issue. "That's a big house, no doubt about," he said, "but we recognize it as a gift from God."

Some people in the community were outraged that a preacher would use the hard-earned tithes and offerings of his flock to build such an expensive place for his family. The pastor countered that complaint by saying the house was purchased mostly from his book royalties, not from his salary with the church.

But the "haters" didn't back down when they heard his "book royalty" argument. They pointed out that the pastor's book royalties were largely attributable to his position at the church. With thousands of people in the congregation and many others who watched his sermons online, the pastor had a huge jump start when any new book was launched.

And weren't his books based mostly on the messages he had preached at the church? Since the messages were prepared during his work with the church, shouldn't the *church* receive the book royalties, rather than the pastor?

Transparency

There was another problem with the pastor's argument that he had built his new home with personal funds rather than from his salary. The haters wanted to know how much his salary was at the church.

If the church were an ordinary nonprofit organization, the salaries of corporate officers are a matter of public disclosure. But churches don't have such a legal requirement. And this pastor (and his church) refused media requests to share his compensation and housing allowance from the church.

This raised a whole new issue: Shouldn't people in a church be able to find out how much the church is paying their pastor? A refusal to provide this information makes it seem like there is something to hide. We live in a society where more transparency is expected.

As the investigative reporters continued to dig into this story, they found out that the pastor's big new home wasn't even in his own name. He had created a trust to purchase the house, so that it wouldn't be something traceable on public records. Apparently this is commonly done by celebrities for purposes of privacy and safety, but it poured even more fuel on the fire. Why were things being done so secretively?

The situation has reenergized critics of pastors' housing allowances and other tax breaks for churches. The original concept of housing allowances was that pastors normally didn't make much money and should at least have their housing expenses paid for by the church. But what about pastors who are making millions of dollars on their book deals today?

The pastor with the big house had always received very favorable media attention. His church gives away more than a million dollars to other ministries and missions, in his own city and beyond. Countless thousands of people have been helped over the years, both spiritually and with their material necessities.

So what's the big deal about the pastor's big house? Are the haters just fueled by envy? Are the pastor's defenders correct when they say the size of his house is no one's business?

The bigger issue, of course, is whether it's okay for preachers of the gospel to be blessed financially, drive expensive cars, and live in nice houses. As a general principle, I believe that is fine. Preachers certainly shouldn't have to take a vow of poverty. If they are telling their congregation that God will be faithful to meet our needs, they shouldn't be driving a broken-down car and living in a shack.

Purpose Driven Abundance

This debate over the proper financial lifestyle of a preacher is unlikely to go away anytime soon. And the issue often gets particularly murky where pastors make a substantial portion of their income from product sales and other sources outside of their salary.

Rick Warren, founding pastor of Saddleback Church, found himself suddenly showered with great wealth when his book, *The Purpose Driven Life*, sold more than fifteen million copies. How would he handle this incredible windfall of millions of dollars?

Warren concluded that God hadn't given him money and notoriety for his own ego or so he could live a life of ease. In spite of all the money coming in, he and his wife Kay amazed their friends by deciding not to change their lifestyle one bit. They made no major purchases and resisted any temptation to flaunt their new prosperity.

Warren's second decision was to stop taking a salary from Saddleback Church. He even added up all that Saddleback had paid him in the twenty-four years since he started it, and he gave it all back. Warren commented, "It was liberating to be able to serve God for free."

Then Warren set up a charitable foundation to fund an initiative called The Peace Plan, focused on planting churches, equipping leaders, assisting the poor, caring for the sick, and educating the next generation.

Rick and Kay Warren are a great example of people who *live* the purpose-driven life, not only write about it. Warren offers us this practical word of challenge:

> We need to ask ourselves: Am I going to live for possessions? Popularity? Am I going to be driven by pressures? Guilt? Bitterness? Materialism? Or am I going to be driven by God's purposes for my life?

Maybe Rick Warren should write a new book called *Purpose Driven Abundance*. In a day when many American preachers are either very poor or very rich, Warren and his wife have set a great example of how to handle God's financial blessings.

As Rick Warren pursued a life driven by a desire to fulfill God's purposes, he also discovered a life of overflowing abundance. Although God's plan for you may not include selling fifteen million books, He wants you to experience His overflowing abundance as well. He wants to bless you more and more, so you can BE a blessing to more and more people. (See Genesis 12:2.)

10

IS THE PROSPERITY GOSPEL HERETICAL?

*"The LORD be magnified, Who delights in the
prosperity of His servant."*

—Psalm 35:27 (NASB)

You've probably heard the "prosperity gospel" vilified, not just by the secular press but by many pastors as well. But I hope you are biblically balanced enough to realize that there is another side to this matter. Money isn't a bad thing. Although the prosperity gospel gets a bad rap, the Bible is clear that God really *does* want to bless His people with abundance, as 3 John 1:2 tells us, *"Beloved, I pray that you may prosper in all things and be in health, just as your soul prospers."*

Notice that the blessings of 3 John 1:2 are not confined to "health and wealth," however. John writes of God desire for His children to *"prosper in all things."* Isn't that fantastic news? Your heavenly Father wants you to prosper in everything you touch—your finances, your family, your health, your peace of mind, and most of all, your intimacy with Him.

But some Christians have picked up the twisted notion that God is a sadist who wants us to undergo continual trials and tribulations in every area of our lives. They warn against being ambitious for a better house or car for your family. They caution that

God may not want to heal broken relationships or protect you from disease.

As in *any* issue we face in life, we must turn to God's Word for guidance. For example, look what David writes about God's goodness:

> *Bless the LORD, O my soul, and forget not all His benefits: Who forgives all your iniquities, Who heals all your diseases, Who redeems your life from destruction, Who crowns you with lovingkindness and tender mercies, Who satisfies your mouth with good things, so that your youth is renewed like the eagle's.* (Psalm 103:2–5)

Don't you think it's pretty clear that God wants to bless you, heal you, and give you good things? Then why not reject the devil's lies that God wants you to be sick, stressed out, and broke?

I find that many Christians actually feel *guilty* about the thought that God may want to bless them with abundance. But let's be clear: The Lord wants to bless you, and there are two distinct reasons for this:

1. *He loves you as His beloved son or daughter.* Do you know any parent who wants their kids to suffer lack and be in poor health? Of course not. If you are in any doubt about this, take a look at Matthew 7:7–11 and Luke 11:9–13.

2. *He wants you to be a blessing to others.* If you're sick and impoverished, how can you be of any real help to others who are in need? Part of our heritage as believers is that, like our spiritual father Abraham, we are called to blessed so we can *be* a blessing. (See Genesis 12:2.) Psalm 67 describes this beautifully:

> *May God be gracious to us and bless us and make his face shine on us—so that your ways may be known on earth, your salvation among all nations….God, our God, blesses us. May*

293

God bless us still, so that all the ends of the earth will fear
him.   (Psalm 67:1–2, 6–7 NIV)

The psalmist here is unashamedly praying for God's favor
and blessings. But he realizes that these will have a ripple effect
in blessing others and spreading the name and fame of the Lord
across the earth. God's ways will be known...His salvation will
spread...and *"all the ends of the earth will fear him."*

Sometimes I run into folks who tell me, "Bishop Bloomer, I
don't need God to bless me with more. I have enough to pay my
bills each month, and I'm content with that."

Do you see how selfish this kind of perspective is? God doesn't
want to bless us with just enough to pay our monthly bills—He
wants to give us *more than enough*! Our prayer should not be just to
survive, for God wants us to *thrive*. He wants to provide *overflowing*
abundance that can bless a needy world and send out the gospel to
the nations.

The Millionaire

Many years ago there was a popular television series called *The*
Millionaire. Each episode showed an extremely wealthy benefactor
anonymously giving a check for a million dollars to someone who
least expected it.

What was interesting about *The Millionaire* series was seeing
how the recipients handled their great financial windfall. Some
used it wisely, bettering not only themselves, but others as well.
Yet other beneficiaries of this extraordinary generosity completely
misused their new fortune, often blowing it in a very short time.
Frequently, they ended up in a worse condition than before receiving the money.

What about you and me? If a wealthy benefactor (God) suddenly gave us a million dollars, what would we do with it? Could

He trust us with such a sum, knowing that we would faithfully use it to further His purposes on the earth? And would our unexpected bonanza turn out to be a true blessing for us, or a curse?

I want to be trustworthy with the Lord's money. Whether He gives me one dollar or one million, I want to be a faithful channel, a good steward. Jesus challenges us to be faithful in little things so He can entrust us with much. (See Luke 16:10–13; Matthew 25:21.) He is looking for some people to whom He can entrust millions or even billions of dollars—not just so they can be interviewed on *Lifestyles of the Rich and Famous*, but so that kingdom projects can be funded.

Friend, the Bible tells us that the eyes of the Lord still move to and fro throughout the whole earth, looking for people to strongly support because their hearts are fully His. (See 2 Chronicles 16:9.) He is still looking for people He can bless so that they might become a blessing.

Yes, the prosperity gospel can be heretical if self-centered people apply it with a bless-me-club mentality, where the prosperity message is preached without the cross. And we also must be careful not to act as if God's blessings are limited to material things, rather than our health, relationships, peace of mind, and intimate personal relationship with Him.

However, the prosperity gospel most of us are preaching today is simply meant to correct the *poverty gospel* that too many pastors and Bible teachers are foolishly advocating. Sure, we need to beware of extremes, but shouldn't err on the side of God's goodness and His desire to bless His people with abundance?

The poverty gospel, in contrast, implies that being poor is a mark of humility and true spirituality. *Nothing* could be more idiotic and heretical than that.

EPILOGUE

CAN WE TURN THINGS AROUND?

"A taste for truth at any cost is a passion which
spares nothing."

—*Albert Camus*

I hope you've been able to hear my heart in the pages of this book. I'm grieved that so few people in today's society are courageous enough to speak out on the hot-button issues of our day. I'm astounded that so many high-profile evangelical preachers consistently duck the issues rather than take a stand.

Throughout the Scriptures, we see leaders who brought transformation to the world through courageously facing obstacles and enemies. Joshua was told he must be *"strong and very courageous"* (Joshua 1:7) in order to lead the Israelites into their Promised Land. When other men of his generation were terrified of facing the Philistine giant Goliath, young David boldly charged into battle, armed only with a slingshot and *"the name of the LORD of hosts, the God of the armies of Israel"* (1 Samuel 17:45).

In more recent times, men like William Wilberforce courageously led a movement to abolish the slave trade. And President Abraham Lincoln signed the Emancipation Proclamation amid a heroic effort to save the union.

The message of history is clear: We will never succeed in turning things around in our nation if we remain emasculated by political correctness. Change is only possible when brave and audacious men and women are willing to confront evil and injustice through their words and their actions.

But the struggle we face today involves more than just political correctness, free speech, and a willingness to state our opinions. You see, our *opinions* are pretty much worthless unless they are based on *God's truth* and *His wisdom*. I'm sure you and I would disagree on some of the issues discussed in this book. That's okay. We just need more revelation of God's truth and wisdom.

And here's the good news: If we're humbly and sincerely following Jesus, He has promised to *show us* the truth—truth that will set us free. (See John 8:32, 8:36.) If we lack wisdom, the Lord has promised to give it to us when we ask. (See James 1:5.)

Are You a Seeker of Truth?

Not everyone really wants to hear the truth. Jesus said it's like casting pearls before pigs to try and convince some people of anything holy and true: *"Do not give what is holy to the dogs; nor cast your pearls before swine, lest they trample them under their feet, and turn and tear you in pieces"* (Matthew 7:6). In other words, don't waste your time arguing with people who don't really care about the facts. Save your breath for interaction with genuine truth-seekers.

But before trying to convince anyone else, we have to make sure that *we've* made a firm decision to seek and hold onto the truth. Solomon instructed us to *"buy the truth, and do not sell it, also wisdom and instruction and understanding"* (Proverbs 23:23). It is all too easy to "sell" the truth these days, trading it for tolerance and political correctness.

And let's face it: The truth is rarely comfortable. It demands that we respond and take action. That's why Ralph Waldo

Emerson wrote, "Every mind must make its choice between truth and repose. It cannot have both."

It's this simple: You must determine whether you want the truth more than personal comfort. Author C. S. Lewis pointed out, "If you look for truth, you may find comfort in the end; if you look for comfort, you will not get either comfort or truth, only soft soap and wishful thinking to begin, and in the end, despair."

President James A. Garfield was right when he said, "The truth will set you free, but first it will make you miserable." Are you willing to endure the painful reality in order to arrive at wisdom and liberation in the end?

Restoring the Plumb Line

While reading the biblical prophet Amos recently, I was struck by his statement that God wanted to show up in the midst of corruption and chaos with a *"plumb line"* (Amos 7:7) in his hand.

In case you're not a carpenter, let me explain what a plumb line is. The dictionary describes it as a cord with a weight attached to one end, enabling the user to determine a straight vertical line. If a wall is sagging or leaning to one side or another, a plumb line will expose the problem.

Since the time of ancient Egypt, construction workers have utilized plumb lines (also known as plumb bobs or plummets) to ensure that their buildings are "plumb" or perfectly vertical. Without this kind of tool, construction would be completely subjective, and you would never end up with straight walls.

The Bible describes God as using a plumb line to help His people discern between what is straight and what is tilted or crooked:

Then he showed me another vision. I saw the LORD standing beside a wall that had been built using a plumb line. He was using a plumb line to see if it was still straight. And the LORD said to me, "Amos, what do you see?" I answered, "A plumb line." And the LORD replied, "I will test my people with this plumb line. I will no longer ignore all their sins."

(Amos 7:7–8 NLT)

You see, the problems in America today are not primarily a matter of right or left, but right and wrong. Despite numerous promises to "drain the swamp" or "clean house" in Washington, neither side of the aisle seems truly willing to apply God's moral plumb line to their behavior or their policies.

We live in a day when politicians called on the carpet for intentionally failing to pay their taxes protest that they're just victims of partisan politics, a witch hunt, or even racism. It's time to cut the crap and pull out the plumb line! No matter what our political leanings may be, why can't we *all* agree on basic principles of truth and falsehood, right and wrong?

And don't get me started on the issue of our massive national debt and annual deficits. You don't have to be an accountant or possess an MBA to realize that our present course is simply unsustainable—and balanced budgets are a *moral* issue, not just a matter of politics.

It's time to face the fact that the political "walls" in Washington are no longer vertical. They're badly tilted, jeopardizing our long-term future as a nation. Will you help me sound an alarm?

The people of God are called to be a plumb line amid a warped and perverse culture. But before that can happen, the Lord has to use His plumb line on *us*. How can we boldly speak out about unrighteousness in our society, when there is still so much unrighteousness in our own lives? How can we challenge a watching world to repent, when they can see hypocrisy and compromise in our churches and families?

This is not a new problem, for Peter addressed it even in his day:

> *The time has come for judgment to begin at the house of God; and if it begins with us first, what will be the end of those who do not obey the gospel of God? Now "If the righteous one is scarcely saved, where will the ungodly and the sinner appear?"* (1 Peter 4:17–18)

This means that before we can rightfully point our finger at sin in our society, we must first allow God to deal with sin in our own lives and in the church. There won't be a spiritual awakening in our nation until there first has been an awakening in the church and the lives of individual Christians.

Impacting Our Culture

We see this same principle in the life of David. Although he was a man of God, he sinned grievously—committing adultery with Bathsheba and then having her husband put to death. But David *repented* when Nathan the prophet exposed his sin in 2 Samuel 12. Think about what would happen in our country if every Christian would sincerely pray a prayer like this:

> *Create in me a clean heart, O God, and renew a steadfast spirit within me. Do not cast me away from Your presence, and do not take Your Holy Spirit from me. Restore to me the joy of Your salvation, and uphold me by Your generous Spirit.* (Psalm 51:10–12)

Immediately after asking for forgiveness and cleansing, David makes a powerful statement about how his repentance will impact people around him: *"Then I will teach transgressors Your ways, and sinners shall be converted to You"* (Psalm 51:13). You see, we can't expect changes in our society unless we are willing to undergo changes in our own hearts and lives.

The people of God will have virtually no impact if we only *point* the way to God's standards of righteousness. The world will merely ignore us or ridicule us as narrow-minded, but they'll never be motivated to seek God or repent. Instead, we must *lead* the way, showing people through our lives that God's plan is truly the best plan.

So, are you ready? Will you not only *speak* to the issues of our day, but also be *salt and light* for a world that desperately needs to see people who are authentically living the Good News?

ABOUT THE AUTHOR

Bishop George Bloomer is a native of Brooklyn, New York. After serving as an evangelist for fourteen years, he began pastoring in 1996. Bloomer is the founder and senior pastor of Bethel Family Worship Center in Durham, North Carolina, but he continues to travel extensively, sharing with others his testimony of how the Lord delivered him from a life of poverty, drug addiction, sexual abuse, and mental anguish. He is the author of a number of books, including the best seller *Witchcraft in the Pews*. He also conducts many seminars dealing with relationships, finances, stress management, and spiritual warfare. Bloomer is founder of Young Witnesses for Christ, a youth evangelistic outreach ministry with several chapters on college campuses through the United States, and bishop of C.L.U.R.T. (Come Let Us Reason Together) International Assemblies, which includes over 80 churches nationwide and abroad.